THE UNITED NATIONS IN A CHANGING WORLD

THE UNITED NATIONS IN
A CHANGING WORLD

LELAND M. GOODRICH

COLUMBIA UNIVERSITY PRESS
New York & London

Library of Congress Cataloging in Publication Data

Goodrich, Leland Matthew, 1899–
    The United Nations in a changing world.

    Includes bibliographical references.
    1. United Nations.   I. Title.
JX1977.G67   341.23   74-893
ISBN 0-231-03824-0 (cloth)
ISBN 0-231-08343-2 (paperback)

Second cloth and first paperback printing.

Copyright © 1974 Columbia University Press
Printed in the United States of America

TO ELEANOR

PREFACE

IT IS NOT THE PURPOSE of this book to sell the United Nations as an international organization that has promise of solving all the world's critical problems if given only half a chance. Nor is it to depreciate the Organization as bound to fail in the achievement of its declared purposes as did the League before it. Rather the purpose is to look objectively at the Organization in its historical context; to recall how it was originally conceived; to examine the changes that have taken place as the result of the changing world environment, the expanded membership of the Organization, the attitudes of its members and the demands made upon it; and to consider what its likely prospects are for the years immediately ahead.

My approach to the task, though hopefully objective, is of course a personal one, influenced by certain preconceptions and attitudes that have been acquired over a period of many years as student and teacher. I suppose that one of my strongest convictions is that institutions, whether in the domestic or the international field, develop most efficiently by an evolutionary process. If one accepts this view, constitutional documents such as the Covenant of the League and the Charter of the United Nations assume less long-term significance as acts of creation and become more significant as acts of codification and consolidation.

There is of course one obvious difficulty in applying to international relations the principle of evolutionary institutional development that appears to have validity in explaining the institutions of the modern state. States are not individuals but rather collections of individual persons constituting organized communities and, in the development of international institutions, physical force has not and cannot reasonably be expected to play the role in the development of a central authority and appropriate organs that it has played in the development of the modern state. Consequently we have the problem of achieving comparable results by consent. Some see the possibility of achieving this result in the long run by expanding and deepening the sense of community and the consequent willingness of peoples and governments to accept increased responsibilities and powers on the part of international agencies. There is some evidence that this may happen on a regional and highly selective basis but little evidence as yet that it will soon, if ever, come about globally.

This raises a serious problem for one who seeks to look into the future and to judge the prospects of global international organization, represented today by the United Nations and its related specialized agencies. If the ultimate goal is some form of world government it is a matter of real doubt whether this goal can be achieved by evolutionary development of the system, based on consent, which we now have. It can indeed be strongly argued that there is a gulf between the present consent system and the future goal that can only be crossed by a development that is truly revolutionary in character. On the other hand, the goal for which we should strive may not be world government with the inevitable danger of excessive centralization of power and bureaucracy but rather some form of institutionalized cooperation between pluralistic communities, with a great variety of institutions, and structural, functional, and procedural arrangements. The active participation in world affairs today of a great variety of participants other than traditional states is one factor which lends support to the greater validity of this goal as our ultimate objective. Furthermore, functionalist theory gives us some grounds for believing that such a goal can be attained.

Though my initial interest in international organization resulted from the study of international law and tended to emphasize its legal basis, I have come to recognize that organizations like the United Nations are more political than legal in that considerations of power and national interest are in the end determinative. From this it follows that ultimate success in the performance of their functions largely depends upon the extent to which responsibility is related to power. The principle of majority rule with each state, irrespective of power, having one vote has no necessary validity in international organizations, valid though it may be in the operations of national representative organs. The success of international organizations largely depends on the support of the major members, importance being measured by the capacity to contribute to the fulfillment of the organization's purposes. It is for that reason, and not because of my being a citizen of the United States, that in assessing the future of the United Nations, I come to the conclusion that for the foreseeable future so much depends on the course followed by the government in Washington.

It is impossible to give detailed acknowledgment of all the assistance that I have received in the writing of this book. I owe a great debt to the teachers, students, and colleagues with whom I have been associated over the years. My thinking has been influenced greatly by specific experiences that I have had, such as being in Geneva on sabbatical leave from Brown University in the early months of 1936, serving as director of the World Peace Foundation during the war years, being a member of the International Secretariat of the San Francisco Conference, and serving for many years on the Board of Editors of *International Organization*. I owe a special debt to the International Studies Programme at the University of Toronto and the Institute of War and Peace Studies at Columbia University for providing me with the opportunity to continue my research and writing under extremely favorable circumstances after my formal retirement at Columbia in 1968. And finally I am greatly indebted to my wife for support and encouragement, and willingness to forego my companionship in order that a manuscript might be completed and published.

Columbia University
January, 1974

L.M.G.

CONTENTS

THE UNITED NATIONS IN A CHANGING WORLD

CHAPTER ONE

FROM LEAGUE TO UNITED NATIONS

FOLLOWING THE CARNAGE of World War I, the League of Nations was established to prevent future wars. Within less than two decades it was clear not only that the League had failed in its primary purpose but that the world was on the eve of a second major conflict. When this second world war was nearing its end in 1945, representatives of the allied nations met in San Francisco to draft and sign the Charter of the United Nations and the new organization became a reality in October of that year. Now, over a quarter of a century later, the United Nations, though far from moribund, has failed to live up to the hopes and expectations of its founders and supporters. This is true not only in the field of international peace and security where its achievements, though substantial, have been profoundly disappointing, but also in the economic and social areas where its programs to promote economic development have not narrowed the gap between rich and poor and its efforts to promote respect for human rights have encountered insuperable obstacles.

From this disappointing record, some would conclude that the United Nations is on its way to much the same fate as the League of Nations. Even though its failure may not be registered in the outbreak of a third world war—from which we may be saved by the effectiveness of modern instruments of destruction—still, according to this view, the organization is likely to gradually pass into disuse, save possibly in dealing with matters of minor importance outside the main interests of the major powers. Others conclude that while its failures in the field of peace and security and the present trends of international relations indicate the likely declining importance of the United Nations as an organization for maintaining international peace and security—a goal that is more likely to be achieved by a return to the old system of balance of power—the United Nations still has an important, though modest, role to play in dealing with problems of a nonpolitical nature, many of which have come to assume critical proportions as the result of technological developments and growing interdependence. Finally, there are those who see the United Nations as performing an increasingly important role in the achievement of common purposes set forth in the Charter and, while disappointed by its inadequacies and failures, see the future in terms of a more effective organization and greater willingness on the part of governments to make use of it.

One thing is fairly certain. So long as the state retains its primacy as a form of social organization, international organization in some form will be necessary for dealing with matters of common concern that cannot be satisfactorily handled by individual state action. The practical question that we face is the form that this organization is to take, the extent of the functions and powers that are to be vested in international agencies, and the responsibilities that states are to assume.

Not only is international organization, in a great variety of forms, an essential and inevitable feature of the modern world scene, but what is equally significant is the degree of continuity of the institutional and conceptual development, extending over a century, that has produced what we have today. The United Nations and the various agencies, related or unrelated, are not the products of sudden inspiration or of a particular time of crisis. They are not hastily adopted devices which can be discarded and replaced by other methods once their use proves inconvenient. They are the product of evolutionary development, the result of decisions taken by responsible governments as to how they can best cope with problems with which they are faced. While the development may appear to be discontinuous and broken because of the intervention of major military conflicts, if we look at the basic concepts and principles that have guided governments in their organized inter-state relations, we find a degree of continuity comparable in many ways to that which we observe in the development of the institutions of the modern state.

If we take the basic concepts and institutional arrangements of the United Nations, including the specialized agencies, we find that they have much in common with those of the League of Nations [1] The differences can be explained, as institutional development is customarily accounted for, by the application of the lessons of experience and changes in institutional environment. At the time the League of Nations was established, many were under the illusion that this organization was an entirely new creation representing a complete break with the past. This view admittedly received strong support from some of its major proponents, especially President Wilson who chose to emphasize the break that the League represented with the discredited ideas and practices of the past. Nevertheless, if one examines closely the process by which the Covenant was drafted and the concepts and institutional arrangements that were incorporated into it, one will find that the Covenant to a large extent simply incorporated and, hopefully, improved upon ideas and practices that had acquired wide acceptance in earlier years.[2]

There were of course many novel features in the League system, some of them of sufficient importance to provide a measure of justification for Wilson's claim. Thus, the establishment of a league of nations with universal membership and global responsibilities to prevent war by the concerted action of its members was unprecedented, though the idea of such a league had been advanced many times in the past by peace advocates and private peace organizations. Similarly, the principle of the guarantee by members of such a league of the political independence and territorial integrity of each member against external aggression—for President Wilson the heart of the Covenant—was a novel concept, though the idea

1. See Leland M. Goodrich, "From League of Nations to United Nations," *International Organization*, I (1947) 3–21.

2. See David Hunter Miller, *The Drafting of the Covenant* (2 vols.; New York: Putnam, 1928); and Alfred Zimmern, *The League of Nations and the Rule of Law* (London: Macmillan, 1936).

was a logical extension of similar guarantees in the past of more limited geographic application. Finally, the use of collective measures—economic, financial, and hopefully military—to defeat aggression was something new, though the recent war and earlier wars had seen the use of collective economic and financial measures in support of military action for winning wars and had demonstrated their effectiveness under war conditions.

But more significant were the elements of the League system which represented the acceptance and adaptation of principles, organs, and practices which long antedated the League. The League Council had as its antecedent the European Concert, in which the major powers assumed special responsibilities for keeping the peace. The League Assembly, like the prewar international conference, provided the opportunity for the wider participation of states, but on a permanent basis with established membership and responsibilities, a development which the two Hague Conferences of 1899 and 1907 clearly anticipated. The Secretariat was the League's counterpart of earlier bureaus of international conferences and public unions. The Permanent Court of International Justice was the fruition of a development going back to the early nineteenth century when third-party decision was recognized as well adapted to the final settlement of certain kinds of international differences. Even though judicial settlement came to be seen as having certain advantages over arbitration, not until the establishment of the League was it possible to resolve the problem of how to choose the judges. Various procedures of peaceful settlement developed and refined in the Covenant and League practice were the common currency of prewar diplomatic practice and treaty undertakings.

While the League of Nations was not in fact a wholly novel approach to the problem of war prevention and to furthering international cooperation in areas of common interest, it was presented by its proponents, particularly in the United States, as a break with past practices which had led the world to disaster, and as holding the promise of a better world in which free people would cooperate to achieve peace, security, and justice. The extravagant hopes that were encouraged were bound to be disappointed, the more so since one of the major assumptions of the League's architects—the participation of the United States—was not realized in practice. It is significant, however, that in spite of the failure of the United States to join, and the devastating blow which this dealt to the League's prospects, there was no serious thought given to putting an end to "the great experiment" then and there. The League was recognized as essential to the performance of numerous functions in connection with the implementation of the peace treaties, the preservation of peace, and dealing with a wide range of economic and social matters. For close to two decades the League was the principal means by which the great majority of states in the world sought to deal with their common problems.[3]

The first decade was a period of relative success in spite of the initial handicap of American abstention. During the first two years of the League's existence it was called upon to deal with a number of questions resulting from the war and, while it was not always successful, it nevertheless established itself as an important influence in international relations.[4] The years 1924 to 1929 were a period of relative peace, characterized by apparent general prosperity and cooperative relations among the major powers with the exception of the Soviet Union. No serious challenges were offered to League principles, and complicated political problems such as disarmament and the more effective organization of peace were tackled with some promise of constructive results. The possibilities of cooperation in the economic and social fields were intelligently explored. However, the League failed to move governments to take the steps required for the solution of basic problems of economic maladjustment and imbalance resulting from the war. Governments were unwilling to face the need of basic adjustments and changes of policy at a time when, superficially, economic conditions appeared good and promising for the future. The years 1930 to 1936 saw a

3. For an authoritative and highly sympathetic account of the League's work, see F. P. Walters, *A History of the League of Nations* (2 vols.; New York: Oxford University Press, 1952).

4. For two fully documented case studies, see James Barros, *The Aaland Islands Question* (New Haven: Yale University Press, 1968); and *The Corfu Incident of 1923* (Princeton: Princeton University Press, 1965).

world-wide depression, the coming of which had been prophesied by many independent experts. During this period, as the result of worsening economic conditions, nationalist movements committed to aggressive and expansionist foreign policies gained strength and eventually succeeded in establishing themselves in power in countries where democratic institutions were insecurely based. The establishment of expansionist authoritarian regimes in Germany and Japan, and the return of the Fascist regime in Italy to more aggressive foreign policies marked the end of the period of international tranquility and foreshadowed new challenges to international peace and security. These challenges the League was unable to cope with due to the strictly limited cooperation of the United States as a non-member and the failure of France and Great Britain to give the necessary support.

The 1930s saw the decisive failure of the League to prevent war and its final demise as a functioning peace organization. The failure of the League to check Japanese aggression in Manchuria in the early thirties was followed in quick succession by the rise of Hitler to power in Germany, the failure of League sanctions against Italy following Mussolini's attack on Ethiopia in October 1935, and German remilitarization of the Rhineland in March 1936 in clear violation of the Treaty of Versailles and the Locarno Pact. It required no great gift of foresight to recognize that these events portended the close approach of another world catastrophe. At a time when the United States was cooperating to an increasing extent with the League in the maintenance of peace and security, those members whose interests clearly lay in the preservation of international peace and security by collective means, in particular France and the United Kingdom, were so obsessed with domestic political, economic, and financial problems, the fear of communism, and the short-range demands of national security that they failed to discharge their responsibilities as League members. After 1936 the League as an organization for the maintenance of peace and security was dead, and its members, instead of looking to the League and its principles for support in organizing their security, sought security by retreat, by isolation, or by closing their eyes to the dangers about them. The expulsion of the Soviet Union in

1939 following its attack on Finland was in a sense the League's last dying, feverish gesture. Efforts to salvage it as an organization for furthering international cooperation in economic and social matters met with some measure of success, and during the war some of the work of the League was continued under hastily improvised arrangements.

The collapse of the League as an organization for the prevention of war in the thirties was clearly shown by the fact that, with war imminent as the result of the Czechoslovakian crisis and the threat to Poland, no attempt was made to use League machinery and procedures to prevent it. Only after war had actually begun and the Soviet Union had embarked on its separate venture at Finland's expense was use temporarily made of the League for the purpose of condemning Soviet action.

It is significant that even though the outbreak of the war had signalled the failure of the League, it was nevertheless recognized early in the conflict that some kind of international organization must be established to take its place. When President Roosevelt and Prime Minister Churchill met at their Atlantic rendezvous in 1941, Churchill expressed the desire that by their joint declaration they should give expression to their hope that some form of international organization would be created to provide a greater sense of security after the war. Once the United States was in the war as the result of the Pearl Harbor attack of December 7, 1941, constructive steps for the establishment of a postwar organization to maintain international peace and security, to carry on the task of the League of Nations, were not long delayed.[5] The initiative was taken by the U.S. Department of State; under the direction of Secretary Hull a draft charter was prepared embodying U.S. proposals.[6] After the governments of China, the USSR, the United Kingdom, and the United States had agreed at Moscow in 1943 on the desirability of establishing "a general international organization . . . for the

5. For a detailed account of the preparation of the UN Charter, see Ruth B. Russell and Jeannette E. Mather, *A History of the United Nations Charter* (Washington: Brookings Institution, 1958).

6. U.S. Department of State, *Post-War Foreign Policy Preparation, 1939–1945,* Publ. 3580 (Washington: Government Printing Office, 1950), pp. 595–606.

maintenance of international peace and security," [7] their representatives met at Dumbarton Oaks in 1944 and agreed on proposals which became the basis of discussions at San Francisco in April–June 1945. The Charter, signed on June 26, 1945 entered into force on October 24 of that year.[8]

DOMINANT CONSIDERATIONS IN THE DRAFTING OF THE CHARTER

In the drafting of the Charter the decisive influence was exercised by those states which were making the chief contribution to the winning of the war. Of these, the United States undoubtedly played a major part, although in a negative sense the influence of the Soviet Union was as decisive since there was general agreement that the two major military powers should be members of the new organization. However, it was the United States that took the initiative in carrying out preliminary studies, preparing working drafts, and pressing for final agreement. Certain considerations were of major importance in determining the final result.

Of these, one that was particularly important so far as the major military powers themselves were concerned was the relation of the proposed organization to the purposes and objectives to which the Allied powers were committed in the war. These purposes had been set forth in general terms in various statements and agreements, and the postwar organization which was in the process of being set up was viewed as a concluding step in the war effort to defeat the forces of aggression and to organize the world in accordance with these objectives. Thus the justification for giving those states that assumed the major role in winning the war permanent membership in the Security Council was to be found not only in their military power but also in their commitment to the achievement of widely accepted goals in the postwar period. It is signifi-

7. U.S. Department of State, *Bulletin,* Vol. 9, p. 308.

8. For details on drafting of the Charter, see Russell and Mather; see also Leland M. Goodrich and Edvard Hambro, *Charter of the United Nations: Commentary and Documents* (Boston: World Peace Foundation, 1946).

cant that a condition of being invited to attend the San Francisco Conference was active participation in the war against the Axis powers. While the eventual goal of the Organization was universality of membership, it was nevertheless clearly recognized at the time the Charter was being drafted that the states which had a special claim to membership in the initial period were those whose commitment during that period was at least helpful to the war effort. While the eventual participation in the Organization of the so-called enemy states was envisaged, it was assumed that these states would have to pass through a test period before their membership would be accepted.

A second consideration that had a decisive influence in determining the nature of the new organization was the belief that the states that had made the chief contribution to the winning of the war and whose cooperation was needed to keep the defeated enemy states under control—more particularly the United States, the Soviet Union, and the United Kingdom—must join and be active participants in the work of the new organization if it were to succeed. One of the conclusions drawn from the experience of the League of Nations was that a global organization could not be successful without the full and active participation of the major powers. Consequently, not only were Charter provisions drafted to assure their becoming members but the new organization was so constructed as to enable each of these major powers to effectively protect its vital interests.

A third consideration was the conviction based upon the experience of the years immediately preceding the war that an organization to maintain the peace must have responsibility for dealing with economic and social problems as well as for the maintenance of peace and security through the avoidance and suppression of the use of force. This view was not initially accepted by the Soviet Union, which desired that the Organization have the single purpose of maintaining peace and security and saw little reason for international cooperation to maintain the viability of an economic system, the validity of which, on ideological grounds, it refused to accept. Nevertheless, in the preliminary discussions before San Francisco the Soviets accepted the broader concept of the Organization's purposes. The likelihood that economic discontent would lead to political instability and the establishment of authoritarian regimes, and that regimes based on the denial of human rights would practice aggression in their foreign relations, were widely accepted conclusions from the prewar experience. Consequently, full recognition was given to the need of creating basic economic and social conditions favorable to peace as well as to the need of effective action in dealing with particular disputes and situations as they arose.

Finally, a decisive influence in the drafting of Charter provisions relating to the structure and powers of organs, particularly those having to do with the maintenance of international peace and security, was the recognition of the need of relating responsibility to power. Under the Covenant of the League of Nations an attempt had been made to establish a system which would operate more or less automatically to bring into operation certain sanctions of an economic and financial nature against any state, irrespective of its military strength, that violated the prohibition of "resort to war." The experience of the League of Nations discouraged any revival of this approach. First of all, it seemed clear that even though states were willing to enter into commitments of this kind for the future, when the actual occasion arose for their fulfillment, governments would be reluctant to perform their legal responsibilities unless they perceived that their national interest in the particular situation justified it. Furthermore, the League system of sanctions, by failing to take into account the special situations of member states, imposed responsibilities upon members that they were not prepared to undertake because of the serious consequences for themselves. Thus, it became quite apparent with the failure of the United States to join the League that any effort to apply the sanctions of Article 16 would have consequences that many members of the League were not prepared to accept. So in the new organization it was, from the beginning, accepted as essential that the responsibility for decisions involving the possible use of military forces should be taken by organs so constituted as to reflect the special interests and responsibilities of the principal contributors.

NATURE OF THE NEW ORGANIZATION

The organization for which the Charter provided, like the League of Nations, was essentially an association of independent states co-operating for the achievement of certain common purposes. Its associational character was demonstrated by the emphasis placed upon the sovereign equality of its members, by the fact that no state would become bound by the Charter until it had deposited its instrument of ratification, by the requirement that other states than those originally participating in the San Francisco Conference would become members only upon formal application and indication of their willingness to accept the obligations of the Charter,[9] and by the recognition at San Francisco that any member might withdraw from the Organization. It is, of course, provided that changes in the Charter may become effective under the amendment procedure without the consent of certain members of the Organization. The admission of the right of withdrawal, however, provides a means by which any member can free itself from being bound by an unacceptable amendment.[10]

The Charter provided for a multipurpose organization. While the maintenance of international peace and security is listed as the first purpose of the Organization, the development of friendly relations, the achievement of international cooperation in dealing with economic and social problems, the promotion of respect for human rights and fundamental freedoms, and the economic, social, and political development of underdeveloped territories are all recognized objectives of the Organization. In a sense these objectives are related to the maintenance of international peace and security, but they also constitute goals which require appropriate action by the members and the organs for which the Charter pro-

9. The only exception was Poland, which did not participate in the work of the Conference because of the inability of the Sponsoring Governments to agree on the government to be recognized, but which as a signatory of the Declaration by the United Nations later signed the Charter and became an original member.

10. On right of withdrawal, see Leland M. Goodrich, Edvard Hambro, and Anne P. Simons, *Charter of the United Nations: Commentary and Documents* (3d rev. ed.; New York: Columbia University Press, 1969), pp. 74–76.

vides, even though the action in question may not be closely related to the maintenance of peace and security in any realistic sense. Consequently, the Organization is not only a peace and security organization but also one committed to the promotion of man's welfare and the fuller realization of his potentialities.

To guide the Organization and its members in the pursuit of these purposes, the Charter set forth certain principles.[11] Strictly speaking, these are not legal rules of the kind that lend themselves to interpretation by a court, but are general principles for the guidance of member states and organs in the policies and programs which they adopt. Consequently, they lend themselves to differences of interpretation in their actual application. These principles fall roughly into two categories: those which establish limits upon the competence of the Organization, and those which indicate positive action which members and the organs are to take to carry out the Organization's purposes. Falling into the first category are the principle of sovereign equality,[12] and the principle that the Organization shall not intervene in any matter falling essentially within the domestic jurisdiction of a state.[13]

The principle of sovereign equality was intended to give assurance that the Organization did not have a supranational character, and that smaller states have equal rights and are not subject to restrictions and limitations that are not equally imposed upon the larger states. The principle of equality was not consistently applied, however, since the major powers were given special rights in the Security Council through permanent membership and the voting procedure on substantive questions.[14]

The domestic jurisdiction principle was taken seriously in the drafting of the Charter and was clearly intended to have a restrictive effect upon the Organization's activities. As formulated in the Charter, the limitation went beyond that incorporated in the Covenant of the League or even that included in the Dumbarton Oaks Proposals in that it applied to all organs of the United Nations in all their activities and not just to the Security Council when discharg-

11. Set forth in Art. 2, but also in other articles, especially Arts. 56, 73, and 76.
12. Art. 2, par. 1.   13. Art. 2, par. 7.   14. Arts. 23 and 27.

ing its function of pacific settlement. What prompted this broad application of the domestic jurisdiction principle was the expanded scope given to the Organization's powers at San Francisco in dealing with economic and social problems. Clearly, the United States delegation, in pressing for this broader application of the domestic jurisdiction principle, was concerned with possible Senate reactions. Though possessing the potentiality of a serious limitation upon the Organization's activities, the principle has not in practice acquired great importance.

The principles of a more positive nature have proved in practice to be much more significant than the negative principles. Some of these relate to the maintenance of international peace and security, and these were the ones regarded as the most important at San Francisco. "All members shall settle their international disputes by peaceful means in such a manner that international peace and security, and justice, are not endangered." [15] Complementing this principle is the requirement that "[a]ll Members shall refrain in their international relations from the threat or use of force against the territorial integrity or political independence of any state, or in any other manner inconsistent with the Purposes of the United Nations." [16] Primarily intended to support the action of the United Nations in the maintenance of peace and security but also capable of wider application is the principle that "[a]ll Members shall give the United Nations every assistance in any action it takes in accordance with the present Charter, and shall refrain from giving assistance to any state against which the United Nations is taking preventive or enforcement action." [17] What might be regarded as revolutionary is the principle that "[t]he Organization shall ensure that states which are not Members of the United Nations act in accordance with these Principles so far as may be necessary for the maintenance of international peace and security." [18]

Not all the basic principles which members are expected to respect and which the organs of the United Nations are expected to implement are set forth in Article 2. Thus, members "pledge them-

15. Art. 2, par. 3.   16. Art. 2, par. 4.   17. Art. 2, par. 5.
18. Art. 2, par. 6.

selves to take joint and separate action in cooperation with the Organization" for the achievement of the economic and social objectives set forth in Article 55.[19] In the administration of non-self-governing territories, members recognize that the interests of the inhabitants of these territories are paramount, accept the obligation "to promote to the utmost, within the system of international peace and security established by the present Charter, the well-being of the inhabitants of these territories," and undertake to ensure the political, economic, social, and educational advancement of the peoples of these territories and to develop self-government.[20] In the case of territories placed under trusteeship, these general principles are given much more detailed application, and procedures for implementation are specified.[21]

STRUCTURE, FUNCTIONS, AND POWERS OF THE PRINCIPAL ORGANS

To carry out the declared purposes of the United Nations, the Charter provided for the establishment of six principal organs and such subsidiary organs as might be found necessary. The six principal organs are the General Assembly, the Security Council, the Economic and Social Council, the Trusteeship Council, the International Court of Justice, and the Secretariat. In establishing these organs and in determining their functions and powers, the authors of the Charter were guided by the principle of functional effectiveness. It was recognized that in a world of independent states with great inequalities, it is necessary and desirable to relate responsibility to power and to achieve in each organ such accommodation of differences of power and interest as will give maximum assurance that the decisions taken will be translated into action. This was considered to be particularly necessary in light of the decision to dispense with the rule of unanimity which had governed decisions of international conferences in the past and to

19. Art. 56.   20. Art. 73.   21. Chaps. XII and XIII.

substitute for it the principle of decision by majority or modified majority vote.

The General Assembly is the organ which most accurately reflects the total membership of the Organization. Since, however, it was conceived as an organ based upon the principle of equality of participation and voting power, it could not realistically be thought of as having truly legislative powers or the power to take binding decisions except in limited areas pertaining chiefly to the internal affairs of the Organization. It was referred to at San Francisco [22]—and has frequently been so characterized—as the "town meeting" of the world. This term quite accurately describes its principal role as envisaged at San Francisco: that of a forum where all members have the equal right to participate, express their views, and take part in the formulation of general principles and policies for the guidance of the Organization. Its functions were conceived as falling under the headings of discussion and recommendation, control of finances, election and admission of new members, and the initiation of proposals for Charter review and amendment. Indeed, its powers of discussion and recommendation were to be very extensive. The principal limitations upon these powers, other than those imposed by the domestic jurisdiction principle, were that in the field of peace and security the Security Council had "primary responsibility," that the Assembly was not to make recommendations with respect to any matter before the Security Council, and that it was to refer to the Security Council any matter upon which "action" was required. In other than peace and security matters, the General Assembly was to have primary responsibility, as the two Councils which were provided with quasi-executive functions—the Economic and Social Council and the Trusteeship Council—were to function under its general authority.

The second principal organ, the Security Council, most fully expressed the concern of the major powers to have their special interests and responsibilities reflected in institutional arrangements. It was thought to be important to the effectiveness of the Organiza-

22. By Senator Vandenberg.

tion in the maintenance of peace and security that there should be one organ with power to take binding decisions in situations where peace and security were directly threatened. To this end, the Security Council was established with composition and voting procedure specifically adapted to making it acceptable to the chief military powers, who were expected to be the major contributors in the maintenance of peace and security. In addition to vesting in the Council this major responsibility,[23] defining in considerable detail the specific powers that the Council might exercise, and placing upon the General Assembly certain limitations with respect to its action in this field, the Charter so defined the composition and voting procedure of the Council that no substantive decisions could be taken without the approval of its permanent members.

In the selection of the permanent members of the Security Council, there was no question of the appropriateness of including the United States, the Soviet Union, and the United Kingdom. While France's role in the war may not have justified her inclusion as a permanent member, her assistance in checking the revival of German expansionist ambitions after the war was accepted as adequate reason. In the case of China, inclusion was dictated by the concern of the United States to have a strong and friendly China as a counterbalance to the revival of Japanese power in the Far East.

The insistence of the Sponsoring Governments and France upon the requirement of concurrence of the permanent members in all nonprocedural decisions of the Council was not easily accepted by the smaller states at San Francisco. These governments, however, insisted that this requirement apply to all the Council's decisions in the exercise of its powers under Chapter VI as well as Chapter VII on the ground that each step in the consideration of a dispute or situation constituted a link in a chain of events which might lead to enforcement action with which all permanent members were admittedly specially concerned.[24] Since the Secretary-General is given special responsibilities in connection with the maintenance of peace

23. Art. 24.

24. See "Statement by the Delegations of the Four Sponsoring Governments on Voting Procedure in the Security Council," Goodrich, Hambro, and Simons, pp. 217–20.

and security and since one of the major obligations of members is to assist in this effort, it was also decided that the Security Council should participate in the appointment of the Secretary-General and in the admission of new members, and that the veto should apply in each case.

The third principal organ of the United Nations was to be the Economic and Social Council. It had no counterpart in the League, although it was anticipated in the recommendation of the Bruce Committee in 1939 that the Assembly establish a special committee responsible to that organ to perform functions of the League Council in the economic and social fields. In the drafting of the Charter it was decided that the quasi-executive functions of the League Council in the whole range of its responsibilities be divided among three councils: the Security Council, the Trusteeship Council, and the Economic and Social Council. However, in the case of the latter, because of the limited nature of its powers of discussion and recommendation and the nature of the activities that the United Nations was likely to undertake, the major powers did not insist that they be given permanent membership or special voting rights. Consequently, unlike the Security Council, part of whose membership was to be permanent and the other part elected by the Assembly, the Economic and Social Council has all members elected by the General Assembly.

In further explanation of the willingness of the major powers to forego any special membership or voting rights in the economic and social field, it should be noted that the Charter envisaged operational activities being carried out principally through specialized intergovernmental agencies with their separate constitutions in which special national interests could be protected, as had already been done in the case of the Bank and the Fund. The functions of the United Nations organs were conceived to be principally the formulation of general principles, the development of programs in general terms, and the coordination of the activities of the various specialized agencies by discussion and recommendation.[25]

The fourth principal organ, the Trusteeship Council, had no

25. See Arts. 57 and 58 of the Charter.

exact counterpart in the League system, although it combines certain of the characteristics of the League Council on the one hand and the Permanent Mandates Commission on the other. Unlike the League Council in its relation to the mandates system, however, it was not the organ given final responsibility for the supervision of trusteeship administration. This responsibility was placed on the General Assembly. The Trusteeship Council was expected to perform functions more akin to those of the Permanent Mandates Commission; however, because it was composed of member states, there was no assurance that the individuals representing those member states would have the special expertise that members of the Permanent Mandates Commission possessed under the League system. Since the administering states under the trusteeship system were expected to see to it that the trust territories played their part in the maintenance of peace and security, the argument was made and accepted at San Francisco that the permanent members of the Security Council had a special interest in the functioning of the trusteeship system and consequently should be members of the Trusteeship Council. Furthermore, it was provided that the membership of the Council should be so constituted that there would be an equal balance between administering and nonadministering states.

The fifth principal organ for which the Charter provided was the International Court of Justice which, unlike the Permanent Court of International Justice which had evolved as a more or less autonomous organ of the League in order to attract United States adherence, was declared to be the principal judicial organ of the United Nations.[26] Its Statute was made an integral part of the United Nations Charter. Except for this formal difference, however, the Court was essentially a continuation of the former Court; it was composed of fifteen judges, elected by the General Assembly and the Security Council voting concurrently. Like the Permanent Court, it was given the twofold function of serving as a tribunal for the final settlement of disputes submitted to it by the parties and acting in an advisory capacity to the General Assembly,

26. Art. 92 of the Charter.

the Security Council, and other organs accorded this right of consultation by vote of the General Assembly, on questions of a legal nature which might be referred to it.

In establishing the sixth principal organ, the Secretariat, the authors of the Charter followed generally what had been the practice of the League of Nations, except in one important respect. There was agreement that the Secretary-General should have the independent right to bring a dispute or situation to the attention of the Security Council.[27] The Covenant did not give the Secretary-General this power, nor had he exercised it in practice. Those who drafted the Charter, however, felt that there might be situations where a government might not be willing to take this initiative and where it might be desirable for the Secretary-General, representing a general interest in the maintenance of peace and security, to have the right to do so. Furthermore, the authors of the Charter specifically envisaged the possibility that important responsibilities were to be conferred upon the Secretary-General under resolutions adopted by the political organs. Regarding the manner in which the members of the Secretariat perform their functions, and the principles governing recruitment of personnel, the authors of the Charter followed closely the principles that had been developed by the first Secretary-General of the League of Nations.

EXPECTATIONS AT SAN FRANCISCO

In light of the disappointments and frustrations of the past twenty-five years, the question naturally arises as to how there could have been any serious expectation that the new organization would be more successful in achieving its purposes than the League before it. What basis was there for believing that an organization based upon the principle of sovereign equality, requiring for its success the voluntary cooperation of states great and small with divergent national interests, would succeed when the League of Nations had failed? Had not the experience of the past shown that grandiose

27. Art. 99.

schemes based on the fragile foundations of cooperation in war and hopes for a better world thereafter would come to grief on the inevitable conflicts and rivalries following military victory?

It must, of course, be recognized that wartime coalitions have in the past tended to disintegrate once the cement of common interest in achieving military victory has disappeared. The coalition which was successful in bringing Napoleon to heel in 1815 survived the end of the war by only a few years before it fell apart on the rocks of conflicting national interests and different concepts of what constituted the peace of Europe and how that peace could best be maintained. Likewise, the Principal Allied and Associated Powers who fought World War I to a successful conclusion soon fell out over the way in which the problems of peace were to be dealt with and the use to be made of the League of Nations. Not only did the United States refuse to ratify the peace treaties and join the League, but the British and French governments, representing the two major members of the League of Nations, disagreed as to the role of the League in the postwar world and more particularly the use to be made of it in coping with postwar problems of peace and security.

In a sense, the United Nations was established under circumstances even less favorable than those which faced the League at its beginning. While there had been maximum cooperation between the United States and the United Kingdom in the conduct of the war, the cooperation of the Soviet Union had been minimal—only to the extent necessary to gain military victory. While the Soviet Union did agree to the establishment of a general international organization for the maintenance of peace and security, it never enthusiastically accepted the views of the Western powers with respect to the scope of the organization's activities, and during the negotiations leading to its establishment doggedly insisted upon preserving its own freedom of action and establishing its right to prevent any decisions from being made which were contrary to its own interests. Furthermore, as a Communist state ideologically committed and with national interests that did not necessarily correspond with those of the other major powers, the Soviet Union could not be expected to share fully with the Western democracies their views regarding policies and programs which the United Nations should pursue for the achievement of its objectives. Realistically, it must be admitted that at the time of the San Francisco Conference there was ample ground for skepticism regarding the likely success of the Organization.

Nevertheless, after the experience of World War II and the destruction that had taken place in Western Europe and especially in Eastern Europe, there was some real ground for believing that, contrary to the experience of the past and notwithstanding the divergencies of interests and values that were likely to reappear in accentuated form once peace had been established, the major victor nations had a sufficient interest in preventing a recurrence of what they had just experienced to cooperate to the extent necessary to make the system work. Furthermore, it should be emphasized that the authors of the Charter, while recognizing the difficulties ahead, believed that the organization that they were establishing, based on the principle of great power cooperation, was the only kind of organization that had any real chance of success. The League approach had failed, and there was no possibility or desire to return to the form of collective security that had once been tried. The method of informal concert of great powers without formal participation of the smaller states had failed to prevent World War I and gave no greater promise of success at the end of World War II; yet, it was recognized that the concert was based on a valid principle. So the drafters of the Charter came to the conclusion that a form of organization that followed the general lines of the League system, but incorporated the concert principle that peace could only be maintained so long as the major powers had an interest and were willing to cooperate in maintaining it, had at least a chance of success.

That the authors of the Charter were not completely certain of the success of their venture is evidenced by some of the safeguards that were introduced. Chief of these was the express reservation of the right of individual and collective self-defense in case of armed attack. This meant that in case the Security Council failed to discharge its responsibilities and, more particularly, in case a major power engaged in aggressive action, other members would have the admitted right to take necessary measures to deal with the situation, admittedly beyond the resources of the Organization itself. Thus, while the authors of the Charter may not have been certain that their new creation would achieve its purposes, they looked upon it as the most promising system of cooperation that could be devised for meeting the perils and challenges of the postwar world.

CHAPTER TWO

THE UNITED NATIONS AS AN EVOLVING POLITICAL SYSTEM

THE CHARTER PROVIDED THE LEGAL BASIS for an international organization devoted to important common purposes. It was necessary from the beginning that the Organization adapt to changing conditions and develop roles and activities which might not have been envisaged by its founders. To meet the needs of a rapidly changing world and to find a significant role in it, adaptation and growth were the alternatives to death and oblivion.

THE LEGAL BASIS AND NATURE OF THE ORGANIZATION

The United Nations Charter is at once an agreement between states and the constitution of a world organization. It is clear that the Organization rests on the consent of its members. It cannot be successfully argued, as was done in the case of the federal government under the Constitution of the United States, that it derives its authority from the people of the member states. While the Charter begins with words which suggest this—"We the peoples of the United Nations . . . have resolved to combine our efforts to accomplish these aims"—it then adopts the more conventional language of international agreements: "Accordingly, our respective Governments, through representatives assembled in the city of San Francisco . . . have agreed to the present Charter of the United

Nations and do hereby establish an international organization to be known as the United Nations." It is clear from this and the remaining provisions of the Charter that the United Nations is the creation of governments.

The Charter, furthermore, makes it quite clear that the organs of the United Nations do not have the kinds of functions and powers that are commonly vested in organs of government. These organs do not have legislative and taxing powers as those powers are generally understood. They cannot directly compel individuals to serve in United Nations armed forces. They deal generally with the governments of member states instead of with their citizens. And in dealing with these governments, they do not have, generally speaking, the kind of powers that the federal government of the United States has in dealing with the constituent states. Only exceptionally can they take substantive decisions that are binding upon members. The special authority vested in the Security Council when dealing with threats to and breaches of the peace stands out as an exceptional grant of power. The exercise of this authority requires the unanimity of the Council's permanent members, and in practice has been seldom used.

While the United Nations must be viewed not as a superstate but rather as a voluntary association of states for certain common purposes, it is something more than the sum of its parts. The United Nations as an international organization has a legal personality of its own. It has recognized responsibilities as defined by the Charter, which establishes organs and determines their composition, powers, and procedures. The decisions of these organs produce certain legal consequences for members of the Organization.

The International Court of Justice asserted in a very forthright manner the international personality of the United Nations in the advisory opinion which it gave April 11, 1949, on the question of *Reparation for Injuries Suffered in the Service of the United Nations*.[1] In giving its opinion on the rather technical point of whether the United Nations had the capacity to bring an international claim against a state, the Court observed that

1. ICJ *Reports,* 1949, pp. 174–220.

[T]he Organization was intended to exercise and enjoy, and is in fact exercising and enjoying, functions and rights which can only be explained on the basis of the possession of a large measure of international personality and the capacity to operate upon an international plane. It is at present the supreme type of international organization, and it could not carry out the intentions of its founders if it was devoid of international personality. It must be acknowledged that its Members, by entrusting certain functions to it, with the attendant duties and responsibilities, have clothed it with the competence required to enable those functions to be effectively discharged.[2]

That the United Nations has an international legal personality and the capacity for performing legal acts is shown by various provisions of the Charter and other international agreements and is illustrated amply from its own experience. Under the Headquarters Agreement with the United States,[3] the United Nations is recognized as having rights to property within the Headquarters district and to take such measures, including the exercise of police authority, as may be necessary to the performance of its functions. Under Article 100 of the Charter, each member undertakes to recognize the "exclusively international character" of the responsibilities of the Secretary-General and his staff. Under the Staff Regulations established by the General Assembly, members of the staff are required to take an oath of loyalty to the United Nations. Contracts of employment are between the United Nations and staff members. These examples amply demonstrate the possession by the United Nations of an international personality and the capacity for performing a wide variety of legal acts.

In addition, the organs of the United Nations are given the power to adopt decisions which produce a variety of legal consequences for members.[4] The General Assembly and the Councils can decide questions of their internal procedure. The General Assembly has certain powers of decision in the election of members of

2. ICJ *Reports*, 1949, p. 179.   3. UN Doc. A/427, Oct. 27, 1947, pp. 9–18.
4. See Jorge Castañeda, *Legal Effects of United Nations Resolutions* (New York: Columbia University Press, 1969).

other organs. Likewise, its decisions regarding the annual budget and the apportionment of expenditures have definite legal effects. The Assembly, on the recommendation of the Security Council, can take legally binding decisions on the admission of new members, and it may also, on like recommendation, suspend or expel a member. Security Council decisions regarding measures to be taken under Articles 41 and 42 to maintain or restore peace in case of a threat to or a breach of the peace are binding upon members, including those not members of the Council.

Within the range of their respective powers, the General Assembly, the Security Council, the Economic and Social Council, and the Trusteeship Council can make recommendations to members with respect to matters properly before them. While these recommendations may not be legally binding, they have important legal consequences for members and in any case are not to be lightly disregarded. Thus, for example, though the Security Council's recommendation of June 27, 1950, to members to give assistance to the Republic of Korea was not binding in a strictly legal sense, it did serve to validate measures taken by members in accordance with that recommendation. With respect to disputes submitted to it by agreement of the parties,[5] the International Court of Justice's decisions are binding on the parties. All these powers of decision or recommendation vested in the United Nations organs can be exercised by a majority or special majority vote. Only in the case of the Security Council is it possible for a particular state, by its sole negative vote, to prevent a decision from being taken, and this "right of veto" is limited to permanent members.

THE UNITED NATIONS AS A COMMITMENT TO COMMON VALUES

The United Nations is more than a legally constituted body with defined powers. While the legal structure of the Organization is important and determines the framework within which its activities

5. This may take the form of a special agreement relating to the particular dispute or of the acceptance of the Court's compulsory jurisdiction by a declaration under Article 36 of the Statute or other act.

may be carried on, by itself it does not provide the driving force, the dynamic quality, which has given to the Organization influence in world affairs. It is because of this dynamic quality, essentially moral in nature, that the United Nations must be viewed as being something more than just the sum of its parts. For this same reason, the United Nations must be viewed as something more than a bit of machinery, a "standing international conference," available to members, which under certain conditions they may use for the furtherance of particular national interests.[6]

The United Nations has importance in the world today as the expression of the common values and interests of the peoples and governments of the member states. Notwithstanding the cultural differences which separate the peoples of the world and which are accentuated by their political and ideological divisions, there are certain common purposes and principles which have wide popular appeal and which governments accept as being not only morally✓ good but also as conforming to the best interests of their respective peoples. These are purposes and principles that have been the result of an evolutionary development over many decades. They have found expression in the writings of philosophers and publicists, in the programs of private organizations, in the laws and policies of governments, and in international agreements. These purposes and principles, as they have developed and have been generally accepted, find expression in the Charter of the United Nations.

What are these common values? In the first place, the members of the United Nations are committed to the goals of peace and security. They accept the desirability of settling disputes peacefully and in conformity with the principles of justice and international law and of avoiding the use of force except for Charter purposes. No government would publicly disassociate itself from the principle, except in self-defense or in furtherance of UN purposes.[7] It is

6. On the dynamic quality of the United Nations, see A. H. Feller, *United Nations and World Community* (Boston: Little, Brown, 1952), and the Introduction to Secretary-General Hammarskjöld's Annual Report, 1960–61, in Wilder Foote (ed.), *Dag Hammarskjöld: Servant of Peace* (New York: Harper & Row, 1962), pp. 354–75.

7. These exceptions leave much room for disagreement, however, and can be used to justify the use of force under questionable circumstances, as for example, Soviet

significant that even the opposing parties in the cold war professed fervently their commitment to peace, protested that they had no aggressive intentions, and justified their armaments solely on the ground of self-defense.

Members of the United Nations recognize the evils of the colonial system under which subject peoples are not free to govern themselves and determine their own future. The Charter places on the Organization and its members the responsibility for assisting these people to achieve self-government or independence.[8] It furthermore asserts the principle of self-determination [9] which has been interpreted by the General Assembly in a resolution adopted by a vote of 89 to 0, with 9 abstentions, to mean that self-determination is a right, and that independence should never be delayed on the ground of lack of preparedness.[10] While there may be some difference of opinion as to how the principle of self-determination is to be interpreted, particularly with respect to timing, it is quite clear that members of the United Nations have been committed from the beginning to ending a system under which peoples have been subject to an alien rule not of their own choosing.

Members states are committed to the principle that the individual has certain basic rights which must be respected, and that the United Nations has an important responsibility in this respect. This recognition finds expression in numerous provisions of the Charter.[11] By the Universal Declaration of Human Rights [12] the General Assembly gave substance to the Charter commitment by defining the human rights for which respect was to be sought. While the attention of members has tended to be focused on one particular abuse of human rights—the denial of racial equality—this does not diminish the basic commitment of members to furthering respect for human rights in general.

---

military intervention in Hungary in 1956, Indian military occupation of Goa in 1961, and U.S. military intervention in Vietnam, especially since 1965.

8. Chaps. XI–XIII.   9. Art. 2, par. 2.

10. Declaration on Granting Independence to Colonial Countries and Peoples (General Assembly Res. 1514 [XV], Dec. 14, 1960).

11. Arts. 1(3), 13, 55, 56, and 76.

12. General Assembly Res. 217 (III), Dec. 10, 1948.

Members share a common commitment to improving the economic and social well-being of peoples.[13] This commitment has many facets, but the one that has received the most serious attention has been assistance in economic and social development. The numerous programs and declarations adopted by the General Assembly for assisting underdeveloped countries bear witness to the depth of this commitment.[14] The lack of progress thus far achieved in narrowing the gap between developed and underdeveloped countries testifies to the complexity of the problem and does not indicate any refusal to recognize the UN commitment.

As the institutional expression of these common values, the United Nations has the opportunity to exercise real influence. Not only in the discussions within the United Nations but also in negotiations and activities carried on outside, members find it necessary to show devotion to these values and to avoid being placed in the position of appearing to violate or disregard them openly.

Of course it must be admitted that the common values which the Charter sets forth are stated in very general terms and that their generality permits much latitude in their interpretation. Furthermore, it must also be granted that the organs of the United Nations, generally speaking, do not have the authority to interpret and apply these principles in any conclusive manner and that, as a result, members are left free to decide not only how these purposes and principles are to be interpreted but also how serious an effort is to be made to apply them. Notwithstanding, there is reason to believe that members of the United Nations have been substantially influenced in their policies and actions by the purposes and principles set forth in the Charter and by the interpretations given them by the organs of the United Nations.

But it is not alone, or primarily, as a system of moral restraints on members that the purposes and principles of the Charter have

13. See particularly Arts. 1(3) and 55.

14. For instance, Expanded Programme of Technical Assistance and Special Fund, now combined in United Nations Development Programme (UNDP), United Nations Conference on Trade and Development, United Nations Industrial Development Organization, and An International Development Strategy for the Second United Nations Development Decade (General Assembly Res. 2626 [XXV], Oct. 24, 1970).

helped to make the United Nations a significant force in international relations. In addition, these purposes and principles have provided the conceptual framework within which United Nations discussions have taken place and have defined the ends toward which United Nations activity has been directed. While delegates may seek to exploit technicalities to their advantage, they do not find it advisable to do so in open disregard of basic principles. More often, these principles and purposes set the tone and direction of discussion and the limits within which an accommodation of national attitudes and interests in terms of a common policy or program becomes possible.

When we think of the United Nations as an institution for dealing constructively with the problems of the modern world we must, therefore, direct our attention to those provisions of the Charter which define the common ends for which members have agreed to cooperate and the principles which they have accepted as guides to their conduct. Without these the machinery of the United Nations would simply provide additional diplomatic tools; with them, the mechanism acquires driving power and direction. Primarily because of these provisions of the Charter, the United Nations has been able to develop a role of vital importance as the expression of the will of a nascent world community.

DEVELOPMENT OF THE UNITED NATIONS

While the provisions of the Charter setting forth purposes and principles define the conceptual framework and direction of world cooperation, and other provisions prescribe the machinery and methods to be used, neither are self-operative. Both require interpretation, adaptation, and even change to meet new situations as they arise and to meet old situations more effectively. The United Nations was conceived to be a permanent international organization, and since it was called upon to function in a highly dynamic and changing world, to be permanent it needed to be adaptable. The Charter consequently could not be thought of as rigid and unchangeable; it must have flexibility and adaptability. This has been achieved by amendment and by interpretation and adaptation.[15]

Amendment

While the Charter provides for formal amendment, this has not been an important method of Charter development and change. The Charter prescribes two methods by which amendments may be proposed: by the vote of two-thirds of the members of the General Assembly, or by two-thirds vote of a general conference called by vote of the General Assembly and the Security Council.[16] The proposed amendment becomes effective when ratified, in accordance with their constitutional procedures, by two-thirds of the members of the Organization, including the permanent members of the Security Council.

This procedure makes it possible for any permanent member of the Security Council to prevent a proposed amendment from entering into force. On the other hand, any other member of the Organization may find itself bound by an amendment which it has refused to ratify. This would appear to constitute a violation of the principle of sovereign equality. It was in part to ease the situation of those members who, on the one hand, might be frustrated by the failure of a proposed amendment which they favored to become effective because of a veto, or, on the other hand, might find themselves in the position of having to accept an objectionable amendment, that the San Francisco Conference adopted a statement approving the right of withdrawal from the Organization.[17]

The amendment procedure has been used sparingly, and only when the Charter provision in question is so specific as to exclude

15. On general subject of Charter development, see Ruth B. Russell, "Changing Patterns of Constitutional Development," *International Organization,* XIX (1965), 410–25.

16. The vote required in the Security Council is the affirmative vote of any nine, originally seven, members. In the General Assembly, a two-thirds vote is required, except that when the question of holding such a conference was automatically placed on the agenda of the General Assembly at its tenth session, a majority was sufficient.

17. See below, p. 44.

any possibility of achieving the desired result by interpretation. Thus, in 1963 the General Assembly approved proposed amendments to Articles 23, 27, and 61 which increased the number of elected members of the Security Council from six to ten, the number of affirmative votes required for a decision of the Council from seven to nine, and the number of members of the Economic and Social Council from eighteen to twenty-seven. The proposed amendments entered into force August 31, 1965. Later, on December 20, 1971, the Assembly approved an amendment further expanding the membership of ECOSOC to fifty-four. In 1965 the General Assembly proposed an amendment to Article 109 increasing the number of affirmative votes required for a Security Council decision on the calling of a review conference to conform to the changed requirement of Article 27. This amendment entered into force on June 12, 1968.

While the question of holding a general conference to review the Charter was placed on the agenda of the tenth session of the General Assembly in 1955, as required by Article 109 of the Charter, there was no substantial support at that time for holding such a conference. Members of the Organization have been reluctant to undertake a general revision of the Charter for fear that issues will be raised upon which agreement will not be possible, with the result that the very future of the Organization will be endangered.

Interpretation and Adaptation

Though interpretation has been the principal method by which the Charter has been adapted to new conditions, there is no specific provision for it in the Charter itself. A number of proposals were made at San Francisco for giving the International Court of Justice or the General Assembly special powers in this connection; none of them was adopted. Instead, a statement was approved by the Conference [18] which accepted the view that each organ would interpret such parts of the Charter as applied to its own functions and that members would be free to use the various methods available to

18. UNCIO, *Documents,* XIII, pp. 709–10. Text is given in Leland M. Goodrich, Edvard Hambro, and Anne P. Simons, *Charter of the United Nations: Commentary and Documents* (3d rev. ed.; New York: Columbia University Press, 1969), p. 14.

them to obtain authoritative interpretations of Charter provisions of special concern to them. Thus, in effect, the Conference left the organs and members of the Organization free to determine for themselves and by such procedures as they might choose the meaning of Charter provisions. The statement concluded with these words:

> It is to be understood, of course, that if an interpretation made by any organ of the Organization or by a committee of jurists is not generally accepted it will be without binding force. In such circumstances, or in cases where it is desired to establish an authoritative interpretation as a precedent for the future, it may be necessary to embody the interpretation in an amendment to the Charter.

This highly decentralized system of Charter interpretation runs counter to widely accepted ideas regarding the requirements of a legal order. The principle of judicial review according to which the courts have a special role in constitutional interpretation is accepted in the United States. This principle, however, is not generally accepted in other countries, and there was little sentiment at San Francisco for giving the Court authority to pass on all questions of Charter interpretation. In fact, even under the United States Constitution, the legislative and executive departments have important responsibilities for constitutional interpretation so far as their own powers and procedures are concerned, and the power of judicial review is exercised only with respect to those questions that can properly be brought before the courts in actual litigation.

Under the Charter there is one possibility of using the Court for Charter interpretation that does not exist under the American constitutional system. The General Assembly, the Security Council, and other organs of the United Nations and the specialized agencies, when authorized by the Assembly, may ask the Court to give advisory opinions on legal questions, including questions of Charter interpretation. This has been done in a number of cases.[19]

19. These include *Conditions of Admission of a State to Membership in the United Nations* (1948); *Reparations for Injuries Suffered in the Service of the United Nations* (1949); *Competence of the General Assembly in the Admission of a State* (1950); *International Status of*

Nevertheless, the Court through its advisory function has played a relatively minor role in the interpretation of the Charter compared with the political organs and the member states themselves.

The responsibility for interpreting the Charter and adapting it to specific situations is shared widely with very limited possibility of a single authoritative interpretation. Furthermore, since the responsibility for interpretation is vested in organs and members alike, the process is more likely to be political than judicial. This means that the view taken of the meaning of the Charter in any particular situation is more often than not the result of a bargaining process or an assertion of voting strength than an attempt to apply Charter provisions by a process of reasoning based on accepted principles of interpretation. Decisions tend to reflect the common interests of members in achieving certain results. Considering that the perceived interests of members change and that the voting alignments of members vary according to the issues presented, this politicization of the interpretation process inevitably produces inconsistencies and confusion in the way the Charter is interpreted and applied.[20]

Unfortunately, perhaps, especially from the point of view of one who attaches importance to the rule of law, important changes in the Charter system have occurred as the result of failure to implement certain provisions or the adoption of a practice that can more easily be justified as informal amendment than as reasonable Charter interpretation.

There can be no question that the United Nations has been given a different character from what was originally intended as the result of the failure or refusal of members and organs to implement certain provisions of the Charter. The most striking example of this has been the failure to conclude the special agreements under

---

South West Africa (1950); Effect of Awards of Compensation made by the United Nations Administrative Tribunal (1954); Certain Expenses of the United Nations (Article 17, paragraph 2 of the Charter) (1962); and Legal Consequences for States of the Continued Presence of South Africa in Namibia (South West Africa), Notwithstanding Security Council Resolution 276 (1970), (1971).

20. On interpretation, see Goodrich, Hambro, and Simons, pp. 12–16.

Article 43 by which members would undertake to place armed forces and facilities at the disposal of the Security Council. As a consequence, the Security Council has not had at its disposal the military forces which it needs to fully exercise its powers to maintain or restore international peace and security. However, it must be admitted that failure to conclude the agreements is not the real cause of the Council's weakness but rather another result of the primary cause, namely, the inability of the permanent members to agree. Another example of nonapplication was the bypassing of the Charter provision requiring that trust agreements be concluded in the first instance between "the states directly concerned." [21]

There are a number of instances where it is somewhat uncertain whether the result has been achieved by interpretation or informal amendment. For example, Article 27 (paragraph 3) provides that nonprocedural decisions in the Security Council shall be taken by the affirmative vote of seven members "including the concurring votes of the permanent members." On the face of it, this phrase would seem to require the affirmative votes of all permanent members, and to exclude the possibility of an abstention being interpreted as other than the absence of concurrence. This interpretation was accepted by the representatives of the four Sponsoring Powers and France at San Francisco.[22] And yet in practice an abstention has not been treated as constituting a veto. Again, the Charter provides in Article 23 that the nonpermanent members of the Council shall be elected by the General Assembly, ". . . due regard being specially paid, in the first instance, to the contribution of Members of the United Nations to the maintenance of international peace and security and to the other purposes of the Organization, and also to equitable geographical distribution." Some would regard the primary attention that is given to equitable geographic distribution as in fact amending this particular provision of the Charter.[23]

21. Art. 79.

22. *Foreign Relations of the United States, 1945* (Washington: Government Printing Office, 1967), I, 1258–60.

23. See General Assembly Res. 1991 (XVIII), Dec. 17, 1963.

PRINCIPLES OF CHARTER INTERPRETATION

In the interpretation of the Charter and the application of its provisions in dealing with particular questions, the members of the
United Nations have tended to adopt one of two competing principles of interpretation, depending to a large extent upon which better serves their particular purposes: restrictive interpretation and
liberal interpretation. They relate to the extent to which the
Charter is interpreted as giving powers to the United Nations and
its organs. In American constitutional law they have their counter-
parts in the doctrine emphasizing the powers reserved to the states,
and that emphasizing the powers vested in the national government. In fact, it has been suggested that Chief Justice Marshall's
famous dictum in the case of *McCulloch vs. Maryland,*

> Let the end be legitimate, let it be within the scope of the Con-
> stitution, and all means that are appropriate, that are plainly
> adapted to that end, and are not prohibited are constitutional,

provides a reasonable standard for determining the powers of
United Nations organs.[24]

From the doctrinal point of view, these two principles of Charter
interpretation reflect differences with respect to the significance to
be attached to the fact that the Charter is the constitution of an international organization in addition to being a treaty between
states. Those who espouse the principle of restrictive interpretation
are more inclined to view the Charter as a treaty—to be interpreted
in accordance with the recognized principles of treaty interpretation.[25] On the other hand, those who adopt the liberal interpretation tend to emphasize the special character of the Charter as a
constitution, and seek to so interpret the detailed provisions of the
Charter as to make the Organization effective in achieving its declared purposes.

The principle of liberal interpretation covers a variety of specific

24. Benjamin V. Cohen, *The United Nations: Constitutional Development, Growth, and
Possibilities* (Cambridge: Harvard University Press, 1961), p. 6.

25. See, for example, Gregory I. Tunkin, "The Legal Nature of the United Nations," in Academie de Droit International, *Recueil des Cours,* CXIX (1966), 18–28.

modes of reasoning used to justify proposed courses of action by the organs of the United Nations. In its opinion on the capacity of the United Nations to bring a claim for damages suffered by an official of the Organization, the International Court of Justice stated:

> [T]he Organization must be deemed to have those powers which, though not expressly provided in the Charter, are conferred upon it by necessary implication as being essential to the performance of its duties.[26]

In this opinion, accepted by the General Assembly, the emphasis was not so much upon the legitimacy of the purpose as upon the ability of the Organization to do those things necessary to the performance of functions expressly given to it by the Charter.

In other instances, reliance has been placed mainly upon the declared purposes of the Organization to justify proposed measures. Thus, the preamble to the Uniting for Peace resolution,[27] after repeating the first two paragraphs of Article 1 of the Charter and affirming the primary responsibility of the Security Council for the maintenance of international peace and security, continues with this paragraph:

> Conscious that the failure of the Security Council to discharge its responsibilities on behalf of the Member States, particularly those responsibilities referred to in the two preceding paragraphs, does not relieve Member States of their obligations or the United Nations of its responsibility under the Charter to maintain international peace and security.

In the *Certain Expenses* case, the International Court expressed the view that

> [W]hen the Organization takes action which warrants the assertion that it was appropriate for the fulfillment of one of the stated purposes of the United Nations, the presumption is that such action is not "ultra vires" the Organization.[28]

26. *Reparations for Injuries Suffered in the Service of the United Nations, Advisory Opinion: ICJ Reports,* 1949, p. 182.

27. General Assembly Res. 377 (V), Nov. 3, 1950.

28. ICJ *Reports,* 1962, p. 168.

In like manner, the purposes of the Organization have been relied on to justify General Assembly resolutions directed against apartheid in the Republic of South Africa and the violation of human rights in other countries. By a somewhat similar mode of reasoning, the International Court of Justice in its advisory opinion of June 21, 1971, held that to deny to the General Assembly the power to terminate the South African mandate amounted "to a complete denial of the remedies available against fundamental breaches of an international undertaking," [29] even though under the Charter the Assembly's power is declared to be that of recommendation and not binding decision.

Those who have adopted the principle of liberal interpretation to justify the assumption of challenged powers by United Nations organs naturally take a restrictive view of those Charter provisions which purport to limit the activities of these organs. The principle of restrictive interpretation is generally employed by those who seek to keep the activities of the Organization within relatively narrow limits, or who are anxious to maintain what they consider to be the original negotiated relationship between the functions and powers of the principal organs. On the question of the respective responsibilities and powers of the General Assembly and the Security Council for the maintenance of international peace and security, the Soviet Union and some other members have quite consistently adopted the restrictive principle and have argued that failure of the Security Council to take a decision does not justify using the General Assembly as an alternative means of achieving the purpose set forth in Article 1, paragraph 1, of the Charter. In his dissenting opinion in the *Certain Expenses* case, Judge Winiarski of Poland stated the reasoning behind this position:

> The Charter has set forth the purposes of the United Nations in very wide, and for that reason too indefinite, terms. But . . . it does not follow, far from it, that the Organization is entitled to seek to achieve those purposes by no matter what means. The fact that an organ of the United Nations is seeking to achieve one of those purposes does not suffice to render its

29. ICJ *Reports,* 1971, p. 49.

action lawful. The Charter, a multilateral treaty which was the result of prolonged and laborious negotiations, carefully created organs and determined their competence and means of action.

The intention of those who drafted it was clearly to abandon the possibility of useful action rather than to sacrifice the balance of carefully established fields of competence, as can be seen, for example, in the case of voting in the Security Council. It is only by such procedures, which were clearly defined, that the United Nations can seek to achieve its purposes.[30]

Generally speaking, the principal organs of the United Nations, with the exception of the Security Council where the requirement of concurrence of the permanent members has assured a more cautious approach, have adopted the liberal principle in interpreting their powers under the Charter. This has resulted in the Organization's taking on a different character in many respects than a reading of the Charter would indicate. But the activity of the Organization, and particularly that of the General Assembly, can be misleading as regards results achieved. Lacking the power that a government normally possesses to implement its decisions, the United Nations runs the risk that its pretentions will far exceed its capacity. Being dependent upon its members for the implementation of its decisions and programs, the development of the responsibilities and decision-making powers of its organs cannot safely go much beyond the limits of the general consensus. This means that a development by liberal interpretation of the Charter that is not generally accepted is likely to have little effectiveness in reality.[31]

30. ICJ *Reports*, 1962, p. 230.

31. How general the acceptance must be for a resolution of the General Assembly to constitute an authoritative interpretation of the Charter is discussed persuasively by Oscar Schachter in "The Relation of Law, Politics and Action in the United Nations," Academie de Droit International, *Recueil des Cours*, CIX (1963), 186.

CHAPTER THREE

MEMBERSHIP AND REPRESENTATION

THE MEMBERSHIP OF THE UNITED NATIONS has been a decisive factor in determining its role in international affairs and its effectiveness in achieving its declared purposes. It is not surprising, therefore, that questions of membership have received a great deal of attention during the years of the Organization's existence. Nor is it perhaps surprising that these questions have been deeply influenced by political considerations, particularly by the calculations and strategies of the major powers who are not insensitive to the pressures mobilized by states less powerful in military means and less privileged in worldly goods.

CONDITIONS OF MEMBERSHIP

The Charter follows the example of the League Covenant in making certain states original members of the United Nations and providing that others may be admitted to membership by decision of the Organization if they satisfy certain conditions.[1] The Charter thus limits membership on a qualitative basis to those states that provide some evidence of capacity, worthy conduct, and intention.

Like the League, the United Nations had its beginnings in a military coalition. At the Yalta Conference in 1945 the heads of gov-

---

1. See Art. 1 of the Covenant, and Art. 4 of the Charter.

ernment of the United Kingdom, United States, and Soviet Union agreed that only states which by March 1 had declared war against one of the major Axis powers would be invited to attend the Conference to draft the Charter. The San Francisco Conference subsequently decided, after an open clash between the Soviet Union and the United States, to permit Argentina, Denmark, and the two Soviet Republics of Byelorussia and the Ukraine to take part in the Conference. The states participating in the work of the Conference, by signing the Charter and subsequently ratifying it, became original members of the United Nations.[2]

As a peace organization, the United Nations had as its principal purpose the maintenance of international peace and security on the basis of the new order resulting from the victory of the Allied powers. Consequently, members were expected to be willing to accept—and join in guaranteeing against change by force—the new postwar order, an important part of which would consist of the arrangements to be decided upon by the principal victor nations.[3] A primary duty of membership would thus be to participate loyally in carrying out such measures as might be found necessary by the Security Council for the maintenance or restoration of international peace and security on this basis. No state could fully perform this duty, it was argued, unless it was prepared to accept the specific obligations of the Charter, and unless its record was such as to justify the belief that it not only subscribed to Charter purposes but was prepared in fact to discharge in full the obligations of membership. There was also wide support at San Francisco for the view that a state whose government gave support to the Axis powers, even though not becoming an "enemy" of any Charter signatory, was not qualified initially for admission to membership.

In the course of preliminary discussions in the United States Department of State there had been considerable support for the idea of universality. This idea also received wide support at San Francisco, particularly from some of the Latin American republics.

2. Poland was not represented at the Conference because of inability of the Big Three to agree on the Polish government to be recognized, but subsequently signed the Charter and became an original member.

3. See Art. 107 of the Charter.

There were certain practical difficulties, however, in the way of achieving this objective immediately, as well as serious objections to the principle. How, for example, could a state which did not at the time desire to participate or which because of war conditions had no effective or generally recognized government be made a fully participating member of the new organization? What authority did the states represented at San Francisco have to declare other states members of the proposed organization against their will or in the absence of an explicit statement of their desires? Faced with practical difficulties of this kind, the exponents of universality limited their efforts to defining the conditions of membership in such a way as to facilitate rather than delay the achievement of the goal.

There was general agreement that membership in the proposed organization should be limited to states, though there was an inclination not to insist on the requirement of full independence. The Covenant had used the phrase "any fully self-governing State, Dominion or Colony," [4] obviously to cover such categories as dominions of the British Commonwealth and colonies possessing a substantial measure of self-government, such as India. It was taken for granted at the time the Charter was being written that India and the Philippines would be original members, even though they were not fully independent at the time, and at the Yalta Conference it had been agreed that at least two of the Soviet republics—certainly not independent—would be accepted as original members. Thus, the principle that states alone would be members of the Organization was never applied in any strict sense.

The four governments which were parties to the Moscow Declaration of October 1943 and which were represented in the Dumbarton Oaks Conversations of August–October 1944 were in agreement that membership in the Organization should be limited to "peace-loving" states. This term had overtones derived from war experience and thinking. States that were engaged in the war on the Axis side or that gave support to or showed sympathy with the Axis cause were clearly not peace-loving, and required reformation before they could qualify for membership. Since there could be

4. Art. 1, par. 2.

no satisfactory objective test of the peace-loving quality other than war participation—which could not be applied for long—and since each state applying for membership would so declare itself, this condition of membership was open to highly subjective interpretation and application. At San Francisco there was wide insistence on some additional test more specific and objective. Thus, the Dumbarton Oaks text, which made this the only qualification, was revised to read:

> Membership in the United Nations is open to all other peace-loving states which accept the obligations contained in the present Charter and, in the judgment of the Organization, are able and willing to carry out these obligations.[5]

It is to be noted that this phraseology expressly reserved to the Organization the right to determine whether in its judgment—and that of course meant the judgment of the responsible organs—the applicant was "able and willing" to carry out the obligations contained in the Charter. Furthermore, the technical committee dealing with the matter, in its report accepted by the Conference, stated that its failure to recommend various elements that should be taken into account in making this decision did not imply that "in passing upon the admission of a new member, considerations of all kinds cannot be brought into account." [6]

In the Department of State consideration of United States proposals as well as in the discussion at Dumbarton Oaks there appears to have been general agreement that new members should not be admitted without the consent of the major powers. This was a departure from the provisions of the League Covenant which provided for the admission of new members by two-thirds vote of the Assembly alone.[7] Since the primary purpose of the proposed organization was to maintain international peace and security, it was reasoned that the major powers, with special responsibilities in this area, should also have a part in determining whether applicants for membership were able and willing to discharge their responsibilities. Furthermore, particular governments had special reasons to insist on the rule of concurrence. The Department of State felt

5. Art. 4, par. 1.   6. UNCIO, *Documents*, VII, p. 326.   7. Art. 1, par. 2.

that the United States should have a veto to head off any attempt to
give separate membership to the Soviet Republics. At San Francisco it was agreed that the Security Council should first consider
an application and decide whether or not to recommend the applicant for admission. It was clearly understood that the General Assembly need not follow the recommendation, but it was equally well
understood that admission could not take place without a favorable
recommendation. Nor was there any real doubt that a decision to
recommend was a decision on a non-procedural question requiring the concurrence of the permanent members.

In addition to the admission of new members, the San Francisco
Conference considered the questions of withdrawal, suspension,
and expulsion. During the drafting of the League Covenant, President Wilson had reluctantly come to the conclusion that it was necessary to have a provision permitting withdrawal in order to get
Senate approval. However, the position of the United States government was that no such provision should be introduced into the
Charter, although the right of withdrawal was to be assumed.
In the end, largely to satisfy those states which were not at all
happy over certain provisions of the Charter that the Sponsoring
Governments insisted must be accepted, notably the provisions
regarding Security Council voting procedure, a declaration was
approved by the Conference which admitted the right of withdrawal.[8]

The discussions at San Francisco on suspension and expulsion
reemphasized the importance that was attached to the peace and
security function of the Organization. Although some states
argued strongly against any provision for expulsion on the ground
that universality should be the goal and that a recalcitrant state
could better be controlled as a member than as a nonmember, the
Conference finally decided to make provision for expulsion as well
as suspension. The Soviet Union was particularly insistent that a
member who persistently violated the principles of the Charter

8. UNCIO, *Documents,* I, 616–17. Indonesia is the only state to have exercised the
right of withdrawal. The government informed the Secretary-General of its decision to withdraw on January 20, 1965. On September 19, 1966 the government informed the Secretary-General that it wished to resume full participation. On September 28 the General Assembly invited the Indonesian delegation to take its seats.

should be treated as "a cancerous growth" and removed from the Organization. Article 6 does not state explicitly that the reference is to the principles set forth in Article 2, but the use of the capitalized form ("Principles") supports this interpretation.

MEMBERSHIP AND THE COLD WAR

From the time that the Security Council's Committee on the Admission of New Members first met at the end of July 1946, until December 1955, when the membership deadlock was finally broken, discussions and decisions with respect to the admission of new members were substantially affected by the purposes and strategies of the principal participants in the cold war. Under the leadership of the United States, the non-Communist members of the United Nations, particularly those most closely associated with that country in efforts to contain communism, were generally inclined to insist on the strict fulfillment by applicants of membership qualifications under the Charter in the context of Western non-Communist values.

The Soviet Union, on the other hand, was generally inclined to use the veto as a means of obtaining the admission of its candidates, and interpreted Charter terms and the terms of other pertinent international agreements in such a way as to disqualify most applicants supported by the West. The increased political role of the General Assembly and the importance attached to the results of General Assembly voting led the foremost protagonists in the cold war increasingly to be influenced by the likely effect on Assembly voting of the admission of particular states. It is not surprising, then, that up to 1955 when the Tenth General Assembly met, the great majority of states applying for admission had been turned down. Only those states that were thought to be "neutral," uncommitted to one side or the other, were able to escape the consequences of either the Soviet veto or the withholding of Western majority support.[9]

9. During the period 1946 to 1955, out of twenty-eight applicants, only nine were favorably recommended by the Security Council and admitted to membership by the General Assembly.

The membership deadlock became a source of growing concern to members of the United Nations in the years following 1950, particularly to those who believed that the effectiveness of the Organization would be increased by greater progress toward universality. The efforts to break the deadlock fell roughly into two categories: legal and political. The principal legal arguments were (1) that the General Assembly had the power to admit new members in the absence of a favorable Security Council recommendation (denied by the Court in an advisory opinion), and (2) that members of the Security Council could only invoke failure to satisfy the specific conditions listed in Article 4 in opposing applications for membership. The Soviet Union, while admitting that Italy and Finland satisfied the qualifications laid down in Article 4, paragraph 1, made its support conditional on the willingness of the Western members to accept Soviet-supported applicants. Though the argument that the Soviet action was in violation of the Charter was supported by the majority of the International Court of Justice in an opinion given at the request of the General Assembly,[10] the Soviet Union continued to maintain its position, arguing that it was political and not a legal question.

Efforts to break the deadlock by political means centered on proposals that the permanent members of the Security Council reconsider their positions, that they consult with a view to reaching agreement on the admission of certain states, or that they agree to refrain from the use of the veto on membership questions. There was no progress toward a political solution until after the death of Stalin. During the Eighth Assembly it was clear that members of the Assembly were becoming restless over failure to move toward a more inclusive membership for the United Nations and that opposition to the Soviet package proposal was weakening. The Assembly appointed a committee of good offices

> to consult with members of the Security Council with the object of exploring the possibilities of reaching an understanding

10. Admission of a State to the United Nations (Charter, Art. 4); Advisory Opinion: ICJ *Reports,* 1948, p. 57.

which would facilitate the admission of new Members in accordance with Article 4 of the Charter.[11]

By the time the tenth session of the Assembly convened in September 1955, the Geneva Conference of heads of governments had met and the tensions of the cold war seemed to be lessened. Opposition to the Soviet package proposal weakened. The Committee of Good Offices reported encouragingly that there were indications that the positions of the permanent members of the Security Council were not immutable. On December 8, 1955, the Assembly by a vote of 52 to 2 with 5 abstentions requested the Security Council "to consider, in the light of the general opinion in favor of the widest possible membership of the United Nations, the pending applications for membership of all those eighteen countries about which no problem of unification arises." [12]

In the Security Council the full implementation of this request was blocked by the Chinese veto of the Mongolian People's Republic; but a new compromise, suggested by the Soviet Union, that excluded Mongolia and Japan from the package was accepted, and on December 14, sixteen new members were admitted by the General Assembly. Thus, the long deadlock was broken by a political arrangement which some members found difficult to harmonize with the specific provisions of Article 4 of the Charter. However, the overwhelming sentiment of the Assembly was favorable since it brought the United Nations substantially nearer to the universality of membership so widely accepted as a desirable goal.

THE MEMBERSHIP EXPLOSION

The breaking of the deadlock in 1955 marked the beginning of a dramatic increase in the membership of the Organization. Between 1956 and 1959 seven new members were admitted. In 1960, pri-

11. General Assembly Res. 718 (VIII), Oct. 23, 1953.

12. General Assembly Res. 918 (X). The eighteen countries were Albania, Mongolian People's Republic, Hungary, Romania, Bulgaria, Jordan, Ireland, Portugal, Italy, Austria, Finland, Ceylon, Nepal, Libya, Cambodia, Japan, Laos, and Spain.

marily as a result of the dissolution of France's African colonial empire, seventeen new members were admitted. Between 1961 and 1971 an additional thirty-two states, former colonies and protectorates that had acquired their full independence, became members of the United Nations.[13] The Organization had started with fifty-one members in 1945. By 1959 total membership had reached eighty-three. By 1972 there were one hundred and thirty-two members, with every prospect of further increase. The admission of the Federal Republic of Germany and the German Democratic Republic, along with the Commonwealth of the Bahamas, in 1973 brought the total to 135.

The new members admitted after 1955 differed in important respects from the states that had formed the bulk of the membership up to that time. Up to 1956, a majority of United Nations members were long-established states with developed political, economic, and social systems, had substantial populations, and were Western in their general orientation. A majority took an anti-Communist position on cold war issues and relatively few professed to be uncommitted. The 1955 package deal marked the beginning of a change. Four of the sixteen states admitted that year were Communist countries and six were Asian or African states. Since 1955, however, change has become even more pronounced. Fifty of the fifty-six new members of the United Nations are African or Asian states. Most have populations of less than 5 million and many under 1 million. With very few exceptions they are new states with little experience in discharging the responsibilities that come with independence. Characteristically, they have underdeveloped economies which their leaders are anxious to modernize. For this

13. The following states became members between 1956 and 1971: *1956:* Japan, Morocco, Sudan, Tunisia; *1957:* Ghana, Malaya; *1958:* Guinea; *1960:* Cameroon, Central African Republic, Chad, Congo (Brazzaville), Congo (Democratic Republic of the), Cyprus, Dahomey, Gabon, Ivory Coast, Madagascar, Mali, Niger, Nigeria, Senegal, Somalia, Togo, Upper Volta; *1961:* Mauritania, Mongolia, Sierra Leone, Tanzania; *1962:* Algeria, Burundi, Jamaica, Rwanda, Trinidad and Tobago, Uganda; *1963:* Kenya, Kuwait; *1964:* Malawi, Malta, Zambia; *1965:* Gambia, Maldive Islands, Singapore; *1966:* Barbados, Botswana, Guyana, Lesotho; *1968:* People's Republic of Southern Yemen, Mauritius, Swaziland, Equatorial Guinea; *1970:* Fiji, *1971:* Bhutan, Bahrain, Oman, Qatar, United Arab Emirate.

purpose they require substantial external financial assistance. Consequently, they are fervent advocates of the expansion of United Nations development and financial aid programs.

The expansion of membership since 1955 has taken place without extensive debate and with few objections being raised or critical questions asked. Leaders of both Eastern and Western blocs have sought to win the good will and support of new states by rapidly welcoming them to United Nations membership. Such discussions as have occurred on the admission of these states have not revealed any consistent attempt to judge whether these states meet the requirements of Article 4, paragraph 1 of the Charter. There has been little effort to determine whether an applicant is "able and willing" to carry out the obligations of the Charter. Statements of intention contained in the applications for membership have been accepted at their face value without any consistent attempt to apply Charter standards on the basis of available evidence.

Of late, the situation resulting from the admission of so many small newly independent states of limited resources and the prospect of more to follow has become a matter of growing concern. The prospect that remaining colonial territories, mostly small and insular, might gain independence and apply for admission has led to consideration of the criteria for United Nations membership that should be enforced, and of feasible arrangements by which miniscule states might enjoy the benefits of membership without all the rights and obligations.[14] Fears have been expressed that the admission of ministates to the United Nations will strain the physical and financial resources of the Organization, overload the already heavy agenda of its principal organs, and further reduce the credibility and influence of General Assembly resolutions. Furthermore, the burdens of membership are often beyond what these small new states can carry. This applies both to the financial costs and the need of making available for UN service and participation in various United Nations meetings personnel that is needed for

14. See Patricia W. Blair, "The Ministate Dilemma," *Occasional Paper Series* No. 6 (New York: Carnegie Endowment for International Peace, 1967); and Jacques Rapaport et al., *Small States and Territories: Status and Problems.* A UNITAR Study (New York: Arno Press, 1971).

domestic purposes. Many of the alleged benefits of membership can in any case be achieved through participation in the work of the specialized agencies, either through membership or by arrangements that many of the agencies provide for some special relationship.

Those supporting the ministates' right to membership in the United Nations argue that these fears are exaggerated. They believe that the interests of populous and wealthy states are protected by the basic fact that the General Assembly can make recommendations only rather than make decisions that are legally binding on governments. Furthermore, the influence of these states in General Assembly decision-making is not measured by the votes they possess. Proponents emphasize that ministates require services which the United Nations is best equipped to provide. Membership in the United Nations is a mark of sovereignty which statesmen in small countries frequently regard as an essential sign of independence. Access to United Nations organs provides small states with an unequalled opportunity to draw attention to their existence and needs. Through the United Nations, ministates can secure a wide range of essential technical assistance. In addition, the United Nations can give the statesmen of small countries the political experience they need to conduct their international relations effectively.

In 1970 the problem was referred by the Security Council to a committee of experts for study. Under consideration are new methods of relating ministates to the United Nations that will permit them to get the benefits that the Organization can bestow without the negative consequences of full membership.[15] Many formulas have been suggested for providing ministates with some measure of participation in the work of the United Nations. A strengthened observer status might be created. Several ministates might as a group be granted membership, having the privileges and duties of one member. A ministate might be granted "limited participation" status as an "associate member," with the right to take part in the work of some specified organs, or for a defined set

15. See "Report of the Secretary-General on the Work of the Organization, 16 June 1969–15 June 1970" (General Assembly, *Official Records,* 25th Sess., Suppl. 1), pp. 77–78.

of agenda items. These limited forms of participation would require smaller financial contributions by ministates than the minimum currently assessed against members. It has also been suggested that a section might be established in the Secretariat which would have the responsibility of providing services of various kinds to small independent states that do not wish to take on the responsibilities of membership.[16]

THE QUESTION OF REPRESENTATION

Distinct from the question of the admission of new members is that of determining the representation of states that are already members. Insofar as effective participation in the United Nations is concerned, the decision of an organ denying the right of a delegation to represent a member state may have the same practical consequences as a decision not to admit the state to membership. For example, from 1950 to 1971, the Chinese people who inhabited mainland China and who were under the effective control of the Peking government were just as effectively debarred from any participation through their representatives in the United Nations as if the Republic of China had not been a member, unless of course one accepted the thesis that the Nationalist government on Taiwan really represented these people.

Normally, the question of representation presents no particular difficulties since the credentials of the representative appointed by the government of the member state are usually accepted by each organ without question. When, however, there are two authorities which claim to be the government of a state, a choice must be made. This problem arose at the time of the San Francisco Conference when Poland, though a signatory of the Declaration by United Nations of January 1, 1942, was not invited to participate in the San Francisco Conference called to draft the Charter because the Sponsoring Governments were unable to agree on the government to be recognized. After the Conference had adjourned, agreement was

16. See Rapaport et al., pp. 177–81.

reached, however, and through the action of the recognized government Poland became an original member by signature and ratification of the Charter.

The question did not arise in the United Nations in acute form until November 1949 when in a cablegram to the President of the General Assembly the Foreign Minister of the government of the People's Republic of China, the Communist regime which had succeeded in driving the Nationalist government from the mainland, stated that his government repudiated the legal status of the delegation headed by T. F. Tsiang, appointed by the Nationalist Government on Taiwan, and held that it did not represent the Republic of China and had no right to speak on behalf of the Chinese people in the United Nations. This stand was repeated in a cablegram to the governments of members of the Security Council on January 8, 1950. It was supported by the Soviet Union, and when the Council refused to accept it the Soviet representative withdrew.[17] At this time the great majority of members of the United Nations, including the United States, France, and the Latin American republics, recognized the Nationalist government as the government of the Republic of China. The Communist members, the United Kingdom, and India were among those that had extended recognition to the Peking government.[18]

After the initial consideration of the question by the Security Council, the Secretary-General requested the preparation of a confidential memorandum on legal aspects of the problem and subsequently made it public.[19] This memorandum argued that the question of representation had been improperly linked with the question of recognition by member governments. The obligations of membership could be carried out only by governments which in fact possessed the power to do so. When a revolutionary govern-

17. Security Council, *Official Records,* Fifth Year, 459th Meeting (Jan. 10, 1950), pp. 1–4.

18. The Nationalist government was recognized by forty-three members and the Communist government by sixteen.

19. UN Doc. S/1466, March 9, 1950. For an excellent discussion of the question see Herbert W. Briggs, "Chinese Representation in the United Nations," *International Organization* VI (1952), 192–209.

ment presented itself as representing a state, in rivalry to an existing government, the question at issue should be: Which of these two governments in fact is in a position to employ the resources and direct the people of the state in fulfillment of the obligations of membership? In essence, this required an inquiry as to whether the new government exercised effective authority within the territory of the state and was habitually obeyed by the bulk of the population. If these facts were established, United Nations organs should accord to the new government the right of representation even though individual members might refuse to accord recognition for political reasons which they considered valid.

The question of Chinese representation was submitted for inclusion in the agenda of the General Assembly every year until 1971, when it was finally resolved by the seating of the Peking delegation and the exclusion of the Nationalists. From 1951 through 1960 the Assembly accepted a United States proposal not to put the question on the agenda. The large majorities supporting the United States position diminished rapidly with the expansion of membership after 1955. After 1960 the United States did not contest placing the item on the agenda. Instead its strategy was to get the General Assembly to decide that the issue was an "important question" requiring a two-thirds majority for a decision. This the Assembly repeatedly did until its twenty-sixth session. In 1970 for the first time the proposal to seat delegates of the Peking government received majority support, there being 51 votes in favor, 49 against, and 25 abstentions.

Through the years the view of the United States had been that a revolutionary government to be recognized for purposes of representation must exercise effective authority, be based on the consent of the population, be able and willing to fulfill its obligations under the Charter and international law, and respect human rights and fundamental freedoms. Members supporting the acceptance of the Peking regime as the lawful government of China had argued that it was the regime which was in effective control of all, or nearly all, of the state's territory and which had the allegiance of the overwhelming majority of the population. They argued that continued isolation of Communist China limited the possibilities of peaceful cooperation and more particularly the effectiveness of the United Nations in achieving its purposes. As more states established diplomatic relations with Communist China, the movement to bring her into active participation in the United Nations gained additional support.

After 1966 there were indications that the position of the United States government might be changing. A growing number of private groups and scholars were expressing the view that the United States government should at least give consideration to the so-called "two-China" solution. According to a proposal made by the National Policy Panel established by the United Nations Association of the United States of America consisting of a number of eminent scholars, lawyers, diplomats, and business executives,[20] the People's Republic of China and the Republic of China (Taiwan) would be accepted as members of the United Nations by right of succession, with membership in the General Assembly. The People's Republic of China would eventually be given the Chinese seat in the Security Council. This represented an essentially political approach based upon a questionable legal premise. It had the merit of taking into account the special problem of Taiwan.

By 1971 the United States government recognized the need of a more realistic approach to the Chinese question and sought to achieve the advantages of bringing mainland China into participation while at the same time protecting the membership of Nationalist China by proposing a two-China solution. At the same time, it sought to defeat the perennial Albanian proposal that the delegation of the People's Republic of China be seated and that the Nationalist delegation be expelled by again requesting that the question be declared an important one requiring a two-thirds vote. This change of policy came too late to serve its purpose. The rush of many Western states to establish diplomatic relations with Peking during the summer and early fall, and the sudden announcement from Washington in early October that the President of the United States was visiting Peking, presumably to prepare the way for the

20. For a text of the Panel report, see *International Organization*, XX (4) (Autumn 1966), 705–23.

establishment of diplomatic relations—and this without previous notice to governments that had given loyal support on the Chinese question—created an atmosphere which made a compromise settlement no longer possible. By a decisive note of 76 to 35 with 17 abstentions, the Albanian proposal was adopted.[21] While this did not constitute a recognition by the General Assembly of the Peking government's claim that Taiwan was a part of China, it did exclude for the foreseeable future any possibility that Taiwan, in the exercise of the right of self-determination, might as an independent state become a separate member of the United Nations.

The recognition of the Peking government as entitled to represent the Republic of China in the United Nations was long overdue. The grounds advanced for its previous exclusion had little justification in the words or theory of the Charter. The question was obviously not one of membership requiring or permitting that the criteria of Article 4 should be applied. Failure to recognize the Peking government meant that many important questions could not be usefully discussed or realistic solutions sought within and through the United Nations. Nor could the United Nations effectively serve what has come to be regarded as one of its primary functions, the harmonization of the actions of nations in the pursuit of common ends.

21. General Assembly Res. 2758 (XXVI), Oct. 27, 1971.

CHAPTER FOUR

THE CHANGING STRUCTURE OF POWER AND INFLUENCE

WRITERS ON INTERNATIONAL RELATIONS are in wide agreement that power viewed as the capacity to influence others is an important factor in relations between states. In this connection, power is not to be thought of solely in terms of military strength. It includes also economic, political, and psychological factors.[1] Under a political system where effective authority is largely centered in separate states, subject to no central control such as exists under a federal form of government, the relative power of each state becomes an important and often decisive influence. The exercise of influence through superior power may take such forms as largely to conceal its use; but regardless of the manner of its exercise, states are likely to resist giving up by formal arrangements the advantages that superior power gives them, except in return for some acceptable *quid pro quo.*

Thus, in the establishment and functioning of international organizations, states are usually reluctant to relinquish substantial power advantages and seek to have the organization so constituted that they will be able to continue to exercise a comparable amount of influence. On the other hand, relatively weak states, which in the absence of special treaty arrangements are at a disadvantage in

1. See E. H. Carr, *The Twenty-Years Crisis, 1919–1939* (New York: Macmillan, 1940), pp. 133 ff.; and Alastair Buchan, *Power and Equilibrium in the Twentieth Century* (New York: Praeger, 1973).

their relations with more powerful states, naturally seek to take advantage of every opportunity to increase their relative power and influence. This they may seek to do by placing limitations on the freedom of action of the major powers and by obtaining institutional arrangements which enable them to maximize their influence in international affairs, particularly with respect to matters of special concern to them. The establishment and maintenance of an acceptable and effective international organization consequently requires a fair accommodation between these competing demands. Since the effectiveness of the organization is dependent on the extent to which its members cooperate in support of its purposes, a reasonable working hypothesis is that structural and procedural arrangements for taking decisions should take into account the differences that exist between states with respect to power and the range of their interests.[2]

EXPERIENCE OF THE LEAGUE

The importance of the power factor was evident in the League of Nations as it had been in the international relations of the previous century. In the drafting of the Covenant, the initiative was taken by the United States and the United Kingdom. In the League of Nations Commission, which was assigned the responsibility at the Paris Peace Conference for drafting the Covenant, the Principal Allied and Associated Powers—the United States, the United Kingdom, France, Italy, and Japan—had the decisive influence.[3] Proposals of the lesser powers were incorporated in the draft Covenant only to the extent that they were acceptable to the "Big Five."

In determining the functions, structure, and powers of League organs, the authors of the Covenant agreed that the major military powers—the principal victor nations in the war just ended—should have a role in the new organization commensurate with their

2. For an insightful development of this theme, see W. W. Kaufmann, "The Organization of Responsibility," *World Politics,* I (1949), 511–32.

3. See David Hunter Miller, *The Drafting of the Covenant* (2 vols.; New York: Putnam, 1928).

power and responsibilities. The initial American–British plan called for a council composed exclusively of the five Principal Allied and Associated Powers. The British and American governments were persuaded, however, by the arguments of General Smuts of South Africa and leaders of other smaller nations, that the lesser powers should be given some representation in the Council. Consequently, in the Covenant as finally approved, the Council was to include, in addition to the five permanent members, four nonpermanent members elected by the Assembly. Since the Council had responsibility not only for preventing war but also for promoting cooperation in economic and social fields and supervising the administration of mandated territories, the privileged position of the major military powers extended to League action in these areas as well.

The Assembly, on the other hand, was so constituted as to provide the lesser states with an opportunity to make their voices heard and, through public discussion and resolutions adopted, to influence the course of League activities. The Covenant defined in exceedingly broad terms the role of the Assembly. Members were given equal opportunity to participate in discussions and equal voting power. While this equality seemed inconsistent with the principle that responsibility should be related to power, and seemed to mark a departure from the hierarchy of power relationships that had previously prevailed, this inconsistency was more apparent than real. The governments of the major powers clearly anticipated that through the Council they would assume a role in the work of the League reflecting their power status. Furthermore, they expected the Assembly to concern itself primarily with general principles of cooperation, leaving to the Council the responsibility of dealing with specific disputes and situations where in matters of special concern to them the lesser powers could be expected to be greatly influenced by major power desires. If necessary, a decision could always be prevented by a negative vote.

In the actual functioning of the League, the pattern of power and influence which the drafters of the Covenant originally envisaged underwent substantial change. For one thing, the failure of the United States to join reduced the authority of the Council as a chosen instrument of the major powers, and successive increases in the number of nonpermanent members detracted further from its special status. The withdrawal of Japan, Germany, and Italy from the League, even though balanced to some extent by the admission of the Soviet Union, weakened further the Council's role as an organ of great power cooperation. As a consequence, the major powers came more and more to deal with problems of special concern to themselves through negotiations outside the League, and the Council progressively lost its capacity to act as a world "concert of powers," as originally intended. While the expanded role of the Assembly did provide the opportunity for the smaller states to make known their views on a wide range of issues, their weakness prevented them from being able to save the League from the consequences of neglect or contempt on the part of the major powers. By becoming increasingly unrelated to the power realities of the contemporary world, the League lost any capability it might otherwise have had for dealing effectively with the critical problems of peace and war.

CHARTER PATTERN OF POWER AND INFLUENCE

Those who were principally involved and influential in writing the Charter were deeply impressed by the importance of power in international relations and the need to take account of the power factor in the construction of the new organization. The outcome of the war then in progress was being determined by the superiority of the military power of the United States, the Soviet Union, and the United Kingdom. It was taken for granted that these same powers would assume the major responsibility for the maintenance of international peace and security in the new world organization.

Recognition of the power factor found expression first in the nature of the Organization itself, and the provisions intended to safeguard the independence and freedom of action of its members. Members, while committed to respect certain principles, are left with great freedom in their interpretation and application. No interpretation of the Charter by an organ is legally binding on a member unless "generally accepted."

Notwithstanding, the principal organs are given certain powers which can be used to influence the conduct of individual members. While these powers do not generally extend to the adoption of binding decisions on substantive issues, they do involve important means of influence such as discussion, investigation, recommendation, and even decisions purporting to enunciate the obligations of members under the Charter and international agreements which, while they may not be technically binding as interpretations, are nevertheless bound to have considerable influence. In view of these possibilities, it was inevitable that considerable attention should be given to the structure, powers, and procedures of the principal organs.

With respect to arrangements for the maintenance of peace and security, there was insistence on the part of the major powers that the allocation of responsibilities among organs and the definition of their powers, composition, and structure should reflect differences of power, with the emphasis on the military element. Their position, clearly set forth in the Dumbarton Oaks Proposals and steadfastly maintained at San Francisco, found detailed expression in the Charter provisions placing on the Security Council primary responsibility for the maintenance of international peace and security and giving them permanent membership and special voting rights in that organ.[4] At San Francisco the lesser powers, with some assistance from certain of the major powers, were able to blur somewhat the line of division between the responsibilities of the Security Council and the General Assembly by getting the conference to approve Article 10 which gives the General Assembly a wide-ranging power of discussion and recommendation with respect to all matters falling within the scope of the Charter.[5]

There was no comparable attempt on the part of the major

4. See Ruth B. Russell, *A History of the United Nations Charter* (Washington: Brookings Institution, 1958), pp. 440–77; 646–776.

5. Also, Article 14 was added giving the General Assembly power to consider less serious situations affecting general welfare or friendly relations.

powers to safeguard their interests in the Assembly by special voting requirements. Apparently most of them were prepared to rely upon the special influence they would be able to exercise on other members in discussions and voting. Furthermore, on most substantive issues the Assembly could only recommend; and though a recommendation on questions relating to international peace and security could be adopted by a two-thirds vote, the major Western powers could have reasoned that, given the composition of United Nations membership, there should not be too great difficulty in mobilizing the necessary support to prevent the adoption of an objectionable recommendation. The Soviet Union was clearly not as convinced of its ability thus to protect its interests, and its strong opposition to expanding the General Assembly's power of discussion and recommendation by Article 10 could only be overcome with difficulty.[6]

When we consider institutional arrangements for promoting economic and social cooperation, including promotion of respect for human rights and fundamental freedoms, we find that very little was done at San Francisco to take into account differences in economic power, degrees of involvement, and capacities for contributing to the achievement of Charter purposes in determining the powers, structure, and procedure of responsible organs. Since the Economic and Social Council and the General Assembly could only recommend, the major powers could well rely for the safeguarding of their interests on the need of their positive participation to make UN policies and programs effective. Furthermore, the major powers could reason that since their support was essential to effective action, they would in practice be elected to membership on the Economic and Social Council, the Organization's quasi-executive organ in economic and social matters, with the consequence that the same result would be achieved as if there was an explicit provision for permanent membership. A further indication that the major powers relied on the need of their cooperation for the protection of their interests is to be found in their willingness to accept the General Assembly as the organ with primary responsibility

6. See Russell, chap. XXIX.

in the promotion of economic and social cooperation. It would appear, however, that the Council was expected to serve as a kind of executive committee with powers under the Charter which would enable it to provide guidance and direction to the Assembly.[7] With the Council so acting, and with the major powers reasonably assured of membership on it, they would have an additional means of exercising influence commensurate with their economic power and the range and importance of their interests.

For discharging the Organization's responsibilities in non-self-governing territories, including those placed under trusteeship, the accommodation that was reached was not primarily between greater and lesser powers, however power might be defined, but rather between the administering and nonadministering members. With regard to non-self-governing territories generally, the Charter specifies certain obligations of member states administering them, but is not explicit as to the powers of any organ to discuss or take any action with respect to questions of fulfillment of Charter obligations. In the case of non-self-governing territories placed under trusteeship, the Charter is more explicit. The General Assembly is the organ primarily responsible, but the Trusteeship Council, even more than in the case of ECOSOC, appears to have been conceived as an organ with important powers and responsibilities of its own. For its composition two requirements were laid down: that the number of administering and nonadministering members should be equal, and that the permanent members of the Security Council should be permanent members. This intrusion of the power factor into Council membership was justified on the ground that one objective of the trusteeship system was "to further international peace and security."

THE UNITED NATIONS OF THE 1970S

In practice, the patterns of power and influence in the United Nations have developed along different lines than initially envisaged.

7. On the relationship between ECOSOC and the General Assembly, see Walter R. Sharp, *The United Nations Economic and Social Council* (New York: Columbia University Press, 1969), chap. 1.

These changes have for the most part taken place without formal Charter amendment in response to developments in the international system. Of these developments, the most important have been the so-called cold war, the precipitate retreat of Western nations from their colonial responsibilities, and the consequent emergence of a host of new states insistent on establishing their national identities.

The most important changes that have taken place in the pattern of power and influence will be discussed under three headings: (1) changes in the composition of organs, (2) the developing relationship between the Security Council and the General Assembly in the maintenance of international peace and security, and (3) the changing priorities of the Organization resulting from expanded membership.

Changes in the Composition of Organs

The General Assembly

The organ that has experienced the most radical and significant change has been the General Assembly. As the result of the expansion of the membership of the Organization, it has grown from a body of fifty-one members to one of one hundred thirty-five, the majority of which are non-Western and underdeveloped, and only recently have arrived at independence.[8] Of the eighty-four new members that have been admitted since the United Nations began to function, sixty-eight are states that have gained their independence since the war. Whereas the UN had eleven original members from Asia and Africa, by 1972 seventy-five members, or close to three-fifths of the total, were from these two regions. As the result of the proportionately greater increase in the number of small, relatively poor, and underdeveloped states, it had become possible by the 1970s for members representing 10 percent of the total population of UN countries and contributing less than 5 percent of the budget to make up the two-thirds majority necessary for the decision of important questions in the General Assembly. Even allowing for the fact that voting equality does not amount to equal-

8. For further details, see above, pp. 47–48.

ity of influence and that the major powers do exercise influence out of proportion to their single votes, the expansion of membership has clearly further weakened the tie between power and influence so far as the General Assembly is concerned.

The Security Council

As the result of pressures within the General Assembly, the composition of the Security Council has assumed in two respects a character different from that originally specified. First, whereas the Charter provides that in the selection of nonpermanent members of the Council due regard should be "specially paid, in the first instance to the contribution of Members of the United Nations to the maintenance of international peace and security and to the other purposes of the Organization," and only secondarily to "equitable geographical distribution," the principle of equitable geographical distribution has tended increasingly to take precedence. During the first decade, the pattern of selection for nonpermanent members was the following: two members from Latin America, one from Western Europe, one from the Middle East, one from the Commonwealth, and one from Eastern Europe. In making regional selections, some attention was given to the principle of ability to contribute. This pattern of regional selection began to break down after 1955 as the result of the admission of new members, particularly Asian and African. The substantial increase in the number of Asian and African members led to their demands for better representation on the Council. Largely to meet this demand, it was decided to increase the number of nonpermanent members from six to ten. In its resolution approving this amendment to the Charter, the General Assembly decided that the seats should be allocated as follows: five for Africa and Asia, one for Eastern Europe, two for Latin America, and two for Western Europe and "other states." [9] By this decision and by the procedure followed in giving effect to it, "geographical distribution" came to mean "regional representation." The states elected to the Council are generally those whose candidacies have the support of the regional groups to which they belong.

9. General Assembly Res. (XVIII), Dec. 17, 1963.

This increase in the size of the Security Council, accompanied by an increase in the number of affirmative votes required for a Council decision, has had the effect of somewhat lessening the importance of the permanent members. Whereas under the original Charter provision it was not possible for a decision, whether procedural or nonprocedural, to be taken without the support of at least one permanent member of the Security Council, under the amended Charter provision a procedural decision can be taken by the affirmative votes of any nine members. Since there are ten nonpermanent members, the concurrence of no one of the permanent members is required. This has a further possible consequence. If the procedure followed in two cases to avoid the "double veto" is again used,[10] it becomes possible for a decision to be taken that a particular matter is procedural by a majority of 9 affirmative votes including only the affirmative votes of nonpermanent members. This of course is not likely to happen because of the influence the permanent members are able to exercise.

The increase in the number of nonpermanent members, accompanied as it has been by an emphasis upon equitable geographical distribution instead of ability to contribute to the purposes of the Organization in the election of nonpermanent members, has created a danger that the Security Council will suffer the same fate that befell the Council of the League of Nations. There is at present no conclusive evidence that the practice of the major powers of conducting important negotiations outside the framework of the United Nations is due to changes in the membership of the Security Council. However, one of the main reasons for vesting in the Security Council a special responsibility for the maintenance of peace and security was that this organ—small, continuously in session, and capable of quick and expeditious action—provided the major powers, i.e., permanent members, with a forum in which their influence would be decisive and their decisions would not be subject to excessive influence by states who were not in the position to assume major responsibilities.

10. Invitation to People's Republic of China, 1950, and appointment of subcommittee on Laos, 1959. See Leland M. Goodrich, Edvard Hambro, and Anne P. Simons, *Charter of the United Nations: Commentary and Documents* (3d rev. ed.; New York: Columbia University Press, 1969), pp. 225–27.

It is not alone through changes in the membership of the Security Council to meet the demands of new and smaller states that the organ is made less reflective of actual power relations. In a changing world a particular pattern established at a given moment must inevitably become less adequate with the passing of time unless changes are made to take account of new developments. The increase in the number of UN members and changes in their geographic distribution have been roughly reflected in the changes of composition already described. Changes in the relative power standing of members of the Organization, especially those of the top rank, have not been taken into account due to the fact that the change would require Charter amendment. No permanent member is likely to voluntarily relinquish its privileged position. Proposals for the radical modification of the composition and voting procedures of the Security Council at the expense of any of the present permanent members are thus bound to encounter serious if not insuperable objections.[11]

The Economic and Social Council

The Charter initially provided that the Economic and Social Council should have eighteen members, to be elected by the General Assembly with no specific guidelines as to the criteria to be followed in their selection. Four major industrial nations have not only been elected but also reelected, as is permitted under the Charter, with the result that for all practical purposes they have the status of permanent members. Until 1965, when the amendment to Article 61 entered into force, the pattern of composition followed with considerable consistency by the General Assembly in the election of members, other than France, the United Kingdom, the United States, and the Soviet Union, was as follows: two members from Western Europe, two from Eastern Europe, two from Africa, four from Latin America, three from Asia, and one from the Commonwealth. In deciding that the size of ECOSOC should be increased to twenty-seven members, the General Assembly de-

11. See, for examples, proposals of Arthur Lall in *The Security Council in a Universal United Nations* (New York: Carnegie Endowment for International Peace, 1971).

cided [12] that the nine additional members should be elected according to the following pattern: seven from African and Asian states, one from Latin American states, and one from Western European and other states. This has resulted in a considerable shift in the geographic balance, and also in the balance as between the more advanced industrial states and the less developed states, as compared with that which existed in the early years when there was little representation of the African continent.[13]

The Economic and Social Council has from the beginning failed to function as an effective executive organ responsible to the General Assembly and exercising substantial influence over the activities of the Organization through its powers of initiative, supervision, and coordination. During the first decade, the Council's weakness was not too apparent since its membership was broadly representative of the total membership of the Organization. From 1955 on, however, the Council became progressively less representative from a regional point of view, and pressures multiplied to increase membership to achieve better representation. It was, in fact, strongly argued that only through expanded membership could the Council acquire the confidence of the total membership which would enable it to discharge its Charter responsibilities satisfactorily. Increasing the membership of the Council instead of achieving better representation within the limits of the original Charter number has had the effect, however, of making the Council increasingly a replica of the Assembly itself and as a consequence bringing into question the need of its existence.

The Trusteeship Council

Changes that have taken place in the Trusteeship Council have reflected the progressive achievement of the purposes of the trust-

12. General Assembly Res. 1991 (XVIII), Dec. 17, 1963.

13. By Resolution 2847 (XXVI), December 20, 1971, the General Assembly approved a Charter amendment doubling the size of the Council to 54, the members to be elected according to the following pattern: 14 African; 11 Asian; 10 Latin American; 13 Western European and other; and 6 Socialist States of Eastern Europe. This was declared by the Assembly to be desirable to provide broad representation of UN membership and to make the Council a more effective organ.

eeship system rather than any deliberate modification of its composition in order to achieve a different balance among its members than originally intended. As trust territories have achieved independence, the number of administering members has been reduced and the number of members elected by the General Assembly has been correspondingly reduced. This development has now reached the point where it is no longer possible to achieve a balance between administering and nonadministering members. The only possibility of achieving the balance is by increasing the number of administering states by the creation of new trust territories, an unlikely development at the present time.

It is significant that when the decision was taken to establish the Ad Hoc Committee on Information from Non-Self-Governing Territories to examine reports made by administering states under the terms of Article 73(e) of the Charter, it was also decided to maintain within the Committee parity between administering and nonadministering states as in the Trusteeship Council. This practice was continued with each renewal of the Committee. However, when in 1961 a special committee was established to supervise the implementation of the Declaration on the Granting of Independence to Colonial Countries and Peoples, the principle of parity was dropped and the majority of the twenty-four members have consistently been nonadministering states. In 1963 this committee took over the duties of the Committee on Information.

The Changing Role of the Security Council and Its Relation to the General Assembly

Since 1946 we have seen the assumption by the General Assembly of an increased role in the maintenance of international peace and security. The Security Council, which was vested by the Charter with the primary responsibility, has in fact been disappointing in its performance. The mechanism has been available; what has been lacking has been the willingness of the permanent members to equip and use it as a chosen instrument of cooperation.

During the years when the cold war was at its height, a reason commonly given for the weakness of the Security Council and its failure to exercise its Charter powers effectively was the abuse of the veto by the Soviet Union. There was undoubtedly an element of truth in this charge. Nevertheless, it greatly oversimplified the actual situation. Until the end of 1955, seventy-nine vetoes were cast, and of these the Soviet Union was alone responsible for all but three.[14] Whether the veto was abused is a question that cannot be decided solely on the basis of the number of times it was used. It is not in itself a misuse of voting power since it is the exercise of the right to dissent recognized in the Charter. Nevertheless, the representatives of the Sponsoring Governments and France at San Francisco did take great pains to explain that the Charter itself "contains an indication of the application of the voting procedures to the various functions of the Council" and that it was not to be assumed that the veto would be used "willfully to obstruct the operation of the Council." [15] Consequently, it is fair to assert that a permanent member should not exercise the veto for small or unsubstantial reasons or for determining a matter to be nonprocedural that the Charter clearly indicates to be procedural. The judgment whether the Soviet use of the veto was for the purpose of defending important interests or for largely propaganda purposes is not easy to make. The atmosphere of the cold war provided a great temptation to use the Security Council for highly partisan purposes and to place less emphasis on reaching a compromise necessary to unanimity than on making a propaganda point.

It was primarily with respect to its functions of peaceful settlement and enforcement action under Chapters VI and VII that the claim was made that the Council, because of the veto, failed to meet its responsibilities. There is no question that in some sense and to a certain extent this was true. The claim assumed, however, that success required a positive decision in every case and that support of a proposal by the necessary majority was a requirement that should normally take precedence over the requirement of concurrence of the permanent members. It is difficult to harmonize these

14. For a list of vetoes in the Security Council through 1966, see Sydney D. Bailey, *Voting in the Security Council* (Bloomington: Indiana University Press, 1969), pp. 28–31.

15. UNCIO, *Documents,* XI, pp. 710–14; and Goodrich, Hambro, and Simons, pp. 217–20.

assumptions with the provisions of the Charter and the statements made in the San Francisco Conference. When the Charter was being drafted, the possibility of a failure on the part of the permanent members to reach agreement on a particular proposal was certainly envisaged. Furthermore, there is nothing to indicate that the Security Council was expected to take positive action in every case. It was assumed, however, that there would be a willingness on the part of the permanent members to adjust their positions and harmonize their views in order to achieve an agreement. In the atmosphere of the cold war this was not done. Consequently, in dealing with those questions which involved conflicting strategic interests of the United States and its allies on the one hand and the Soviet Union and its allies on the other, the Council was often unable to reach decisions. In dealing with the Greek question in 1947, it was incapable of reaching a decision on the report of its Committee of Investigation. It was blocked by Soviet vetoes when it attempted to deal with the complaint of Soviet intervention in Czechoslovakia in 1948. Though the Council had some successes during these early years in dealing with situations where the interests of the major powers tended to converge,—as in Palestine and in Indonesia—the limited value of the Council in dealing with questions involving the direct and important interests of the major powers contributed to its progressive decline in relation to the General Assembly.

From the discussions at San Francisco it might have been expected that the initiative in asserting the role of the General Assembly would be taken by the smaller states, who would see in such a development an increase in their relative influence in the Organization. This was true to some extent in the early period but much more so later with the great expansion of membership to include a large number of non-Western states. The principal initiative, however, in the early years, was taken not by the smaller states but by the major powers themselves. In fact, the building up of the role of the General Assembly during the first decade was primarily a by-product of the cold war and reflected an effort by the parties, particularly the Western powers under the leadership of the United States, to use the General Assembly as a platform for obtaining broad support for their national policies and objectives and as a means of legitimizing courses of action which their national interests dictated and which seemed to them consistent with the purposes and principles of the Charter. Though the General Assembly could only recommend, this was not viewed as a particularly serious handicap since the Security Council could only recommend when exercising its function of peaceful settlement. Furthermore, it was prevented from taking enforcement measures by the absence of special military agreements under Article 43 and by the inability of the permanent members to agree.

Until the middle of 1948, though increasing use was being made of the General Assembly, the Security Council was still active in dealing with specific disputes and situations. But by late 1948 there was a marked reduction in the number of meetings of the Council and a decline in the number of political questions considered by that organ in comparison with the General Assembly. During the remainder of the United Nations' first decade the trend was definitely in the direction of the declining use of the Council accompanied by increased use of the Assembly for peace and security purposes.[16]

The Charter provides that the General Assembly, either before or after discussion but in any case before making a recommendation, must refer a question on which "action" is necessary to the Security Council.[17] From this it might be assumed that the shift that occurred applied only to questions where there was no necessity or expectation of collective measures being taken. As a matter of fact, the General Assembly equally encroached upon this sphere of Security Council activity. In 1946 it recommended to members that collective political measures be taken against Spain,[18] and in 1949, that direct military assistance be withheld from the countries that were assisting guerrilla forces in Greece.[19] In 1950, when it became clear that the return of the Soviet representative to the Security

16. See Leland M. Goodrich, "The UN Security Council," in James Barros (ed.), *The United Nations: Past, Present and Future* (New York: Free Press, 1972), pp. 16–63; and Table 1.

17. Art. 11, par. 2.   18. General Assembly Res. 39 (I), Dec. 12, 1946.

19. General Assembly Res. 288 (IV), Dec. 5, 1949.

Table 1   MEETINGS OF THE SECURITY COUNCIL

Period	Number of Meetings
1946	88
1947	137
1948	171
1949	62
1950	72
1951	39
1952	42
1953	43
1954	32
1955	23
1956	50
1957	49
1958	34
1959	4
1960	50
1961	21
1962	30
1963	59
1964	104
1965	81
1966	70
1967	46
1968	76
1969	65
1970	38
1971	51

Council prevented that organ from taking further decisions in connection with collective measures in Korea, the United States proposed that the General Assembly explicitly assume the responsibility for dealing with threats to the peace, breaches of the peace, and acts of aggression in case the Council was prevented by the veto from acting. By its resolution,[20] the General Assembly asserted its right to exercise a residual responsibility in case of any threat to or breach of the peace, and, in case the Security Council was prevented from exercising its primary responsibility by the veto, to

20. General Assembly Res. 377 (V), Nov. 3, 1950.

consider the matter with a view to making appropriate recommendations for collective measures, including the use of armed force in the case of a breach of the peace or act of aggression.

The Uniting for Peace resolution had hardly been adopted when it became clear that the General Assembly would be an undependable instrument for initiating collective measures in a cold war situation. When the question of Chinese Communist military intervention in Korea was brought before the General Assembly in December 1950—technically not under the terms of the resolution since the Korean question was already on the agenda of the Assembly—the United States soon discovered that even those members of the United Nations on whom it had been able to depend most reliably for support on cold war issues were unwilling to support decisions by the Assembly invoking collective measures against Communist China until all possibilities of peaceful accommodation had been exhausted.[21] It was nearly two months before the United States was able to get a resolution adopted, by the desired majority, declaring Communist China to be the aggressor as the result of its intervention, and it was over two months later before the General Assembly could be brought to recommend modest economic sanctions against Communist China.[22]

This experience did much to remove any hopes that the United States government might have had that, through appeals from the Security Council to the General Assembly, it would be able to mobilize support for collective measures to resist aggressive action by the Communist states. Though the Uniting for Peace resolution was invoked in 1956 following the invasion of Egyptian territory by Israeli forces and the military intervention of France and the United Kingdom, it is significant to note that in this case the United States and the Soviet Union were in accord on the object to be achieved and that the action taken by the General Assembly was not the invocation of collective measures to restrain aggression but rather the establishment of a United Nations force to observe and

21. See Leland M. Goodrich, *Korea: A Study of U.S. Foreign Policy in the United Nations* (New York: Council on Foreign Relations, 1956), pp. 156–67.

22. See Goodrich, *Korea*, pp. 167–73.

police the agreed withdrawal of troops. Furthermore, though the Uniting for Peace resolution was invoked following Soviet military intervention in Hungary, there was no proposal made to initiate collective measures for the purpose of defeating this intervention. The activity of the General Assembly was limited to debate, publicity, and efforts to achieve clarification of the situation to provide the basis for more effective condemnation. When the Soviet Union requested the General Assembly to consider the Middle East situation in June 1967, it invoked Article 11 of the Charter and not the Uniting for Peace resolution, though the request for a special emergency session came under a procedural rule adopted for the implementation of that resolution.

Though the purpose that motivated the United States in building up the role of the General Assembly in the early years lost much of its appeal in the late fifties and the years following, other members found reasons of their own for making use of the General Assembly in situations in which it would be claimed that international peace and security were being threatened. After the membership deadlock was broken in 1955, pressures mounted in support of independence movements, first within the French colonial empire and later within the British and other remaining colonial empires. The new Asian and African states, with support from other groups, were insistent that colonialism be completely liquidated at once; to that end they invoked the principle of self-determination. Closely related was their demand that racial discrimination be eliminated, a practice which in their minds was closely associated with colonialism. To achieve their purposes these new states were prepared to make use of their voting strength in the General Assembly and to use the General Assembly to the limit of its Charter powers. For their purposes the uses made of the General Assembly in the cold war served as helpful precedents. They were not averse to making use of the Security Council when that action best served their purposes. If the General Assembly was not in session, time could be gained by bringing the matter before the Council on the plea that international peace and security was threatened. Also, as in the cases of Southern Rhodesia and South Africa, recourse to the Security Council provided the only possibility of getting enforcement action. However, the possibility of a "veto," not by the Soviet Union but by a Western power, always had to be considered. In the General Assembly this possibility did not exist. Though the Assembly resolutions were not legally binding, if adopted by large majorities they could have considerable political influence and even some legal force as authoritative interpretations of Charter commitments.

Changing Priorities and the Role of the General Assembly

The past two decades have witnessed important changes in the priorities of the United Nations, with significant consequences for the roles of its organs, particularly the General Assembly. Chiefly as the result of the expansion of membership of the Organization and the interests of the new members, the Organization has come to give higher priority to economic and social development, decolonization, and the elimination of racial discrimination than to the maintenance of international peace and security—partly, no doubt, because of frustrations experienced in the latter field. United Nations action in dealing with these matters is primarily the responsibility of the General Assembly. This means that in dealing with matters to which the highest priority is being given, members enjoy equal opportunity to express their views and equal voting power irrespective of degree of power, range of interests, and capacity to contribute to the achievement of UN purposes.

Initial expectations that, in dealing with problems in the economic and social fields, the Economic and Social Council would act as a quasi-executive organ and give guidance and direction to the General Assembly, have failed to materialize. In these areas the General Assembly has utilized its broad powers of discussion and recommendation under the Charter not only to pass upon the recommendations made by ECOSOC and to give directives to that organ but also to initiate, discuss, and decide, without reference to ECOSOC except for purposes of implementation, many important matters and to discuss at great length matters to which ECOSOC has given initial consideration.[23] Increasing the size of the Eco-

23. On relations of the Economic and Social Council to the General Assembly, see Sharp.

nomic and Social Council and making it more representative of the total membership of the United Nations has reduced the chances of serious disagreement between it and the General Assembly, without giving it a more independent role.

The assertion by the General Assembly of its power and independent responsibility in the economic and social field has been particularly manifested in connection with the consideration given to developmental problems. During the first decade of the United Nations, programs of technical assistance were adopted and put into operation with substantial support from the more advanced industrial nations. Particularly since the expansion of membership in the late fifties and early sixties, there has been growing pressure on the advanced industrial nations to accept programs for assistance to the developing countries which did not, at least initially, have their approval. In some instances the pressure has succeeded in producing voluntary concessions by these countries, as for example in the establishment of the International Development Association which has come to play an important part in the United Nations development effort. In other cases, as for example in the establishment of the United Nations Conference on Trade and Development, the United Nations Organization for Industrial Development, and the United Nations Capital Development Fund, the initial reluctance of the more advanced members did not prevent the General Assembly from acting with results that have not on the whole been encouraging; the necessary cooperation has not been forthcoming from the wealthier and more economically advanced members.

The very fact of the establishment of these agencies and the opportunities they provide for concerted action have represented some degree of success for the underdeveloped countries. However, this use of the General Assembly clearly has its limitations so far as the achievement of practical results is concerned, as is illustrated by the failure of the United Nations Capital Development Fund to get off the ground because of lack of funds. Consequently, one must conclude that use of the General Assembly to achieve certain ends by majority vote does not assure solid achievement. What has been found in practice to be necessary is general agreement on the part of all members whose cooperation is necessary to success. This is not guaranteed by majority votes in the General Assembly.

It has been particularly with respect to non-self-governing territories not placed under trusteeship that the General Assembly has asserted its powers. Until1960 this was done principally by invoking the right of the General Assembly to discuss and make recommendations with respect to the provisions of Chapter XI, even though that particular chapter made no specific provision for the General Assembly to play a supervisory role of any kind whatever. Beginning in 1960 the emphasis shifted from Chapter XI to the self-determination principle set forth in Article 1. By the 1960 Declaration on the Granting of Independence to Colonial Countries and Peoples, the General Assembly proclaimed the new principle that non-self-governing territories should be given independence immediately without regard to degree of readiness. To implement this principle the General Assembly established a committee that in its composition broke completely with the principle of parity between administering and nonadministering states and was clearly intended to be a means of carrying out the will of the majority of members. As a protest against committee excesses, some of the more important administering states have withdrawn from participation, further weakening and depreciating the committee's effectiveness and value.

Consequences of the General Assembly's New Role

That the General Assembly has come to occupy a central, and in many respects, a dominant position in the United Nations does not mean of course that differences in power between members are no longer of any consequence. The members with superior military, economic, and political resources are capable of exercising greater influence in the General Assembly on most questions than the smaller and weaker states. But this greater influence is not fully expressed in institutional arrangements.

The methods by which influence can be exercised and the effectiveness of these methods vary greatly. The Soviet Union, for example, has been quite successful in influencing and, in effect, controlling the voting conduct of the parties to the Warsaw Pact on most questions, and not alone on those relating to peace and security. This degree of success is no doubt due in part to the dependence of the lesser states upon the protection and economic support of the Soviet Union. The major factor, however, is the common membership in a Communist bloc, controlled with varying degrees of effectiveness through a party structure centered in Moscow. Outside of what might be called the Warsaw bloc, Soviet influence depends very much upon the nature of the question. In questions relating to the liquidation of colonialism, which from the beginning has been one of the major objectives of Soviet policy, the Soviet Union can be quite certain of a large amount of support from countries that have an interest in achieving the same result. It would be going too far to say that these states vote in the Assembly as they do because of Soviet influence; rather, the explanation is that their interest in decolonization happens to be shared by the Soviets. On occasion they find Soviet initiatives more of an embarrassment than a help, and generally they see an advantage in achieving a broader consensus than agreement with the Soviet bloc.[24]

United States influence takes a variety of forms and is due to a variety of considerations. During the first decade in particular, countries that were fearful of Communist aggression looked to the United States as the most powerful guarantor of their security, and were consequently prepared to support the United States on issues arising in the context of the cold war. Furthermore, these countries were often willing to follow the United States' lead on other issues either to assure themselves of the United States' goodwill and support or because the United States was successful in identifying itself with commonly accepted principles. But when it comes to questions of national self-determination, racial discrimination, and the economic development of developing countries, the United States is in a less favorable position to exercise influence because its interests are often more complex than those of new and developing countries, and it is consequently not prepared to accept simple and clear-cut formulae. Here the United States does not have the same

24. As illustrated by the way Khruschev's initiative in the 1960 Assembly was taken up and used by newly independent members. See David Kay, "The Impact of African States in the United Nations," *International Organization*, XXIII (1969), 20–47.

leverage as on cold war issues, and along with the United Kingdom and France often finds itself in the position of being outvoted. That the Soviet Union is more often on the winning side on these issues is due not to its superior power but rather because it is able to take positions on these issues that correspond more closely to the interests of the less developed and less powerful states, particularly those in Asia and Africa.

A study of the voting behavior on peace and security questions in the General Assembly [25] shows that the United States has had a high degree of success in getting the necessary support for its proposals and positions, although in recent years it has more frequently faced the necessity of making important concessions in order to get the desired support and even accepting defeats. In 1951, for example, it saw the necessity of conceding to the members of the General Assembly the opportunity to discuss the China question on its merits, and ten years later it was actually outvoted in its opposition to seating the Communist Chinese in place of the Nationalist Chinese. In August 1958, following the landing of American Marines in Lebanon at the request of President Chamoun, the United States found the task of getting the necessary two-thirds majority for its proposals so difficult that it was willing to settle for a resolution of a stop-gap nature, which in effect denied it much of what it had wanted. More recently, on proposals relating to apartheid in South Africa, the situation in Southern Rhodesia, the refusal of South Africa to relinquish control of Southwest Africa, and the future of Portugese colonies, the United States, along with certain other Western countries, has found itself in a minority position or, if not in open opposition, abstaining from voting to avoid being so placed.

No one of the permanent members of the Security Council can be said to be certain that the General Assembly will take a position consistent with its national preferences. Of the four, the United

25. On voting behavior in the General Assembly, see Margaret Ball, "Bloc Voting in the General Assembly," *International Organization,* V (1951), 3–31; Thomas Hovet, Jr., *Bloc Politics in the United Nations* (Cambridge: Harvard University Press, 1960); Hayward R. Alker and Bruce M. Russett, *World Politics in the General Assembly* (New Haven: Yale University Press, 1965); and Robert O. Keohane, "Political Influence in the General Assembly," *International Conciliation* (March 1966).

States has been the most successful; the United Kingdom has shared in the success to a certain extent as a result of the influence that the United States has been able to exercise, though with the members of the Commonwealth it has some small measure of independent influence. On many issues France is able to exercise effective influence over the voting of its former colonies, though this does not generally extend to matters of self-determination, human rights, or economic development.

There is considerable evidence in the current debates in the Assembly and in the resolutions adopted by that organ that many members think of the Assembly as having something approaching legislative power, and conclude that the resolutions that it adopts have a legal force derived from approval by majority votes. If the General Assembly is to be regarded as having powers that are quasi-legislative in nature, then the question can be seriously raised as to whether its voting arrangements should not be altered to give its decisions a more responsible character. Is it reasonable that a member with a population of 100 million should have the same vote as one with a population of 500,000, even making allowances for the possibility of informal influence? Proposals for weighted voting [26] have been made which take into account various factors such as population, gross national product, and military strength, but there is little likelihood that any formula can be found which will receive the necessary measure of support to permit its adoption. This particular approach to the resolution of the problem therefore seems unpromising.

A more promising approach would seem to be to drop all pretense that the General Assembly is a legislative organ capable of reaching binding decisions by a special majority vote, and to recognize instead that the effectiveness of its decisions depends more upon the establishment of a general consensus than on the mobilization of a majority. There is some evidence that this is coming to be recognized. The new states, for example, who have the voting power to secure the adoption of draft resolutions as they are pro-

26. For a discussion of possibilities, see Francis O. Wilcox and Carl M. Marcy, *Proposals for Changes in the United Nations* (Washington: Brookings Institution, 1955), chap. XI.

posed, have recognized the need of something more than a majority if General Assembly decisions are to have substantial results.
They furthermore recognize the importance of the support of the
major powers. This was clearly illustrated at the time of the adoption of the Declaration on the Granting of Independence to Colonial Countries and Peoples. The initial proposal of the Asian and
African states based on a proposal made by the Soviet Union could
undoubtedly have been adopted by the necessary majority without
amendment, but the sponsors of the resolution saw the need of
broader support and were consequently willing to make some concessions in order to achieve it. Unfortunately, this awareness of the
need of broader support has not always been shown, but certainly
experience suggests that if practical results are to follow the adoption of legal texts, the effort must be made to establish a broad consensus in support of them. While, as former Secretary-General
Hammarskjöld observed, the United Nations is something more
than a standing conference, the Assembly is nearer to being a
standing conference than a legislative body and must so remain as
long as its composition and procedures fail to take account of the
inequalities of member states in their capacities to contribute to
United Nations purposes.

CHAPTER FIVE

THE SECRETARY-GENERAL AND HIS STAFF

UNTIL THE TIME OF THE ESTABLISHMENT of the League of Nations, nothing that could truly be regarded as an international civil service had ever existed. Even when plans were being considered for the organization of the League Secretariat, it was an open question whether the Secretariat should be composed of officials assigned by their respective governments or of persons recruited on the basis of personal qualification to serve the international organization exclusively. Sir Eric Drummond, designated in the Covenant as the first Secretary-General of the League, was responsible for the decision to organize the Secretariat as an international civil service. As Frank P. Walters has written: "The creation of a secretariat international alike in its structure, its spirit, and its personnel, was without doubt one of the most important events in the history of international politics—important not only in itself, but as the indisputable proof of possibilities which had hitherto been confidently denied." [1]

Though the League Secretariat was originally planned and organized to perform a modest role in the work of the Organization, various factors combined to increase its importance and make it an indispensable part of the League machine: [2] The Secretariat

1. Frank P. Walters, *A History of the League of Nations* (London: Oxford University Press, 1952), Vol. I, 76.

2. On the League Secretariat, see E. F. Ranshofen-Wertheimer, *The International Secretariat: A Great Experiment in International Administration* (Washington: Carnegie Endowment for International Peace, 1945).

provided the only continuing element in the Organization; a great deal of expertise was developed in the Secretariat and made available to representatives of governments; the representatives of member governments in the Council and Assembly and on various League committees were dependent on expert guidance; and the political organs needed a vast amount of documentation which the Secretariat alone was equipped to provide.

To a large degree such successes as the League enjoyed, particularly in the field of economic and social cooperation and in the administration of the mandates system, but also in dealing with a variety of political questions, were due to the high quality of the work of the secretariat. With this background of experience it was not surprising that in the drafting of the Charter of the United Nations, the desirability—in fact the necessity—of having a Secretariat modeled on that of the League was taken for granted. The only open questions were the extent of its political powers and the degree to which the Secretariat should be brought under some measure of control by member governments insofar as the top positions were concerned.

It is clear from an examination of the Charter and from a review of the discussions that took place in its drafting that the Secretariat, i.e., the Secretary-General and his staff, was viewed from the beginning as having a role of great importance in the work of the Organization. The Secretariat is declared to be one of the principal organs of the United Nations. Members of the Organization undertake to respect the exclusively international character of the responsibilities of the Secretary-General and his staff, and they in turn must refrain from any action which "might reflect on their position as international officials responsible only to the Organization." [3] The full implications of the Secretariat's position as the only organ, other than the Court, comprising expert personnel continuously on the job, and pledged to serve exclusively the interests of the Organization, were not fully spelled out by the authors of the Charter, but it was assumed that League precedents would be followed, as indeed has been the case.[4]

3. Art. 100.

4. For details, see *Report of the Preparatory Commission of the United Nations* (PC/20, Dec. 23, 1945), and *Staff Rules and Regulations* (ST/SGB/Staff Rules/1).

THE SECRETARY-GENERAL

The Covenant of the League had little to say about the Secretary-General's duties other than that he "shall act in that capacity at all meetings of the Assembly and of the Council." Other provisions of the Covenant giving him specific duties to perform left him little opportunity for discretion and did little to provide the basis for the important role which he developed. For the most part, the influence of the Secretary-General was built up in the course of the day to day work of the Organization and in response to practical needs and opportunities. Though Sir Eric Drummond and his successor, Joseph Avenol, refrained from public statements and interventions, they nevertheless took advantage of confidential relationships with government ministers and representatives on League bodies to take initiatives and give advice, which often had important political results.[5]

When, during World War II, the shape of a new international organization to succeed the League was being considered, much attention was given to the role of the Secretary-General. From the experience of the League and the International Labour Organization, some drew the conclusion that what was needed was an executive head who would provide the leadership which Albert Thomas had given the ILO in its early years.[6] In the discussions in the U.S. Department of State during the period of postwar planning, there was general agreement that the chief administrative officer of the proposed international organization should have a more important political role than his League counterpart. At Dumbarton Oaks the four governments agreed that he should be given the right to bring to the attention of the Security Council "any matter which in his opinion may threaten international peace and security."[7] The

---

5. See Arthur W. Rovine, *The First Fifty Years: The Secretary-General in World Politics, 1920–1970* (Leyden: Sijthoff, 1970), chaps. I–III; and James Barros, *Betrayal from Within: Joseph Avenol, Secretary-General of the League of Nations, 1933–1940* (New Haven: Yale University Press, 1969).

6. For an account and assessment of this leadership, see E. J. Phelan, *Yes and Albert Thomas* (London: Cresset Press, 1936).

7. Chapter X of the Dumbarton Oaks Proposals.

Secretary-General, it was felt, would be free of those inhibitions which might prevent a state from acting, or acting in proper time, to have a serious dispute or situation considered by the world organization.

Qualifications and Method of Appointment

At San Francisco the major powers insisted that the important political responsibilities of the Secretary-General, especially in the exercise of his "special right" under Article 99, required that the Security Council be given a decisive role in the choice of the person to fill the office. If the Secretary-General was to be effective in his political role, it was argued, he should have the confidence of that organ, especially its permanent members. It was decided therefore that while the General Assembly should make the appointment, this should be done on the recommendation of the Security Council. Appointment is by simple majority, unless the Assembly should itself decide that a two-thirds majority is necessary; the Security Council makes its recommendation by a nonprocedural vote, the concurrence of the permanent members being required.

The League Covenant listed the name of the first Secretary-General, namely, Sir Eric Drummond, who was a British national and had served in the British foreign office. His successor, Joseph Avenol, was a French national. In fact, until the time of the outbreak of war, when the League ceased, for all practical purposes, to function, it was generally accepted that the Secretary-General should be the national of a major power. The practice of the United Nations has been quite different. Partly, no doubt, because of the political importance of the office and the unwillingness of any of the permanent members to accord one of their number the opportunity for special political influence, and partly because the interests of the major powers were thought to be adequately protected through the participation of the Security Council in the process of appointment, there was agreement from the beginning that the Secretary-General should be a national of one of the smaller member states.

The Secretaries-General of the League of Nations came to their positions after experience as civil servants in the governments of their states and generally lacked previous experience in politics. The UN Secretaries-General have generally had extensive political experience, though Dag Hammarskjöld, the second Secretary-General, came closer to conforming to the League model. The first Secretary-General, Trygve Lie, had participated actively in the politics of his country, and had, as Foreign Minister, headed Norway's delegation to the San Francisco Conference. The third Secretary-General, U Thant, had participated in his country's politics and represented his country as permanent representative to the United Nations. His successor, Kurt Waldheim, had been active in party politics, having been an unsuccessful candidate for president of Austria, and at the time of his appointment was permanent representative of Austria to the United Nations.

The pattern to be followed in the appointment of the Secretary-General was pretty much established when the General Assembly and the Security Council met in London in January 1946. The first choice of neither the Western powers nor the Soviet Union was acceptable to the other. After Paul Spaak, the Belgian foreign minister, had been elected President of the General Assembly, Trygve Lie, the foreign minister of Norway who had been Spaak's principal rival for the presidency, was accepted by the permanent members as a candidate to be recommended for appointment by the General Assembly. Lie was from a country which had played an active role in the war on the Allied side. He was acceptable to both the Soviet Union and the Western powers as one who, from the point of view of his war record, personal convictions, and nationality, was likely to follow a course as Secretary-General which would not be unduly prejudicial to the interests of either. When the Security Council was considering the choice of a successor to Lie on the expiration of his first term of five years, the cold war had developed to such a pitch that it was impossible for the permanent members initially to agree upon a candidate. Faced with the deadlock in the Council, the General Assembly, on the initiative of the United States, extended Trygve Lie's term of office for a period of three years. The refusal of the Soviet Union to recognize the validity of this action and its refusal to have any dealings with Trygve Lie as Secretary-General created a situation which convinced Lie that, in the interest of the Organization, he should resign.[8] The name of Dag Hammarskjöld was brought forward for consideration at this time and proved to be acceptable to all the members of the Council.

Hammarskjöld's personal qualities and public record assured the major powers that in the conduct of the office he would pursue a course of impartiality and noncommitment. Like Lie, he was a national of a state uncommitted in the East-West confrontation and his previous record was thought to assure the desired objectivity in the discharge of his responsibilities. Unlike Lie, however, he gave promise of being less outspoken in commenting on controversial issues, and his previous conduct even suggested that he might be inclined to model his conduct to some extent on that of the first Secretary-General of the League of Nations, exercising his influence more through private discussions and behind-the-scene negotiations than through public pronouncements.[9]

When Hammarskjöld met his death in 1961 he had been the object of violent attack by the Soviet Union over his conduct of the United Nations Operation in the Congo. The attack was accompanied by a demand that the office of Secretary-General be reorganized so as to provide, through structural and procedural arrangements, the impartiality which, the Soviet Union claimed, had been impossible to achieve in a single person. The refusal of members of the Organization to accept this proposal led the Soviet Union finally to agree to the appointment of U Thant, first as Acting Secretary-General and one year later as Secretary-General. Thant accepted on the condition that the integrity of his office under the Charter should be fully respected. It is significant, however, that considerations similar to those operative earlier were decisive in the selection of Thant. He was a national of a country which was neutral in the confrontation between East and West. His previous record had indicated qualities of independence and impartiality in dealing with issues dividing the major powers, and his previous experience gave promise that he would be able to per-

8. See Trygve, Lie, *In the Cause of Peace* (New York: Macmillan, 1954), pp. 367–419.

9. For a detailed, informed, and sympathetic account of Hammarskjöld's conduct of the office, see Brian Urquhart, *Hammarskjold* (New York: Knopf, 1972).

form the political responsibilities attached to the office in a manner acceptable to the permanent members of the Council.

When Thant refused to consider a third term and it became necessary to choose a successor in 1971, considerations similar to those that had dictated his selection and the choice of his predecessors were decisive in the choice of his successor. Kurt Waldheim was a national of a small country with a policy of nonalignment whose neutrality was assured not only by its own choice but also by the guarantee of four of the permanent members of the Council. Furthermore, as Austria's permanent representative to the United Nations he had demonstrated qualities of character and understanding that gave reasonable assurance to the permanent members that he would act responsibly and with proper appreciation of the Secretary-General's role.

Functions and Powers of the Secretary-General

While there are various ways of categorizing the responsibilities and powers of the Secretary-General, there are certain advantages for purposes of analysis in adopting a classification which parallels to some extent the usual manner of classifying the powers of a president or a prime minister, so long as the analogy is not taken too seriously. So viewed, the powers of the Secretary-General can be thought of as coming under three heads: (1) as the principal administrative head of the Organization; (2) as the chief executive of the Organization; and (3) as the coordinator of a family of more or less autonomous agencies which together constitute the United Nations system.[10]

As the chief administrative officer of the United Nations, the Secretary-General has functions and powers which are of an essentially managerial nature. He has responsibility for seeing that necessary secretarial services are provided for the General Assembly, the Security Council, ECOSOC, the Trusteeship Council, and the large number of subsidiary organs and special bodies set up to do the work of the United Nations. In addition, he is responsible for directing and supervising a wide range of technical services such as

10. "The United Nations Secretariat," *United Nations Studies*, No. 4 (New York: Carnegie Endowment for International Peace, 1950), p. 19.

the preparation of background papers, the preparation of reports and periodical publications, and a multitude of other special technical tasks which the Secretariat may be asked to perform by the General Assembly or the Council. Furthermore, he is responsible for personnel administration, including appointments, promotions, and disciplinary action. He must oversee the administration of the finances of the Organization. While these tasks do not in all cases require the personal attention of the Secretary-General, since responsibility for their performance is commonly delegated to department heads, the responsibility for their proper discharge is necessarily his.

Under the United Nations Charter no attempt is made to bring all important cooperative efforts in the economic and social fields within one organization. Rather the approach is a much more decentralized one, involving the establishment of a number of autonomous organizations, each with its own constitution and organizational structure to deal with particular aspects of the larger field of economic and social cooperation, such as the improvement of labor standards, the improvement of health conditions, or the safety of civil aviation. While the central responsibility for achieving coordination of the policies and activities of the United Nations itself and the various specialized agencies is placed on the General Assembly and the Economic and Social Council, acting under its authority, in practice it has been found necessary that a major part of this responsibility should be delegated to the Secretary-General. Thus, his responsibilities as chief coordinator are of the greatest importance in making the Organization effective in dealing with the wide range of economic, social, and technological problems which assume increased importance with each passing day.

It is the Secretary-General's broader political powers which provide the contrast between the role of the United Nations Secretary-General and that of the League Secretary-General.[11] That the Secretary-General should have an important political role was clearly desired by those who wrote the Charter, but what was not

11. On the political role of the Secretary-General, see Leon Gordenker, *The UN Secretary-General and the Maintenance of Peace* (New York: Columbia University Press, 1967).

and could not be anticipated was the exact form that role would assume. A number of factors have contributed to its definition in practice: (1) the Secretary-General's position as the permanent, top-ranking, full-time official able to speak for the Organization as a whole; (2) the advantages he enjoys in his relations with the political organs as the result of the expertise and detailed knowledge that he commands; (3) the limitations imposed on the Security Council by the difficulty its permanent members have in reaching detailed agreements; (4) the inherent inability of the Assembly to perform executive functions; (5) the degree of confidence that occupants of the office have inspired in the manner in which they have discharged responsibilities placed upon them; and (6) the willingness of member governments to entrust important functions to the United Nations and its organs.

The Secretary-General is able to exercise important political influence in a number of ways: (1) as the official representative of the United Nations; (2) as the official vested with specific responsibilities under resolutions of the General Assembly and the Councils; (3) as the possessor of a special right under Article 99; and (4) as the head of one of the principal organs responsible for implementing the purposes and principles of the Charter.

The Secretary-General represents the Organization in its relations with member governments and in its external relations generally. In his relations with member governments he serves as a useful source of information, an advisor, and a stimulator of policies and action in support of United Nations purposes and principles. He makes contact with governments both by visits to member capitals and by receiving member officials at headquarters; but even more important, in contrast to the League practice, are the opportunities provided at headquarters for easy and continuing contacts with the permanent representatives of member governments.[12] In addition, formal agreements with governments and other organi-

12. While League Secretaries-General tended to discourage the practice of permanent representation of members at headquarters, the practice has been encouraged by UN Secretaries-General and has provided them with useful contacts and channels of influence.

zations are concluded by the Secretary-General, although as a rule they require the approval of the General Assembly.

The Secretary-General also acts as spokesman of the Organization in reporting on its work and making suggestions for its greater effectiveness. The Charter provides (Article 98) that the Secretary-General "shall make an annual report to the General Assembly on the work of the Organization." This follows League practice, but the UN Secretary-General has gone much beyond his League counterpart in using the occasion of the report to express his views on a wide range of subjects. This he does in his "Introduction to the Annual Report" which is made available to members before the annual Assembly session, following submission of the "Report," which is factual in nature. Trygve Lie used the occasion of the annual report to express his views with considerable force on controversial issues, usually however without very much influence. In 1949, for example, he expressed the view that "it is impossible to obtain lasting security from war by any arrangement that leaves out any of the Great Powers." [13] Dag Hammarskjöld used the annual report as the occasion for discussing in more theoretical terms the role of his office, the nature of the United Nations, and its future lines of development.[14] All the occupants of the office have used press conferences and public addresses as means of informing the wider public regarding the work of the Organization in critical situations facing it, and hopes and prospects for the future.

The Secretary-General has been entrusted with the performance of a variety of functions by the General Assembly and the three Councils. The Charter explicitly provides for this in Article 98. While the power of the Secretary-General in performing these duties is circumscribed by the terms of the relevant resolutions, it almost inevitably happens that a considerable amount of discretion

13. This was an obvious reference to the North Atlantic Treaty. *Annual Report of the Secretary-General on the Work of the Organization, 1 July 1948–30 June 1949* (Doc. A/930), Introduction, p. ix.

14. See Mark Zacher, *Dag Hammarskjöld's United Nations* (New York: Columbia University Press, 1970); and Wilder Foote (ed.), *Dag Hammarskjöld: Servant of Peace* (New York: Columbia University Press, 1962).

is involved in the carrying out of these assignments. This has been particularly true in the field of peace and security, where the Secretary-General has been asked to perform such tasks as the appointment of observers to report on violations of cease-fire agreements, the supervision of United Nations peace-keeping operations established to facilitate compliance by states with cease-fire agreements, the conduct of negotiations with a view to bringing about the withdrawal of forces from occupied territory, and the working out of satisfactory arrangements for ending existing tensions between states. The amount of discretion vested in the Secretary-General has to a large extent been determined by the amount of trust which members of the Organization place in the Secretary-General.[15] It reached its height during the Secretary-Generalship of Dag Hammarskjöld when, for example, in the Congo operation he was asked to carry out a complicated peace-keeping operation involving the restoration of peace and stability within the territory of a newly independent state with only general guidance from the political organs as to how the task was to be performed.[16]

While the Assembly and the Security Council do have a choice of means to be used in carrying out their resolutions and have on occasion resorted to the device of appointing individual states, individuals, or committees to do the work, there has been a natural inclination to look to the Secretary-General for the performance of these tasks because of his recognized skill, experience, impartiality, and the resources and information at his command. Since the Congo crisis, however, some of the permanent members of the Council have insisted on keeping the Secretary-General under a very tight rein and thereby preventing him from exercising the amount of discretion practised by Hammarskjöld.

As we have seen, the Charter's major innovation as regards the

15. Since the Soviet Union attacked Hammarskjöld for misuse of powers, that government has been particularly insistent on clear definition and strict interpretation of powers given under Security Council resolutions.

16. For Hammarskjöld's defense against Soviet claims that he had misused his powers, see his Oxford University lecture, "The International Civil Servant in Law and Fact," in Wilder Foote (ed.), pp. 329–53. For detailed account of his handling of the Congo affair, see Urquhart, pp. 389–589.

powers of the Secretary-General is contained in Article 99 which gives him the right "to bring to the attention of the Security Council any matter which in his opinion may threaten the maintenance of international peace and security." The importance of this article lies not so much in the specific power that is given as in its implication that the Secretary-General, unlike his League counterpart, is to have an important responsibility for making the Organization effective in its primary purpose—the maintenance of international peace and security.

In a strict sense, this right has been used only once—in 1960—when Hammarskjöld requested a meeting of the Security Council after receiving requests from the President and Prime Minister of the Republic of the Congo for assistance in dealing with the situation created by the disintegration of domestic security and the landing of Belgian paratroopers. The possession of this right has been used, however, on a number of occasions to justify particular political initiatives intended to safeguard peace and security. Relying upon this right, the Secretary-General has insisted that he may send a personal representative to a troubled area on the invitation of the government to ascertain the facts in order that he may be in a better position to discharge his responsibility under Article 99. Also, the Secretary-General has justified visiting a particular country at the request of the government to familiarize himself with conditions there as an appropriate means of providing the information needed for making a determination under this article.[17] Furthermore, in line with this broad concept of his responsibilities, the Secretary-General has on occasion taken the initiative in intervening in discussions in the political organs to express his views on the issues involved and has on more than one occasion presented a memorandum in an attempt to clarify some legal aspect of the matter under consideration.

Apart from the powers that are given to the Secretariat by the explicit provisions of the Charter, the Secretary-General has, as the head of one of the principal organs, asserted the right and duty to take certain initiatives to achieve the purposes of the Organization,

17. For Hammarskjöld's justification of visits to Laos in 1959 and Tunisia in 1961, See Urquhart, pp. 329–67, 530–44.

particularly in the maintenance of peace and security. In this connection he has offered his services as mediator when such an offer, in his judgment, is likely to provide an acceptable procedure for the settlement or accommodation of an existing dispute or tension. During the course of the dispute between the United Arab Republic and Saudi Arabia over Yemen, the Secretary-General took the initiative in arranging a cease-fire, and on his own responsibility sent observers to assist in checking on compliance. More recently, in 1970 Secretary-General Thant was asked by Iran and the United Kingdom to exercise his good offices with a view to ascertaining the wishes of the people to Bahrain with respect to the future status of the islands. The conclusion of the Secretary-General's Personal Representative that the people of Bahrain desired independence was accepted by Iran and the United Kingdom, and subsequently ratified by the Security Council.[18] During his first term Hammarskjöld was authorized by a General Assembly resolution to proceed to Communist China to conduct conversations with a view to securing the freedom of certain American aviators that had fallen into Communist hands during the Korean fighting. The Peking government indicated its unwillingness to discuss the matter with Hammarskjöld if he was acting under Assembly authorization. However, when he proposed that he should discuss the matter in his capacity as Secretary-General without relying on the authority conferred by the General Assembly, the Peking government indicated its willingness. The negotiations resulted in a substantial degree of success.[19]

The clearest statement of what might be defined as the inherent power of the Secretary-General by virtue of his office to take those steps that he considers necessary to the maintenance of peace and security was made by Hammarskjöld at the time of his second election. In accepting the appointment of the General Assembly, he stated:

> I do not believe that the Secretary-General should be asked to act, by the Member States, if no guidance for his action is to be

18. See *Report of the Secretary-General on the Work of the Organization, 16 June, 1969–15 June, 1970* (General Assembly, *Official Records*, 25th Sess., Suppl. 1), pp. 70–4.

19. See Joseph P. Lash, "Hammarskjöld's Conception of His Office," *International Organization*, XVI (1962), 548; and Urquhart, pp. 86–131.

found either in the Charter or in the decisions of the main organs of the United Nations; within the limits thus set, however, I believe it to be his duty to use his office and, indeed, the machinery of the Organization to its utmost capacity and to the full extent permitted at each stage by practical circumstances.

On the other hand, I believe that it is in keeping with the philosophy of the Charter that the Secretary-General should be expected to act also without such guidance, should this appear to him necessary in order to help in filling any vacuum that may appear in the systems which the Charter and traditional diplomacy provide for the safeguarding of peace and security.[20]

This statement appears to have passed largely unnoticed at the time, but the position that he took was again repeated during the Congo crisis when in his Oxford University address he explained why he considered it necessary to proceed with his own interpretation of his mission in the Congo, when the Security Council and the General Assembly failed to provide him with directives covering the situations that he had to face. This view has been challenged by some permanent members of the Security Council who insist on the exclusive responsibility of that organ to act for the United Nations.

From experience to date, it is quite clear that one of the most significant innovations of the Charter was in laying the basis for the development of the political role of the Secretary-General. This is not to belittle the role of the League Secretary-General, which was important although not always visible. The United Nations Secretary-General has assumed a much more conspicuous public role and has been an important factor in making the Organization something more than a standing conference of the states which constitute its membership. This is not to say, however, that the United Nations is much more than that, because it is still the member governments which in the last analysis determine what the Organization can do.

For that reason it is dangerous to exaggerate the importance of the political role of the Secretary-General and to press too far the analogy to the chief executive officer of a state. The differences are

20. Wilder Foote (ed.), p. 150.

important and decisive. Perhaps most important of all is the fact that while the President of the United States has an important constituency to which he can appeal in case of conflict with the legislative body, the Secretary-General is practically isolated if the governments of member states, particularly the governments of the major powers, turn against him. The success of his undertakings is largely dependent upon the support of a wide consensus of member states, though the exact extent and composition of that consensus may vary from question to question. On questions of peace and security, however, the support or at least tolerance of the major military powers in matters of particular concern to them is essential. It is doubtful that Hammarskjöld, if he had lived, would have had success in countering the attacks he received from the Soviet Union by mobilizing the support of the smaller states. The resources of the Secretary-General's office therefore are limited, and in the discharge of his responsibilities he must be careful not to use them too freely.

THE SECRETARY-GENERAL'S STAFF

According to the Charter, the Secretariat consists of the Secretary-General "and such staff as the Organization may require." [21] The staff needs of the Secretary-General were recognized from the very beginning to be greatly in excess of those of his League predecessor. With the expansion of the Organization's activities and the growth of its membership to over one hundred and thirty (as compared with the League's maximum membership at any one time of half that number), the staff has at least kept step. If Parkinson's law applies, it could be expected to have grown even faster. In any case, by 1970 it numbered some 10,000 men and women at New York Headquarters, in Geneva, in Vienna, and at the seats of the regional economic commissions.

In recent years, in line with the decentralization that has taken place within the total organization of the United Nations, particu-

21. Art. 98.

larly in the performance of those functions related to economic and social development, there has been a considerable decentralization of the Secretariat itself both in functional and in geographic terms. The secretariats of the regional economic commissions have been considerably enlarged and their duties expanded though they have remained administratively within the Department of Economic and Social Affairs. In addition, with the establishment of subsidiary bodies possessing extensive autonomy and with headquarters in many cases far removed from New York City, there has been both geographic and functional decentralization. Thus separate staffs serve the following subsidiary bodies established by the General Assembly: the United Nations Children's Fund (UNICEF), located in New York; the United Nations Development Program (UNDP), in New York; the Office of the United Nations High Commissioner for Refugees (UNHCR), in Geneva; the United Nations Relief and Works Agency for Palestine Refugees (UNRWA), in Beirut; the United Nations Institute for Training and Research (UNITAR), in New York; the United Nations Conference on Trade and Development (UNCTAD), in Geneva; the United Nations Industrial Development Organization (UNIDO), in Vienna; and the United Nations Environment Programme (UNEP), in Nairobi, Kenya. In addition, a portion of the United Nations' regular Secretariat is located in Geneva. This decentralization has created difficulties of effective administrative control that are only in part alleviated by improved and speedier means of communication and travel now available.

As the result of League experience, there was general agreement at San Francisco and in the Preparatory Commission at London that the Secretariat should be organized and function in accordance with certain principles which would ensure its efficiency, independence, and international character. These principles are either specifically enunciated or clearly implied in the provisions of the Charter. They might be briefly summarized as follows: (1) members of the staff should be chosen on the basis of their qualifications to do the work required of them, efficiently and satisfactorily, account being taken of the desirability of having a secretariat that is international in composition to reflect the diversity of the cultures and outlooks of member states; (2) they should loyally serve the United Nations, refrain from any action inconsistent with their status as international officials, and be protected against political pressures by governments; and (3) they should be assured reasonable security of tenure, adequate compensation, opportunities for advancement on the basis of merit, and other benefits adequate to attract and keep highly competent personnel.

Article 101 of the Charter explicitly states that the paramount consideration in the employment of the staff and in the determination of the conditions of service shall be the necessity of securing the highest standards of efficiency, competence, and integrity, and that "[d]ue regard shall be paid to the importance of recruiting the staff on as wide a geographical basis as possible." These words suggest that positions in the Secretariat are to be filled primarily on the basis of the personal qualifications of candidates. It was recognized from the beginning that League staff members should be representative of the major cultures of the world. For this reason and because of pressures exercised by member governments that their nationals should be included in the Secretariat, account was taken of the principle of geographic distribution in the appointment of personnel, particularly in appointments to positions at the higher levels within the Secretariat. Since this principle is explicitly incorporated into the Charter of the United Nations, it becomes mandatory for the Secretary-General to take account of this consideration, although the exact degree to which this should be done is not specified.[22]

In the initial staffing of the Secretariat, carried out under the necessity of recruiting a large staff within a period of a few weeks, Secretary-General Lie drew heavily upon personnel readily available in Western Europe, the United Kingdom, the Commonwealth countries, and the United States. The location of UN Headquarters in the United States and the extensive use of persons employed in the Secretariat of the San Francisco Conference resulted in an initial disproportionate recruitment of U.S. citizens. Consequently, in

22. The Preparatory Commission thought the two principles could "in large measure be reconciled." *Report*, p. 85.

the beginning the staff composition hardly met the requirements of wide geographic distribution.

Responding to a General Assembly request [23] that consideration be given to making the Secretariat more widely representative, the Secretary-General in 1948 set forth his understanding of the principle of geographic distribution and the criteria which he proposed to adopt in applying it.[24] He interpreted the principle as not requiring that nationals of a particular state should have a specified number of posts at a particular level, or that they should receive a particular percentage of a total outlay of salaries; rather, he interpreted it as meaning that "the administration should be satisfied that the Secretariat is enriched by the experience and culture which each Member nation can furnish and that each Member nation should, in its turn, be satisfied that its own culture and philosophy make a full contribution to the Secretariat." From the time of the formulation of this policy until the late fifties, the Secretary-General directed his efforts to the implementation of this principle, and the results which he achieved met with general acceptance by the members of the Organization.

It was not until the great expansion of United Nations membership from 1955 on, and particularly the admission of new states which had previously been colonies in 1960, that there was a revival of dissatisfaction with the composition of the Secretariat and renewed insistence that efforts be made to achieve a more equitable geographic distribution. This demand received strong additional support from the Soviet Union which, as the result of the Congo experience, came to recognize the important role that the Secretariat might play in dealing with matters in which it was specially interested. Up until 1960 there had been relatively few Soviet nationals in the Secretariat, and this did not appear to be a matter of serious concern to the Soviet leaders. The result was an intensive reconsideration of recruitment standards and procedures, and insistent demands upon the Secretary-General that necessary measures be

23. General Assembly Res. 153 (II), Nov. 15, 1947.

24. General Assembly, *Official Records*, 3d Sess., Plenary, Annexes, A/652.

taken to achieve more equitable geographic distribution of staff personnel.

After extended discussion of the matter during its sixteenth session, the General Assembly requested the Secretary-General to present his views to the Assembly at its next session. On the basis of his recommendations,[25] the General Assembly in its seventeenth session recommended that the Secretary-General

> be guided in his efforts to achieve a more equitable geographical distribution, within the general framework of his report, by the following principles and factors:
> (a) In the recruitment of all staff, due regard shall be paid to securing as wide a geographical distribution as possible;
> (b) In the Secretariat proper, an equitable geographical distribution should take into account the fact of membership, Members' contributions and their populations as outlined in the Secretary-General's report, particularly paragraph 69 (b) thereof; no Member State should be considered "over-represented" if it has no more than five of its nationals on the staff by virtue of its membership;
> (c) The relative importance of posts at different levels;
> (d) The need for a more balanced regional composition of the staff at levels of D-1 and above;
> (e) In career appointments, particular account should be taken of the need to reduce "under-representation." [26]

Pursuant to the General Assembly's recommendations, the Secretary-General developed a new formula for determining the desirable range of posts, which took account not only of the financial contribution of member states, but also the population factor and the factor of membership in the Organization.[27]

The Charter contains no provision regarding language requirements for members of the Secretariat. During the early years En-

25. UN Doc. A/5063, Dec. 18, 1961.

26. See UN Doc. A/5270, Oct. 24, 1962, and General Assembly Res. 1852 (XVII), Dec. 19, 1962.

27. See *Composition of the Secretariat*, UN Doc. A/C.5/987, Oct. 11, 1963. For later statistics on composition of the Secretariat, see UN Doc. A/8831, Oct. 6, 1972.

glish was the language commonly used, and although French was accepted as a working language, proficiency in a second language was not required. Beginning with the 1960s which saw a great increase in the number of non-English speaking member states, there was a demand for a more equitable linguistic balance. While there was concern expressed by the Secretary-General and some governments over the possible unfavorable effects of the requirement of proficiency in a second language on recruitment and promotion within the service, there was general recognition of the desirability of proficiency in more than one language if this could be achieved without injustice to otherwise qualified individuals and without denying to the Organization the services of specially qualified personnel. After extended discussion the General Assembly in 1968 approved a plan under which the minimum requirement for recruitment was to be ability to use one of the working languages of the Secretariat, and that beginning January 1, 1972, all promotions should be conditional on adequate knowledge of one of the official languages of the General Assembly, subject to a limited right of the Secretary-General to make exceptions.[28]

While the Charter does not specify what the term of appointment of staff members shall be, implicit in the concept of an international civil service is the notion that staff members should have the opportunity to make the service a career, and that opportunity for advancement on the basis of quality of service should exist. This implies that newly recruited staff members, after a period of probation, should receive appointments that are permanent in the sense of assuring the staff member a career opportunity, subject of course to the usual grounds for termination or dismissal. In its report, the Preparatory Commission emphasized that for the Secretariat to function efficiently it needed a solid core of permanent officials. It recognized, however, that under certain conditions fixed-term appointments might be desirable, but recommended that the proportion of fixed-term appointments should be kept at a comparatively low level—not more than twenty-five percent of the total staff.

28. General Assembly Res. 2480B (XXIII), Dec. 21, 1968. On progress made in the implementation of these two principles, see UN Doc. A/8831, Oct. 6, 1972.

In practice it has not been possible to keep within this limit.[29] A number of considerations have contributed to this result. Not all members of the United Nations have accepted the concept of an international civil service. Instead, some have insisted that the Secretariat is an intergovernmental service and that staff members should be nominated by their governments to serve for limited periods of time. The Soviet Union has been conspicuous in taking this position and has insisted that its nationals be given fixed-term appointments. Many members, especially the new states, insist that their nationals take fixed-term appointments for other reasons. Though insistent on having equitable "representation" in the Secretariat, their personnel resources are not adequate to permit them to forego the services of their better qualified people for long periods of time. Consequently, fixed-term appointments better suit their needs. Another consideration that has contributed greatly in recent years to increasing the proportion of fixed-term appointments has been the insistence on the part of "under-represented" states that such appointments be used to achieve wider geographic representation quickly. Finally, in many cases where positions requiring highly technical competence are to be filled, it has been found necessary to use fixed-term appointments to obtain the services of persons with special qualifications who are unwilling to commit themselves to a career in the international civil service. These persons may be regularly employed by governments, by private industry, or by educational and research institutions, and are often unwilling permanently to relinquish such employment. They are only willing to accept Secretariat appointments if it is possible after a period of service to return to their former or comparable positions.

Clearly it is impossible, and indeed undesirable, to eliminate fixed-term appointments in the interest of a pure career service. In fact, renewable fixed-term appointments, particularly for higher positions, may have positive merit in a career service if used to provide the opportunity to review and assess the work of officials

29. The Secretary-General's 1972 report on the composition of the Secretariat indicated that overall proportion of staff holding fixed-term appointments stood at 34.6 percent. UN Doc. A/8831, Oct. 6, 1972 p. 4.

and to introduce fresh blood and new ideas. Also, in the case of the new and developing members, the Organization performs a useful and desirable service in giving their people experience and training which will benefit them when they return to national service. Fixed-term appointments may become a serious threat to the integrity and efficiency of the international service when used to permit governments to assign persons in their own government service to the Secretariat for limited periods of time with the understanding that they will return to that service at the expiration of the designated period, if not before. This practice, known as "secondment," constitutes at least a potential threat, not so much because of the time element as because of the divided loyalty that is likely to result. As the Preparatory Commission observed, staff members on assignment from their governments cannot be "expected fully to subordinate the special interests of their country to the international interest if they are merely detached temporarily from national administrations and remain dependent upon them for the future." [30]

The practice of secondment is not without its defenders, however. Those who view the Secretariat as a form of intergovernmental service regard it as normal and desirable, as providing assurance that Secretariat officials will retain their national character and an appropriate sensitivity to national attitudes and interests. Those who view the Secretariat as an international service understandably see the Secretariat official under great temptation to subordinate his international loyalty to national loyalty if he is shortly to return to national service and look to his national government for future rewards. On the basis of empirical evidence, one must conclude, however, that the practice has not produced uniformly bad results, and that in many situations seconded officials contribute to the vitality and effectiveness of the international service.[31] In fact, the case can be made with some justification that where the task of the Secretariat official is to assist in preparing the basis for cooperative

---

30. *Report of the Preparatory Commission,* p. 92.

31. For a balanced assessment, see Robert Rhodes James, "Staffing of the United Nations Secretariat," *ISIO Monographs,* 1st Series, No. 2, pp. 19–23.

action between national administrations in economic and social matters, seconded personnel can be particularly effective since they will be able to anticipate government reactions in performing their secretarial functions, and will later be in the position as national officials to implement agreed programs and policies more effectively by virtue of their previous United Nations experience.[32]

While a case can be made for fixed-term appointments—even secondment—under certain conditions, it still remains true that the integrity of the international service concept requires that the Secretariat should possess a solid core and a substantial predominance of personnel on permanent appointments. Only if this is true can one be assured of the development of a tradition of United Nations service, the availability of the skills and experience required for efficient administration, the subordination of national loyalties to the purposes of the Organization, and a willingness on the part of the individual to regard service to the Organization as a useful and rewarding career.

LOYALTY OF INTERNATIONAL OFFICIALS

For an international Secretariat to be truly international it is necessary that its loyalty and devotion to the Organization be assured. Beginning in 1932, members of the League Secretariat were required to make a declaration by which each member undertook to "exercise in all loyalty, discretion and conscience" the functions entrusted to him. Article 100 of the United Nations Charter provides that the Secretary-General and his staff "shall not seek or receive instructions from any government or from any other authority external to the Organization," and that they shall "refrain from any action which might reflect on their position as international officials responsible only to the Organization." Under the Staff Regulations, each member of the Secretariat subscribes to the following oath or declaration:

32. See David Kay, "Secondment in the United Nations Secretariat: An Alternative View," *International Organization*, XX (Winter 1966), 63–75.

I solemnly swear (undertake, affirm, promise) to exercise in all loyalty, discretion and conscience the functions entrusted to me as an international civil servant of the United Nations, to discharge those functions and regulate my conduct with the interests of the United Nations only in view, and not to seek or accept instructions in regard to the performance of my duties from any government or other authority external to the Organization.[33]

There are two aspects of the position of the international official which require special consideration: his duties as an international official and his obligations to the state of his allegiance. The Staff Regulations require that members of the Secretariat conduct themselves at all times in a manner befitting their status as international officials. They must avoid any action and, in particular, any kind of public statement which may reflect adversely on that status or on the integrity, independence, and impartiality which are required of them. While not expected to give up their national sentiments or their political and religious convictions, they are required to exercise the reserve and tact incumbent upon them as international officials, and specifically not to engage in any political activity inconsistent with it. Membership in a political party is permitted if it does not entail action or the obligation to action, public support or criticism of party platforms or candidates, or public criticism or support of the policies or actions of national governments.

A question of perhaps greater difficulty arises in connection with possible conflict between the status of a member of the Secretariat and his loyalty to the state of which he is a national. This question may become particularly serious if the Secretariat official is called upon to perform his service within the territory of the state of his nationality. The question arose in connection with certain U.S. nationals—members of the Secretariat—who, during hearings before a special federal grand jury and the Internal Security Sub-Committee of the Senate Judiciary Committee in 1952, either admitted being members of the Communist party or when asked whether

33. Staff Regulation, 1.9.

they had been members or had engaged in subversive activities, invoked the Fifth Amendment of the United States Constitution which provides protection against self-incrimination. The Secretary-General, on the basis of a report of a committee of jurists,[34] treated these acts as incompatible with the international status of the officials in question, and therefore affording grounds for removal. Considerations of political expediency influenced Secretary-General Lie and his advisers to adopt a course of action that would not offend public opinion, and in particular congressional opinion, in the United States. Dag Hammarskjöld, on succeeding Lie, took a more positive line in defense of the rights of staff members, and his actions, combined with UN Administrative Tribunal decisions in individual cases and General Assembly support, went far to restore Secretariat morale and respect for the position of the international civil servant.[35]

A national of the host state may have obligations as a member of the Secretariat which require conduct in conflict with what his government demands. Furthermore, his status as an international civil servant should give him protection against acts of his government inconsistent with that status. This is not because the United Nations is a superstate but rather because every member state by virtue of acceptance of the Charter has agreed in advance to recognize Secretariat officials as having an international status entitling them to certain rights, privileges, and immunities, including protection in the faithful discharge of their official duties.

CONCLUSIONS

More than any other organ, the Secretariat is responsible for giving to the United Nations a character that places it above the diplomatic machinery of the past. The Secretary-General has the responsibility for determining the nature of that contribution. In his

34. *Report of the Secretary-General on Personnel Policy* (A/2364, Jan. 30, 1953), pp. 21–3.

35. See Urquhart, pp. 56–70.

discrete way, the first Secretary-General of the League recognized the responsibility placed upon him and discharged his responsibilities in such a manner as to create precedents and expectations which were to be decisive in the writing of the Charter. The authors of the Charter took the important decision of placing upon the Secretary-General an additional responsibility and opportunity to make the Organization effective in achieving its purposes. The four Secretaries-General of the United Nations have, in their own individual ways, discharged this responsibility; but they have nevertheless been forced to recognize that while the Secretary-General has important responsibilities and opportunities, he cannot be too far out in front of the members of the Organization that he serves. Their governments in a real sense constitute his constituency, and it is therefore necessary for him, in the initiatives and decisions that he takes, to bring them along with him. Given the role of the major powers in the Organization, it is particularly necessary that the Secretary-General has their support in initiatives and decisions that he takes in the field of peace and security. This does not mean that he must merely be their instrument; he can also be their instructor and, within limits, their leader, but he must recognize that his power of leadership in the last analysis is qualified by their willingness to follow.

If the Secretary-General is to perform his duties in the spirit of the Charter, he must be supported by a staff which is competent, independent of the political influence of member governments, and, like its chief, loyal to the principles and purposes of the Organization. The Organization provides adequate opportunities for adjustments and accommodations to be worked out between the responsible representatives of member governments without introducing the representational principle into the Secretariat itself. While it is desirable, the world being what it is, that the Secretary-General and his principal advisers have the confidence of the major powers, there is no sound reason why even these officials should be viewed in any sense as the representatives of member governments. The permanent missions which members maintain at Headquarters can and should perform that function.

If the staff is to meet the requirements of a truly international civil service, it is necessary that every effort be made to secure highly qualified personnel, to provide attractive conditions of employment and reasonable incentives for well-qualified men and women to take positions in the Secretariat, and to protect members of the Secretariat against improper influences that will detract in any way from the loyal performance of their duties. At the present time the future of the Secretariat is far from clear. This uncertainty is a reflection of the troubled state of international relations and the unwillingness of governments to accord the United Nations a major role. Too often, member governments have failed to use their influence to strengthen the Secretariat by giving their assistance in the recruitment of the best people and creating the best working conditions. If the Secretary-General and his staff are to provide the Organization with the kind of leadership and service required to make the United Nations a vital force, member governments must be prepared to place confidence in them and make it possible for the kind of people to be recruited in whom confidence can be placed.

CHAPTER SIX

MAINTAINING PEACE AND SECURITY

WHEN THE UNITED NATIONS was being established, the maintenance of international peace and security was viewed as its primary purpose and function. Charter provisions for the performance of that function were thought to be a great improvement over those of the League Covenant. In fact, it was the enforcement capacity of the new organization that was most emphasized by its promoters and supporters. In the years that have elapsed since San Francisco, a different view regarding the relative importance of the peace and security role of the Organization has come to be accepted, reflecting not only new demands that have been made upon it but also the failure to perform that function with the effectiveness that had been hoped. This failure has been largely the result of the inability of the major powers to agree on important issues, and their disinclination, particularly of late, to make use to the full of the resources of the Organization, even when in agreement.

THE CHARTER SYSTEM FOR THE MAINTENANCE OF INTERNATIONAL PEACE AND SECURITY

The Charter specifies different approaches to the maintenance of international peace and security. First, members of the United Nations undertake to "refrain in their international relations from the threat or use of force against the territorial integrity or political independence of any state, or in any other manner inconsistent with the Purposes of the United Nations." [1] This goes considerably further than the League Covenant which required members not to "resort to war" under certain specified conditions, but not all. The ambiguity of the term "resort to war" was a factor in reducing the effectiveness of the League commitment.

Second, the Charter requires that "all Members shall settle their international disputes by peaceful means in such a manner that international peace and security, and justice, are not endangered." [2] Nevertheless, it does not provide any complete assurance that peaceful settlement will be achieved. Use of the organs and procedures of the United Nations depends almost entirely on the initiative of states, and is with few exceptions voluntary. Even the jurisdiction of the Court remains voluntary except insofar as states may exercise the option of accepting it on a compulsory basis for certain kinds of disputes.

Third, the Charter provides for enforcement measures to be taken under certain circumstances. In this respect the Charter approach differs from that of the Covenant. The Covenant obligated members of the League to apply forthwith sweeping economic and financial sanctions against any member resorting to war in violation of its obligations under the Covenant. Furthermore, the Covenant contained in' Article 10 an undertaking on the part of members to provide mutual protection against external aggression. The Charter is more selective and more political in that it places upon the Security Council—a political body—the responsibility for determining whether a threat to the peace, a breach of the peace, or act of aggression exists, and what measures are to be taken once the determination is made. [3] The only limitation upon the freedom of decision of the members is that the Council "act in accordance with the Purposes and Principles of the United Nations." [4] At San Francisco the smaller states made a strong effort to get some further limitation on the discretion of the Council included in the Charter, but the Sponsoring Powers and France successfully resisted these efforts.

1. Art. 2, par. 4.   2. Art. 2, par. 3.   3. Art. 39.   4. Art. 24.

Fourth, the Charter envisages the regulation of national armaments as an important feature of a system for peace and security, and directs the Security Council to prepare plans for submission to members. Unlike the Covenant which treated disarmament as an important and independent means of preventing war, the Charter views the regulation of armaments as something to be undertaken after the security provisions have been fully implemented. In fact, the emphasis of the Charter is upon the maintenance of a floor for national armaments, as well as a ceiling, the theory being that it is important that adequate armaments be available for the maintenance of peace.

Finally, the Charter emphasizes the importance of public discussion and multilateral diplomacy [5] as means of achieving the peaceful adjustment of unsatisfactory situations and the acceptance of principles of cooperation and rules of conduct which will contribute to international peace and security. The General Assembly, by virtue of its composition, is particularly well suited for performing this function, which amounts to serving as a sort of "town meeting of the world."

The Charter places primary responsibility for the maintenance of international peace and security on the Security Council. The particular measures which the Council may take and the procedure that it is to follow are defined in considerable detail. However, the Council is given very wide discretion in the evaluation of circumstances, the choice of means, and the timing of its actions. Acting under Chapter VI of the Charter, it may investigate the dispute or situation and make recommendations to the parties regarding the methods and terms of settlement and adjustment. It was made clear at San Francisco, however, that the recommendations which the Council might make for the peaceful settlement of disputes were not to be treated as binding, and that consequently the Council could not in the name of peace "in our time" impose upon any small state the kind of treatment that the major European powers meted out to Czechoslovakia at Munich in 1938.

Under Chapter VII the Security Council is given extensive

5. What has come to be referred to as "parliamentary diplomacy."

powers for dealing with any dispute or situation which has reached the point where a threat to the peace, breach of the peace, or act of aggression is found to exist. It has the power, and in fact is duty-bound, to make a determination when such a condition exists [6] and, having made the decision, it must decide on the basis of its evaluation of the situation what course should be followed to maintain or restore international peace and security. There are three possible courses available to it in such order or combination as the Council may decide: It may choose to act under Chapter VI in an effort to achieve a peaceful settlement or accommodation; acting under Article 40, it may call upon parties to comply with provisional measures intended to prevent the aggravation of the situation; and acting under Articles 41 and 42, it may require members of take such political, economic, and financial measures as may be necessary to restore international peace and security.

However, before members may be required to take military measures they must agree to make available on call designated military contingents under special agreements concluded with the Council. These agreements govern "the numbers and types of forces, their degree of readiness and general location, and the nature of the facilities and assistance to be provided." [7] Until such military agreements are concluded as enable the Council to exercise its responsibilities under Article 42, the permanent members of the Security Council are to consult with each other with a view to taking such joint action on behalf of the United Nations as may be necessary to maintain international peace and security.[8]

IMPACT OF THE DEVELOPING WORLD SITUATION

The success of the Charter system depended primarily on the co-operation of the permanent members of the Security Council. At the time the Charter was written its authors hoped, and had some reason to expect, that the major victors would find it in their interest to cooperate to make the Charter system effective in order to

6. Art. 39.   7. Art. 43.   8. Art. 106.

prevent the recurrence of another disastrous world conflict. It soon became apparent, however, that the Soviet Union and the Western powers, under the leadership of the United States, had conflicting views regarding the necessary conditions of peace and security and did not share a common conviction regarding the role which the United Nations should play. Initially at least, the Western powers sought to make extensive use of the United Nations for restoring conditions of peace and security in the war-torn world, reserving, as had been agreed, the treatment of the defeated enemy powers for decision of the major victors. The Soviet Union, on the other hand, relying on its military strength, the Communist party organization, and the appeal of Communist ideology to provide for its own national security, looked upon the United Nations, and the Security Council in particular, more as means to be used to prevent action inimical to its own interests than as means of cooperation for common purposes. Frequently the uses which the Western powers sought to make of the United Nations were viewed by the Soviet Union as direct threats to its security and therefore to be prevented by the use of the veto in the Security Council.

Failure to implement the enforcement provisions of the Charter by the conclusion of agreements making available to the Security Council the forces and facilities necessary to the full discharge of its responsibilities was the first major blow to the Charter system. Early in 1946 the Security Council requested the Military Staff Committee to examine and report on the question of military agreements under Article 43. The report which the Committee submitted on April 30 showed agreement on twenty-five articles and failure to achieve agreement on sixteen others.[9] The sixteen, unfortunately, concerned matters of a critical nature not adequately covered by the Charter which had to be decided before agreements under Article 43 could be concluded. They related to such matters as size and composition of the armed forces to be contributed by the permanent members, the provision of bases, the location of forces when not in action, and the time of their withdrawal. Generally speaking, the United States favored a large force

9. Security Council, *Official Records,* 2d year, 1947, Special Suppl. 1.

with great striking power, flexibly composed, and so organized and located as to be readily available. The Soviet Union, on the other hand, saw no need of a large force, insisted that the principle of equality should govern contributions, and demanded clear definition of the conditions under which the force could be used. It was obvious from the discussions in the Committee and subsequently in the Security Council that the disagreements resulted primarily from lack of confidence on the part of the Soviet Union and the United States in each other's good faith and intentions. The differences, therefore, were political and not technical.

That military forces and facilities were not made available to the Security Council, permitting it to take measures under Article 42, did not of itself mean that the Council could not exercise extensive powers under other provisions of the Charter. Without military forces at its disposal, it could still recommend procedures and terms of settlement, call upon the parties to adopt provisional measures under Article 40, order collective measures of a nonmilitary nature, and take other measures under its general responsibility for maintaining peace and security. That in practice it was prevented in many instances from taking these measures, even when the necessary majority support was forthcoming, led many participants and outside observers to conclude that the Council was failing to discharge its responsibilities because of the obstructive tactics of the Soviet Union.

This overly simplistic view failed to take account of the fact that the Charter system assumed a relationship of positive cooperation for common purposes among the permanent members of the Council that did not exist under cold war conditions. The Charter system assumed that it would be possible for the permanent members to agree on effective courses of action in situations such as faced the Council when it was called upon to deal with the Greek and Palestine questions. Given attitudes such as were characteristic of the cold war—fear, mutual distrust, lack of confidence in the good faith of the other side—this was not possible, at least in those situations where vital security interests of a permanent member appeared to be threatened. Under such conditions, what is surprising is that the Council was able to achieve as much as it did.

The United States and other Western powers became convinced that the Security Council was an unreliable instrument for providing collective security and maintaining peace, especially in the cold war situation when the major threats seen by them came from a state that was able by its negative vote to prevent any action from being taken. Alternative means of providing this additional security were sought in two directions: (1) the inherent right of individual or collective self-defense recognized by Article 51, and (2) the use of the General Assembly as an alternative means of dealing with serious situations in which the peace was threatened or actually violated.

Of these two alternatives, the first was the one upon which chief reliance was placed. On the Western side, the North Atlantic Treaty of April 4, 1949 became the basis for organized defense cooperation among Western European powers and the United States and Canada, and the principal collective means by which these states faced their major external threat in the years of the cold war. The Warsaw Pact of May 1955 served the same purpose for the Soviet Union and its socialist allies, though they had earlier relied on a system of bilateral agreements justified as "regional arrangements directed against the renewal of aggressive policy" on the part of an enemy state.[10] The success of these self-defense arrangements is a matter of opinion, but there is substantial basis for the belief that they have contributed to the stabilization of an unsettled and dangerous postwar situation and may have made an important contribution to the later development of a spirit of detente in place of the cold war tension.

The use of the General Assembly as an alternative to the Security Council, in case the latter was prevented from taking a decision by a veto, had special appeal for the United States so long as it was reasonably assured of the necessary majority support in that organization. When, in June 1950, North Korean forces invaded the Republic of Korea, the absence of the Soviet representative from the meetings of the Council made it possible for that organ to take decisions initiating collective measures in support of the Republic

10. Art. 53 of the Charter.

of Korea. The resumption by the Soviet representative of his place in the Council on August 1 made it impossible for the Council to continue as the UN director of the collective military operation, and led the United States to introduce proposals in the General Assembly which were subsequently adopted in somewhat modified form as the Uniting for Peace resolution.[11] By the terms of this resolution, the General Assembly assumed the right to consider threats to and actual violations of the peace in case the Security Council failed to discharge its responsibilities because of the exercise of the veto and, in case of violations, to recommend the use of necessary means—including military—to restore peace. The clear purpose of this assumption of power by the General Assembly was not only to make possible the circumvention of the veto in the Security Council but also to change the character of the UN collective security system to resemble more closely that of the League: it would permit the taking of collective measures, under UN auspices and with U.N. approval, against a permanent member of the Council. While a resolution of the Assembly would not be binding upon members, it would have considerable political influence, particularly if adopted by a large majority, and would serve to "legitimize" measures which otherwise might be viewed as contrary to the Charter.[12]

This assumption of powers by the General Assembly on the urging of the United States and other Western members had no sooner been consummated than it became apparent that the purpose of its authors was not to be realized. When Communist China intervened in Korea, and Security Council action was blocked by the Soviet veto, the matter was brought to the attention of the General Assembly; but the United States was unable to get a decision even recommending economic measures until after a long delay due to the unwillingness of members, even close allies of the United States, to take steps which would risk a major conflict.[13]

11. General Assembly Res. 377 (V), Nov. 5, 1950.

12. Inis L. Claude, Jr., *Swords into Plowshares* (4th ed.; New York: Random House, 1971), pp. 268–72.

13. See Leland M. Goodrich, *Korea: A Study of U.S. Policy in the United Nations* (New York: Council on Foreign Relations, 1956), pp. 149–77.

Since 1951 it has been clear that the provisions of the Uniting for Peace resolution cannot be used to coerce a major power or to initiate collective measures in situations where a major power—a permanent member of the Council—would feel its vital interests threatened. The principal use of the resolution has been to achieve quicker consideration by the General Assembly, but not the exercise by that body of powers to which a permanent member objects. Thus, in 1956, while the General Assembly was able to take prompt constructive measures based on general consent in dealing with the Middle East situation, it was unwilling to take any steps beyond investigation and expression of disapproval in dealing with Soviet intervention in Hungary.

The Charter system, as we have seen, recognized a place for the regulation of national armaments in the total scheme of things but, unlike the Covenant, subordinated it to the organization of security. The explosion of an atomic device at a time of growing distrust between East and West had a profound effect on the approach taken in practice. In the West—and especially in the United States—there was widespread concern over the possible consequences of the uncontrolled development and use of atomic energy for destructive purposes. With the agreement of the United States, the United Kingdom, and the Soviet Union the question of international regulation of atomic energy was placed on the agenda of the General Assembly, which established by resolution of January 24, 1946 the United Nations Atomic Energy Commission to make proposals for consideration by the Security Council and member governments. The plan submitted by the United States called for wide international control with safeguards against violation.[14]

The plan, if adopted, would have left the United States, for an indeterminate period, in sole possession of the bomb, but held out the promise of effective international control which would assure the use of atomic energy for exclusively peaceful purposes. In a situation of mutual confidence and trust, the United States might have been satisfied with less far-reaching guarantees of compliance

14. U.S. Department of State, *The International Control of Atomic Energy: Growth of Policy,* Publ. 2702 (1946).

and a definite limit to the period of its exclusive possession of the weapon, and the Soviet Union might have been prepared to accept temporary inequality and even some inspection arrangements to assure compliance. However, in the worsening state of East-West relations, the Soviet response was to change the terms of the debate in order to be able to take a more popular stand, one that would receive wider support. The initial Soviet response was to demand the complete prohibition of the production and employment of atomic weapons; later, when the question came before the General Assembly for consideration, it raised the old much-debated question of general disarmament. As a result the United Nations has been involved from the very beginning in what was essentially the League approach—an effort to achieve disarmament by international agreement as an independent means of assuring peace. The results have been limited, as might have been anticipated in the light of the League experience, and such agreements as have been reached have been negotiated for the most part by the major military powers with the United Nations serving primarily as a facility and the General Assembly as a goad.

The overall impact of the cold war on the Charter system for the maintenance of peace and security was to weaken and distort it during its early years. When the cold war showed some signs of subsiding in the middle fifties and there were indications of an emerging detente, other influences operated to prevent the United Nations from assuming the importance and the special role which its founders had envisioned in the maintenance of international peace and security. The expansion of membership from 1955 on, accompanied by the substantial increase in the number of members "uncommitted" in the cold war, reduced the value of the Organization—and the General Assembly in particular—as a means by which the non-Communist members might mobilize support for their positions and maintain pressure on the Soviet Union and its bloc of Communist states. At the same time, the increased influence of the new, underdeveloped, non-Western states in the Organization led to a shift in Organization priorities, with increasing attention being given to problems of decolonization, racial discrimination, and economic and social development. Even disarmament came to be viewed by the new majority primarily as a means of making more funds available for development purposes.

For a period of a half-dozen years following the death of Stalin in 1953, when tension between East and West seemed to be lessening and Hammarskjöld was able to inspire confidence in the possibilities of a constructive UN role, it seemed that the Organization had the chance to become an important factor in the maintenance of international peace and security, especially through its peace-keeping operations. This prospect was for the time being removed by the Soviet attack on Hammarskjöld over his conduct of the Congo operation, the ensuing financial crisis of the Organization, and second thoughts of the African members regarding the role the Organization should play in the affairs of that continent. Further dimming the prospects of early revival of the UN's role in maintaining peace and security has been the change in the character of the Organization as the result of admission of new states without the military and economic means to contribute responsibly to that goal, yet insistent on a greater degree of participation in decisions.[15] Not unrelated to this development has been the recent decline in U.S. interest in the peace and security capabilities of the United Nations.

THE CHARTER SYSTEM IN ACTION

In the introduction to his last annual report as Secretary-General, Dag Hammarskjöld called attention to two different concepts of the United Nations that have special significance in connection with its work in the maintenance of international peace and security. According to one concept, the United Nations serves as static conference machinery for resolving conflicts of interests and ideologies with a view to peaceful coexistence. According to the second concept, the Organization serves as "a dynamic instrument of governments" through which they seek not only reconciliation but also forms of executive action, undertaken on behalf of all members

15. See chap. 3.

and aiming at forestalling conflicts and resolving them once they have arisen by appropriate diplomatic or political means.[16]

The principal factor in determining which of these two concepts prevails is the extent to which the Secretary-General succeeds in providing effective leadership. As Hammarskjöld rightly pointed out, "it has been and is clearly for the governments, members of the Organization, and for these governments only, to make their choice and decide on the direction in which they wish the Organization to develop." While Hammarskjöld was able, during his tenure of office, to move the Organization somewhat away from the first concept and create the impression, misleading in the light of subsequent events, that a substantial institutional development was in progress, over the years the model of static conference machinery has come closer to describing the United Nations at work than the model of dynamic instrument of governments under an international executive.

GETTING THE UNITED NATIONS INVOLVED

Apart from the right which the Secretary-General possesses under the Charter to bring matters to the attention of the Security Council and the General Assembly—a right which he exercises with some caution because of his weak political position—the initiative in bringing a matter to the attention of the United Nations (Security Council, General Assembly, or International Court of Justice) must be taken directly or indirectly by a state or states. The considerations which influence and determine the decision to take this initiative are varied in nature. They range from legal considerations, such as the provisions of the Charter or other agreements and understandings, to more selfish motives, such as the desire to bring political pressure to bear in an adversary situation or to achieve more effectively a national purpose through international cooperation. Not every question of international peace and security receives UN consideration.

16. *Introduction to the Annual Report of the Secretary-General on the Work of the Organization, 16 June 1960–15 June 1961* (General Assembly, *Official Records*, 16th sess., Suppl. 1A), p. 1.

At San Francisco there was agreement of the Sponsoring Powers and France—the future permanent members of the Security Council—that questions relating to the treatment of the enemy powers in the war then in progress should be reserved for their consideration and should not be matters for the United Nations to consider. While there has been some disagreement among the permanent members on the extent and interpretation of this understanding,[17] it has been generally followed and, as a result, except with the agreement of the powers themselves as on the question of Italian colonies, questions relating to the treatment of the enemy powers in World War II have, with few exceptions, been excluded from UN consideration. This has had consequences not wholly favorable to the Organization. While on the one hand it has disassociated the United Nations from arrangements imposed on the defeated powers that might be regarded as unjust and contrary to UN principles, it has removed from UN consideration important questions of peace and security and, by denying a role to the United Nations in their settlement, has prevented the Organization from playing a part in achieving conditions essential to its own effective functioning. It cannot be denied that deadlocks and delays in reaching agreement on these questions, especially the German question, have contributed to the inability of the permanent members to cooperate within the UN itself.

A second category of questions that in principle is excluded from UN consideration consists of all matters essentially within the domestic jurisdiction of any state, subject only to the qualification that this does not apply to enforcement action.[18] This limitation, of course, applies to all activities of the United Nations, but historically and in practice it has special importance in connection with activities in the peace and security field. While intended to protect a reserve area against UN intervention, it has been interpreted in practice to limit very little, if at all, what organs of the United Nations may do.[19] In particular, notwithstanding the limitation, the United Nations has dealt many times with domestic vio-

17. See Art. 107, and commentary in Leland M. Goodrich, Edvard Hambro, and Anne P. Simons, *Charter of the United Nations: Commentary and Documents* (3d. rev. ed.; New York: Columbia University Press, 1969), pp. 633–37.

18. Art. 2, par. 7.   19. See Goodrich, Hambro, and Simons, pp. 60-72.

lence and internal conditions threatening violence on the basis of their international consequences.

Which organ will be chosen to consider a particular question is also determined in most instances by the decision of a member state. This may be largely dictated by Charter provisions determining the competence of UN organs. More commonly, however, alternatives exist, and in this case the choice is likely to be dictated by what the initiating state is seeking. If it seeks support for a right claimed under treaty or customary law, and the parties involved have accepted the compulsory jurisdiction of the Court,[20] it may choose the Court, the organ which is obligated by its Statute to apply international law in its decisions. On the other hand, a Communist or non-Western state may not find the Court an attractive body because of lack of confidence in the law it applies or in the impartiality of the judges. In situations where colonial rule is being challenged or racial discrimination on the part of white regimes is alleged, the General Assembly is likely to be the organ of choice since members most firmly committed to the principles of self-determination and racial equality constitute a large and assured majority in that organ. Only in such cases when time is of the essence or action is sought that only the Security Council can take is an appeal to that organ likely. When, as in the early days of the cold war, the will of the majority in the Security Council is blocked by the negative vote of a permanent member, or this result seems likely, appeal is made to the General Assembly to get a decision which, though not binding, at least legitimizes and gives support to the desired course of action.

WHAT THE UNITED NATIONS HAS ACCOMPLISHED

Peaceful settlement

Of all the approaches to peace, peaceful settlement has the longest history; it is characterized by the development and use of a variety of methods and the conclusion of innumerable agreements for

20. Under Art. 36 of the Statute.

their use. These methods have been based generally on certain assumptions regarding the nature of international conflict; however, the record of their use has not been such as to inspire complete confidence in the adequacy of the underlying assumptions.[21] Nevertheless, efforts to improve the prospects of peaceful settlement have made use of these traditional methods. The League system provided a permanent international court and institutionalized the practices of mediation and conciliation. The Charter system continued this development. Its particular contributions were to stress the initial responsibility of members to use peaceful methods of their own choice, to make the Court an integral part of the UN system, to relate the UN's responsibilities for peaceful settlement more directly to the preservation of peace and security, and to emphasize the responsibilities of the major military powers.

As has been the case in most of its fields of activity, the United Nations has been called upon to perform its peaceful settlement functions under conditions quite different from those encountered in the past or envisaged at the time the Charter was written. The disputes and situations that the League was asked to deal with concerned largely the interpretation and application of the peace treaties and other international agreements, territorial claims, claims for damages suffered, and other differences of a traditional nature. The parties involved were states, and for the most part states with the same Western traditions. Significantly, the claims that the League was not able to cope with successfully were those that challenged the existing order in the cause of a revolutionary ideology.

The United Nations has had to perform this function in a much more unsettled, divided, and basically revolutionary world. The failure to conclude peace treaties or to achieve agreement between the major victor nations with respect to the treatment of the defeated enemy states left large and important areas of international relations in an unsettled state. The cold war of clashing ideologies and conflicting strategic interests was conducted in part by subversive activities and forms of indirect aggression, which traditional methods had difficulty in coping with. The revolt of Asian and Af-

21. For fuller discussion, see Claude, chap. 11.

rican peoples against colonial rule and racial discrimination produced situations of internal violence with international repercussions which did not lend themselves to treatment by traditional methods of peaceful settlement. Finally, the emergence of new Asian and African states as the result of decolonization has produced a diversified world society. These new states, along with the Communist states of Eastern Europe and Asia, find Western international law unacceptable in important respects and are unwilling to utilize those institutions and procedures that rely upon it. Finally, the authority which the Organization was expected to possess and exercise by virtue of major power agreement in the Security Council has been absent or reduced to a minimum by their divergent interests.

Given these conditions it is not surprising that the record of the Organization in peaceful settlement and accommodation has been disappointing. The International Court of Justice—"the principal judicial organ of the United Nations" [22]—has had only limited use and on the whole has not played as important a role as its predecessor, the Permanent Court of International Justice. While it has given (as of August 1972) thirty-two judgments and fourteen advisory opinions,[23] a substantial number of the judgments have been on preliminary questions and few of the opinions have been on aspects of disputes being considered by other UN organs. In no case has a Communist state taken the initiative and brought a dispute to the Court. Also, the new states of Asia and Africa have shown little interest in using the Court.

In dealing with disputes and situations in which the parties—one or more of them—make claims which they are not willing to submit to binding third-party judgment, the political organs of the United Nations have had only limited success in achieving peaceful settlements or accommodation, although they have been instrumental in reducing the amount of violence. One explanation of this is to be found in the fact that the United Nations is usually brought into the dispute or situation at a fairly advanced stage of its develop-

22. Art. 92 of the Charter.
23. ICJ, *Yearbook, 1971–1972* (The Hague, 1972), p. 12.

ment when firm positions have been taken and violence has often already been resorted to. In part this results from the Charter requirement that the parties must first seek a peaceful settlement by means of their own choice. In situations where claims to independence are advanced, it may only be after there has been resort to violence that a convincing case can be made that a legitimate ground for international concern exists. Until then the state whose authority is challenged has often succeeded in denying the UN competence by invoking the domestic jurisdiction principle. Finally, the effectiveness of both the Security Council and the General Assembly as organs of mediation and conciliation have been reduced by the tendency of the two superpowers to introduce their own divergent ideological and strategic interests. As Paul Hasluck wrote at an earlier time, the Security Council consideration of a dispute all too often

> develops into an argument between the members of the Council and the argument is conducted in a way that gives more attention to the differences between members of the Council than to the differences between the parties to the dispute.[24]

In dealing with disputes and situations with a view to peaceful settlement or accommodation, the United Nations organs have utilized a variety of methods.[25] Some of these are different than, if not improvements on, those utilized by the League. For better or worse, public discussion has been a conspicuous feature of the procedure of both the Security Council and General Assembly. A possible disadvantage of this is that by giving the interested parties the opportunity to present their cases publicly and in great detail at the very beginning, positions become fixed and compromise becomes more difficult. On the other hand, considering the fact that the dispute or situation usually comes to the UN organ at a fairly advanced stage and that positions have generally already been firmly taken and are widely known, thanks to the efficiency of modern

24. Paul Hasluck, *Workshop of Security* (Melbourne: F. W. Cheshire, 1948), p. 94.

25. See Leland M. Goodrich and Anne P. Simons, *The United Nations and the Maintenance of International Peace and Security* (Washington: Brookings Institution, 1955), pp. 207–340, for detailed discussion.

media of communication, public discussion in the UN organ may not add much to the already established rigidity of party positions.

In those cases where fighting has already broken out, the UN organ has initially sought to achieve an agreement to end the fighting as a necessary condition to the fruitful consideration of terms of settlement. The techniques developed for achieving cease-fires and establishing conditions favorable to further substantive discussions have been the major contributions of the United Nations to the methodology of peace maintenance. They will be discussed at length in chapter 7. It must, however, be recognized that these techniques, while effective in reducing if not completely eliminating violence, have not in practice provided any assurance of improvement in relations between the interested parties or satisfactory settlement of their differences. If the cease-fire is effectively maintained, however, it does keep open the possibility that the causes of disagreement will in time become subordinated to other concerns of a more constructive nature.

Efforts to achieve peaceful settlement by methods of mediation and conciliation, usually through a designated individual or group, have had only limited success. When fighting broke out in Indonesia in 1947 between Dutch forces and forces of the self-styled Republic of Indonesia, the Security Council was able not only to achieve a cease-fire but also to play a useful mediatory role in bringing about a final settlement based on recognition of Indonesia's independence.[26] That this success could be achieved was largely due to the fact the United States and other Western members of the Council were prepared to accept and to bring pressure upon the Netherlands to accept a solution which the Soviet Union, in view of its advocacy of independence for colonial peoples, was not prepared to veto.[27] In other situations where large-scale violence has occurred even though a cease-fire has been achieved, efforts to get a final settlement through mediation or conciliation have not succeeded in large degree due to the failure

26. Alastair M. Taylor, *Indonesian Independence and the United Nations* (Ithaca, N.Y.: Cornell University Press, 1960).

27. Taylor, pp. 374–400.

of the major powers themselves to agree on appropriate procedures or terms of settlement or their unwillingness to bring to bear
on the parties the necessary pressure to achieve agreement. A decisive factor has often been the conflicting interests and purposes of
the United States and the USSR. Thus, following the resumption
of large-scale fighting in the Middle East in 1967, though a cease-
fire was achieved and agreement reached on the principles to govern a settlement and the appointment of a mediator to assist the
parties in doing so,[28] efforts to get a settlement have been stalled
not only by the unwillingness of the parties to compromise but also
by the failure of the United States and the USSR to agree on terms
which they are prepared to press their protegés to accept. In
Southeast Asia the intrusion of cold war considerations was one
factor preventing the United Nations from playing a role either in
ending hostilities or achieving a political solution. In both of these
situations, developments during 1973 and 1974 showed that
agreement, or at least lessening of tension, between the United
States and the USSR can effectively contribute to improved prospects of accommodation in the areas of conflict.

While the Security Council and the General Assembly have been
less than successful in performing mediatory and conciliatory roles,
the Secretary-General has on occasion used his powers under the
Charter to assist in reaching agreements. It has not been in mediat-
ing the more serious disputes and situations where the Council and
Assembly have failed that the Secretary-General has succeeded, but
rather in dealing with cases in which violence has not yet been
resorted to, major power interests are not deeply involved, and the
parties are in agreement in accepting the Secretary-General's mediation as a trusted third party.[29]

Enforcement Action

As we have seen, those primarily responsible for drafting the
Charter stressed the enforcement capacity of the new organization

28. See Arthur Lall, *The UN and the Middle East Crisis* (New York: Columbia University Press, 1968).

29. For further discussion, see above, pp. 93–94.

as its most distinctive and promising feature. By this was meant the power given to the Security Council by Chapter VII of the Charter to adopt decisions requiring the use of collective measures, ranging from the severance of diplomatic relations to the use of military force to maintain or restore international peace and security in those cases where a threat to or violation of the peace is found to exist. This power, though it appears promising on paper, has failed to be developed and used in practice, except to a very limited extent and in circumstances other than those originally foreseen.

Inability of the permanent members of the Security Council to agree on the principles governing the special agreements under Article 43 [30] or to agree on measures to be taken under Article 106 pending the coming into force of such agreements precluded from the beginning the taking of collective military measures. The ideological and strategic confrontations of the cold war also made impossible decisions ordering lesser measures of coercion. The use under UN auspices of collective military measures in Korea in 1950 was made possible by a special circumstance not likely to recur: the voluntary absence of the representative of a permanent member who, if present, would have cast a negative vote. While this was an example of collective measures used with considerable effectiveness, it was not a case of ordered military action since the Security Council only recommended. The effect of the Council decision was to legitimize rather than obligate in a legal sense.[31] The Korean operation had the further significance that it involved collective measures under UN auspices against a state having the support of a permanent member—a result which the Charter provisions were intended to prevent and which became possible only because of the absence of the Soviet representative. The formalization of this possibility by the General Assembly's assumption of power to recommend collective measures, including military, was ineffective, due in large measure to the unwillingness of member states to run the risk of a major world conflict.[32]

In recent years there has been a revival of interest in the enforce-

30. See chap. 5.   31. See Goodrich, *Korea*, pp.102–25.

32. See Goodrich, *Korea*, pp. 156–73, and Claude, pp. 269–72. Also see previous discussion, p. 73.

ment provisions of the Charter and pressure to use them for achieving compliance with Charter obligations in the field of human rights. Whereas the original Charter concept was that collective measures should be used, as a policeman uses force, to maintain a condition of peace or to restore a condition of peace once violence had occurred, the new concept in effect is that collective measures should be used as a sanction to assure respect for international commitments other than the obligation to refrain from the use of force. Thus in the cases of apartheid in the Republic of South Africa, the refusal of South Africa to accept General Assembly and Security Council resolutions regarding South West Africa (Namibia), and the Smith regime in Rhodesia, it is not in fact the threat to peace or the actual breach of the peace which is the real occasion for collective measures being ordered or recommended but rather the alleged violation of the principles of racial equality and self-determination as set forth in the Charter and resolutions of the General Assembly. This new emphasis in the use of collective measures has resulted from the changed composition of the United Nations and the pressure mounted by the new majority. While it is too early to enter a final judgment regarding their effectiveness, the reluctance of many members, including some of the major powers, to support strong collective measures makes the prospect of success extremely doubtful.[33]

Disarmament and the Regulation of Armaments

The experience of the United Nations in dealing with this problem has provided only limited encouragement for those supporting the "direct" as against the "indirect" approach.[34] This experience would seem to confirm the lesson of earlier efforts that until states make some progress in settling their differences or have openly or tacitly agreed, with confidence in each other's good faith and inten-

33. See Margaret Doxey, "International Sanctions: A Framework for Analysis with Special Reference to the U.N. and Southern Africa," *International Organization*, XXVI (1972), 527–50. See also chap.8, below.

34. For explanation of terms and defense of indirect approach on basis of League experience, see Salvador de Madariaga, *Disarmament* (New York: Coward-McCann, 1929).

tions, to renounce the use of force in settling their differences, the chances of reaching an agreement on the substantial limitation and reduction of national armaments are very poor. The authors of the Charter accepted this view and intended that the collective security system should be fully implemented and that the peaceful settlement or adjustment of disputes and conflict situations should be reasonably assured before a general system of armament limitation or reduction would be possible. Unfortunately the atomic bomb and the cold war upset the Charter sequence, with the result that there have been long discussions with small results, measured by the size and costs of postwar national armaments and the variety and destructive capacity of the weaponry developed and maintained.[35]

As soon as the disarmament discussions got under way within the context of developing postwar international relations—the cold war, divided Germany, divided Europe, the two superpowers in armed confrontation—it was clear that neither the United States nor the USSR would agree to any terms that seriously weakened its position of relative strength or restricted its ability to redress a position of relative weakness. Thus the United States was unwilling to yield its atomic superiority and the Soviet Union was unwilling to renounce its right to achieve atomic parity or to yield its superiority in conventional arms. Thus, efforts to achieve the international control of atomic energy on the basis of U.S. proposals [36] were successfully blocked by the Soviet Union. Though agreement was reached on the general principles for the regulation and reduction of armaments,[37] subsequent efforts to apply these principles failed. On the major issues, the Soviet Union and the Western Powers took opposite positions. The Soviet position was that nuclear disarmament should come before disarmament of conventional forces, that agreement on concrete disarmament measures should have

35. On the early course of UN efforts, see Bernhard G. Bechhoefer, *Post-war Negotiations for Arms Control* (Washington: Brookings Institution, 1961).

36. U.S. Department of State, *The International Control of Atomic Energy: Growth of a Policy*, Publ. 2702 (1946).

37. General Assembly Res. 41 (I), Dec. 14, 1946.

priority over effective control, that agreement on disarmament measures should not wait on political settlements and increased international security, and that agreement on general and complete disarmament should be sought instead of agreement on first steps and specific details. On all these issues the Western powers generally took reverse positions.[38]

With the lessening of cold war tension from the middle fifties on, the achievement by the Soviet Union of atomic parity, recognition by both sides of the unacceptable consequences of atomic war, and some encouraging progress in the improvement of political relations,[39] it became possible to make limited progress in reducing by international agreement the rivalry in national armaments between the two superpowers and, incidentally, among other states as well.

The agreements concluded fall into roughly three categories: (1) agreements prohibiting the use of certain materials or measures (the 1963 Nuclear Test-Ban Treaty and the 1971 Convention on the Prohibition of the Development, Production and Stockpiling of Bacteriological [Biological] and Toxic Weapons and on their Destruction); (2) agreements excluding weapons or practices from certain areas (the 1959 Antarctica Treaty; the 1967 Treaty on Principles Governing the Activities of States in the Exploration and Use of Outer Space; the 1968 Non-Proliferation Treaty; the 1971 Treaty on the Prohibition of the Emplacement of Nuclear and Other Weapons of Mass Destruction on the Sea-Bed and the Ocean Floor and the Sub-Soil Thereof); and (3) agreements limiting the size of national armaments (the U.S.–USSR Treaty to Limit Anti-Ballistic Missiles, and Interim Agreement on Offensive Missiles, 1972).

A number of considerations have made possible the conclusion of these agreements. In the case of the Antarctica, Outer Space, and Sea-Bed agreements, it was not a matter of limiting or eliminating armaments already in place or in advanced stage of development

38. See Bechhoefer; see also, William Ekstein, *Disarmament: Twenty-Five Years of Effort* (Canadian Institute of International Affairs, 1971).

39. As evidenced recently by agreements on Berlin, acceptance of the status quo in Eastern Europe, and the Nixon–Brezhnev Declaration and the Joint Communique concluding President Nixon's Moscow visit of May 1972.

but rather of preventing armament rivalry from being extended to these areas. Furthermore, there were varying degrees of doubt on the part of national governments as to the strategic value of doing what the agreements prohibited. In the case of the Bacteriological Convention, there was not only doubt as to the strategic value of the use of the materials in question but also a long history of the nonuse of such materials even when available. It is significant that it was not possible at the same time to reach agreement on the prohibition of chemical weapons. In the Limited Test Ban Treaty, the United States, the Soviet Union, and the United Kingdom, under pressure from the nonatomic states, gave up practices that were potentially injurious to peoples outside their borders while retaining the right to continue underground tests which, considering the advanced state of their technology, were considered adequate for further weapon development. By the Non-Proliferation Treaty these same powers achieved certain assurances that their own special positions would be preserved, while allegedly reducing the prospect of nuclear war by limiting the number of states with nuclear weapons. Finally, the U.S.–USSR Moscow Agreements represented the first modest step in the fulfillment of the promise made to nonnuclear states to get their acceptance of the non-proliferation commitment. While providing quantitative limitation of certain weapons and means of delivery, these agreements did not provide for reduction of weapons, placed no limits on qualitative improvement, and at least in the United States were followed by increased rather than decreased armament expenditures.

The role of the United Nations in achieving these limited successes has been important but uneven. Apart from its early unsuccessful efforts in dealing with the international control of atomic energy, the Security Council has given little attention and made no significant contribution to the development of agreements reached, except for limited security assurance given to nonnuclear parties to the Non-Proliferation Treaty.[40] It has not formulated a plan "for the establishment of a system for the regulation of armaments" as Article 26 of the Charter defines its responsibility.

40. Security Council Res. 255 (1968), June 19, 1968.

The General Assembly, on the other hand, has been very active and has served as a valuable forum for keeping the disarmament issue in the forefront of public awareness and for providing governments of member states with the opportunity to express their concern, to formulate their common desires, and to bring pressure to bear upon the major powers to take practical steps to limit and reduce armaments. Considering the amount of time and energy devoted to the topic and the volume of supporting documentation, the results must appear meagre. Nonetheless, a fair judgment must be that Assembly action has produced some results. The Limited Test-Ban Treaty clearly was in large measure the result of Assembly pressure. The Assembly and its subsidiary organs played a significant role in the formulation and acceptance of a number of agreements such as the Outer Space, Sea-Bed, and Bacteriological Weapons agreements which imposed important restraints upon military activities even though they did not result in armament reduction. While the major military powers have been largely impervious to Assembly pressures for the limitation and reduction of their armaments, and have conducted their more serious negotiations substantially outside the United Nations, they clearly have been influenced by Assembly pressure to conduct serious discussions, even though they have shown limited willingness to allow these pressures to influence their national judgments on the terms of the bargains they will accept.

Development of Principles and Methods of Cooperation

A major part of the total activity of the United Nations in the peace and security field has taken the form of developing general principles, rules, and procedures. This has been the special responsibility and contribution of the General Assembly which, under the terms of the Charter, is the organ that is given the responsibility for considering "general principles of cooperation in the maintenance of international peace and security," "promoting international cooperation in the political field," and "encouraging the progressive development of international law and its codification." [41] The Gen-

41. Arts. 11 and 13 of the Charter.

eral Assembly is well suited to the discharge of this responsibility since its inclusion of all members of the Organization gives maximum assurance that all points of view will be presented. A general consensus is essential if General Assembly resolutions are to have practical consequences. This is not assured, however, by the voting procedure of the Assembly which permits resolutions to be adopted by a two-thirds majority of the members present and voting.[42] For this reason proponents of particular proposals usually are anxious to achieve unanimity, or a close approximation to it, and usually are prepared to make concessions to achieve this result.[43]

General Assembly activity in the development of principles of cooperation has chiefly taken the form of discussions and resolutions on (1) general principles for the guidance of member states in their political relations, including principles and procedures for achieving disarmament; (2) the existing rules of international law and its further development; and (3) the strengthening of UN organization and procedures for maintaining international peace and security.

Of these various forms of activity, the efforts to strengthen organizational arrangements and procedures have been the least frequent and on the whole probably the least effective. Partly this has been due to the fact that the major attempts have been made in a cold war context and have not been supported by a sufficiently wide consensus to assure effective results.[44] The attempt in 1947 to increase the effectiveness of the General Assembly by establishing the Interim Committee to discharge certain of its functions while it was not in session failed to achieve its purpose primarily because of the noncooperation of the Soviet Union. As we have seen, the 1950 Uniting for Peace resolution did not achieve its principal purpose because members were not prepared to face the possible consequences of collective measures against a permanent member,

42. Art. 18 of the Charter.

43. On the question of the legal consequences of General Assembly resolutions, see Jorge Castaneda, *Legal Effects of United Nations Resolutions* (New York: Columbia University Press, 1969), chaps. 3 and 7.

44. See Goodrich and Simons, pp. 218–20.

though it did provide the means whereby the General Assembly could meet more expeditiously to consider urgent matters. Efforts to achieve agreement on the principles governing the initiation and conduct of peace-keeping operations have thus far been unsuccessful.

The distinction between principles for the guidance of states in their political relations and rules of international law relating to international peace and security is not a clear-cut one. It is in part a matter of the generality of the first and the specificity or concreteness of the second. It has in fact been much easier to achieve agreement on general principles than to get states to agree on specific rules giving effect to the general principles. Thus, for example, the Charter declares that states "shall refrain in their international relations from the threat or use of force against the territorial integrity or political independence of a state," and in the further development of this principle, the General Assembly has proclaimed that "[a] war of aggression constitutes a crime against peace." [45] Repeated efforts to reach an agreement on the definition of aggression have thus far failed.[46] Most of the work of the General Assembly in promoting the development and codification of international law has been in those areas where national security interests have not been greatly involved. With the assistance of the International Law Commission and the Secretariat, the Assembly has contributed substantially to the development and clarification of the law on important topics, including treaties, diplomatic and consular relations, nationality, and the high seas and territorial waters.[47]

The activities of the General Assembly in developing general principles for the guidance of member states in the maintenance of peace and security can be categorized as follows: (1) activities directed to the improvement of relations between the permanent members, particularly at the time when the cold war was having its

45. General Assembly Res. 2625 (XXV), Oct. 24, 1970.

46. See Benjamin B. Ferencz, "Defining Aggression: Where it Stands and Where It's Going," *American Journal of International Law,* LXVI (1972), 491–508.

47. See Herbert W. Briggs, *The International Law Commission* (Ithaca, N.Y.: Cornell University Press, 1965).

most serious consequences for the Organization; (2) activities concerned with advancing the prospects of disarmament and the international control of atomic energy; and (3) activities directed more widely to the membership of the Organization and concerned with achieving conduct consistent with its purposes and fundamental principles. The Soviet Union has been more frequently than any other member an initiator of proposals for the enunciation of general principles. Particularly during the first decade this may well have been viewed as a useful propaganda tactic in the cold war. In more recent years it has been an effective device for mobilizing the support of the new members of the Organization. The wide support that these General Assembly resolutions [48] have received in the voting does not accurately measure the willingness of member states to give practical applications to the principles in question. The provisions of these resolutions are often ambiguous and contradictory, and the generality of their language permits states to give them voting support for political reasons while each state reserves the right to interpret their terms in accordance with its desires and interests.[49]

The value of what the General Assembly has done in the consideration and formulation of general principles of cooperation is not easily measured. Most informed people would agree that the General Assembly has made a useful contribution to the development of international law, though opinions differ on the extent and nature of that contribution insofar as the legal effects of declarations on general principles of cooperation are concerned.[50] The enunciation by the General Assembly of principles of cooperation has un-

48. For example, the Declaration on Granting Independence to Colonial Countries and Peoples (1960) and the Declaration on the Inadmissibility of Intervention in the Domestic Affairs of States and the Protection of Their Independence and Security (1965).

49. On the ambiguities and contradictions of the 1960 Declaration, see Rupert Emerson, "Self-Determination," *American Journal of International Law*, LXV (1971) 459–75.

50. For two divergent views, see Rosalyn Higgins, "The United Nations and Law-Making: The Political Organs," *American Journal of International Law*, LXIV (Sept. 1970), 37–48, and Leo Gross, "The United Nations and the Role of Law," *International Organization*, XIX (1965), 537–61.

doubtedly had some effect on the actual conduct of states. Even the major powers clearly prefer to act in accord with the general will of the membership as expressed by the General Assembly, unless major national interests appear to dictate a different course. United States intervention in the Dominican Republic in 1965 and Soviet intervention in Czechoslovakia in 1968 illustrate the limitations of such restraints. One cannot avoid the feeling that much of the General Assembly's activity in the discussion and formulation of general principles of cooperation is devoid of any practical, useful results. In part this is due to the unfortunate emphasis that is placed upon getting items on the agenda and getting proposals adopted by the necessary majorities without too much regard to whether a general consensus favorable to action is thereby being achieved. As a result, resolutions are often adopted in the face of substantial opposition. In the effort to achieve wide agreement, ambiguous and contradictory provisions are included. To achieve the semblance of an important result, agreement is proclaimed on principles already accepted in the Charter. Such repetitiveness does little to improve the credibility of the Charter itself or contribute to the effectiveness of the General Assembly in the discharge of its Charter responsibilities.

CHAPTER SEVEN

PEACE-KEEPING

THE "PEACE-KEEPING" OPERATIONS of the United Nations have been the most controversial, the most highly publicized, and in many respects the most constructive and successful of its peace and security activities. Yet the word "peace-keeping" does not appear in the Charter, and considerable discussion has taken place on whether operations of this character are authorized by the Charter and, if so, by which chapter and which articles. In fact, the suggestion has been made that it is necessary to invent a Chapter 6½ to provide a legal basis. As will shortly be argued, this suggestion hardly seems necessary.

The term "peace-keeping," to describe a special form of United Nations activity, came into vogue with the establishment of the United Nations Emergency Force in the Middle East in 1956. The term has been generally used to describe this and subsequent operations such as the United Nations Observer Group in Lebanon (UNOGIL), the United Nations Operation in the Congo (ONUC), and the United Nations Force in Cyprus (UNFICYP). These operations have been differentiated from enforcement action by the fact that military forces are used solely on the basis of consent of all parties concerned, and not for coercive purposes, though the Congo experience has tended to blur this distinction in the minds of some observers. On the other hand, peace-keeping operations have been differentiated from peaceful settlement, though they definitely envisage such settlement, are intended to prepare the way for it, and may be accompanied by efforts in that direction, as in the case of Cyprus.

The Charter specifies two means of maintaining international peace and security: the use of collective measures of coercion to prevent or suppress breaches of the peace, and the use of peaceful methods of settlement or adjustment. However, the Security Council is expressly authorized,[1] in order to prevent a worsening of the situation, to "call upon the parties concerned to comply with such provisional measures as it deems necessary or desirable. Such provisional measures shall be without prejudice to the rights, claims, or position of the parties concerned," though the Security Council "shall duly take account" of failure to comply with such measures. The use of military personnel on a consent basis can easily be justified as a reasonable means of carrying out the expressly authorized power of the Security Council under Article 40. The purpose of such use clearly is to prevent situations from deteriorating, and to achieve a stabilization of relations between parties in conflict, which will permit renewed efforts at peaceful settlement.[2]

The Charter basis of peace-keeping operations initiated by the General Assembly is different. The Assembly's powers in the maintenance of international peace and security, though limited to discussion and recommendation, are wide-ranging with respect to what can actually be discussed or recommended. The limitations which the Charter imposes result primarily from the grants of power to the Security Council, and it is over the extent to which the Council has been given exclusive competence to act that the controversy with respect to the Assembly's power to initiate and direct peace-keeping operations has developed. The contention of some members, including the Soviet Union and France, is that only the Security Council has competence to adopt decisions on the use of organized military units.

1. Art. 40.

2. For analysis of actions taken, either expressly or by reasonable inference, under the provisions of Article 40, see Leland M. Goodrich and Anne P. Simons, *The United Nations and the Maintenance of International Peace and Security* (Washington: Brookings Institution, 1955), chap. 15; and Leland M. Goodrich, Edvard Hambro, and Anne P. Simons, *Charter of the United Nations: Commentary and Documents* (3d rev. ed.; New York: Columbia University Press, 1969), pp. 302–11.

VARIATIONS IN PEACE-KEEPING

Though the operation in its totality may be comparatively new, its elements are indeed old. "Cease-fires," "truces," and "armistice agreements" are established means of bringing armed conflict to an end. The use of observers for the purpose of checking on compliance or of commissions of inquiry for establishing facts preliminary to further international action has a long history.[3] The use of organized military units under international auspices was accomplished with conspicuous success by the League of Nations in the Saar Basin in 1935.[4]

An early example of United Nations peace-keeping was the United Nations Truce Supervisory Organization (UNTSO) in the Middle East. After refusing to implement by force the General Assembly's 1947 recommendation for the partition of Palestine,[5] the Security Council on April 23, 1948, established a Truce Commission for Palestine, made up of those members of the Council, other than Syria, with career consuls in Jerusalem.[6] The Commission was established to persuade the parties to the hostilities then in progress to agree to a truce which the Commission would then observe. It was unsuccessful. On May 14 the General Assembly established the office of UN Mediator.[7] On the following day the British mandate expired and the Provisional Government of Israel proclaimed its independence. Armed forces of the neighboring Arab states immediately invaded Israel, and what had been a condition of internal violence within the mandated territory became a breach of international peace.[8]

3. For detailed account, see David W. Wainhouse and Associates, *International Peace Observation: A History and Forecast* (Baltimore: Johns Hopkins Press, 1966).

4. F. P. Walters, *A History of the League of Nations* (London: Oxford University Press, 1952), II, 586–98.

5. General Assembly Res. 181A (II), Nov. 29, 1947.

6. UN Doc. S/727, April 23, 1948.

7. General Assembly Res. 186, May 14, 1948.

8. For details, see Jacob C. Hurewitz, *The Struggle for Palestine* (New York: Norton, 1950).

On May 29 the Council called on the parties to order a four-week truce to be supervised by the Mediator in conjunction with the Truce Commission with the assistance of military observers.[9] The sixty-three observers, drawn from the three countries' members of the Commission, were supplanted by fifty-one guards from UN Headquarters and about seventy auxiliary personnel. They were subsequently joined by ten more officers from each of the members of the Truce Commission. Count Bernadotte, the Mediator, secured five Swedish officers to act as his personal representatives, and one of these was designated Chief of Staff for truce supervision. The task of the observers was to engage in routine observation, investigate incidents and complaints, and endeavor to settle them on the spot.

The Mediator was unsuccessful in his efforts to get the parties to extend the truce, and when hostilities broke out, the observers were withdrawn. On July 15 the Security Council ordered a cease-fire and instructed the Mediator to supervise the observance of the new truce.[10] This he did by reviving and strengthening the truce organization. However, there were major violations of the truce, and full-scale fighting occurred before the parties became convinced that a negotiated cessation of hostilities was to their advantage. Later, in November, the Council decided to establish an armistice and called upon the parties to conduct negotiations to that end.[11] Negotiations, conducted with the assistance of Acting Mediator Ralph Bunche, led to the conclusion of armistice agreements which utilized the previously established Truce Supervisory Organization for assuring compliance with their terms. Each armistice agreement provided for the supervision of the execution of its terms by the Mixed Armistice Commission under the chairmanship of the UNTSO Chief of Staff, and each Commission was empowered to employ observers from UNTSO's military personnel who were to remain under the command of the Chief of Staff while so employed. To assist in the maintenance of the armistice agreements, the Council asked the Secretary-General to arrange for the

9. UN Doc. S/801, May 29, 1948.   10. UN Doc. S/902, July15, 1948.

11. UN Doc. S/1080, Nov. 16, 1948.

continued service of such UNTSO personnel as was necessary. It instructed UNTSO to observe and maintain the cease-fire and report back to it from time to time.[12] During the period 1949 to 1956 UNTSO was not wholly successful in preventing serious violations of the agreements from occurring, but it did succeed in preventing these incidents from escalating.[13] Clearly, this early employment of military personnel for maintaining peace contained many of the elements of future peace-keeping operations.

The situation leading to the establishment of the United Nations Emergency Force (UNEF) in 1956 was of an even more serious character than that which existed in Palestine in 1948 to 1949. It had one common element—conflict between Israel and her Arab neighbors—but the situation was made more serious by the military intervention of France and the United Kingdom, professedly to protect the Suez Canal, and the threat of intervention by the Soviet Union. Action by the Security Council was prevented by the negative votes of France and the United Kingdom. As a consequence, the Uniting for Peace resolution was used to bring the matter before the General Assembly in a special emergency session. On November 2 the Assembly adopted a resolution calling for an immediate cease-fire, a halt to the movement of military forces into the area, and the prompt withdrawal of forces behind the armistice lines by parties to the armistice agreements.[14] Under the terms of the Uniting for Peace resolution, refusal of the British, French, and Israelis to agree to a cease-fire and to withdraw their forces could have been followed by a recommendation of collective measures, including the use of armed force, to achieve that result. It was not necessary to consider this course of action since the invading states, under considerable pressure, did agree to do as requested.

The withdrawal of British and French forces, and the eventual withdrawal of Israeli forces, were facilitated by a Canadian initiative looking to the establishment of an international force to be introduced into the area for purposes which the British and French

12. UN Doc. S/1376, Aug. 11, 1949.

13. Alan James, *The Politics of Peace-Keeping* (New York: Praeger, 1969), p. 285.

14. General Assembly Res. 997 (ES-1), Nov. 2, 1956.

professed to be serving. The first step taken by the Assembly to implement this idea was to request the Secretary-General to submit "within forty-eight hours a plan for the setting up, with the consent of the nations concerned, of an emergency international United Nations Force to secure and supervise the cessation of hostilities," in accordance with the terms of the November 2 resolution.[15] Following the submission by the Secretary-General of a report giving the details of such a plan, the General Assembly established the United Nations Command for an "emergency international force to secure and supervise the cessation of hostilities," appointed Major-General E. L. M. Burns, Chief of Staff of the United Nations Truce Supervisory Organization, as Chief of the Command, authorized him to recruit the officers needed, and invited the Secretary-General "to take such administrative measures as may be necessary for the prompt execution of the actions envisaged in the present resolution." [16] At the time of its maximum strength, the Force consisted of some 6000 officers and men contributed by ten member states. After the completion of the withdrawal of Israeli forces in March 1957, the Force continued to perform observation and supervision functions along the Egyptian-Israeli armistice demarcation line, though restricted to Egyptian territory.[17]

Though it contained many of the elements of UNTSO, UNEF represented a considerable further development of the peace-keeping idea and came to be regarded as a prototype of successful peace-keeping operations until the time of its withdrawal on the request of the Government of the United Arab Republic in May 1967. Unlike UNTSO, it was composed of organized military units contributed by member governments. By virtue of its size, composition, and function, it involved a much more extensive limitation of the host state's freedom of action and a more serious in-

15. General Assembly Res. 998 (ES-1), Nov. 4, 1956.

16. General Assembly Res. 1000 (ES-1), Nov. 5, 1956.

17. For a detailed study of UNEF, see Gabriella Rosner, *The United Nations Emergency Force* (New York: Columbia University Press, 1963). See also E. L. M. Burns, *Between Arab and Israeli* (New York: Ivan Obolensky, 1963); Terrence Robertson, *Crisis: The Inside Story of the Suez Conspiracy* (New York: Atheneum, 1965); and Brian Urquhart, *Hammarskjold* (New York: Knoff, 1972), pp. 159–230.

trusion upon its normal territorial jurisdiction. The cost of maintaining the force was considerable; it was decided not to include it in the regular budget. The setting up of a separate account, as was done later in the case of the Congo operation, tended to emphasize the special character of peace-keeping operations.

The success of UNEF in achieving its initial purpose and the confidence which the Secretary-General was able to inspire in his impartiality and skill were important factors in leading the Security Council to engage in another peace-keeping operation of a more limited type. In 1958 the Lebanese government accused the U.A.R., recently formed by the union of Egypt and Syria, of "massive, illegal, and unprovoked intervention," threatening its national security. On the proposal of Sweden, the Council decided to send an "observation group" to Lebanon "to insure that there is no illegal infiltration of personnel or supply of arms or other *materiel* across the Lebanese borders." [18] The Secretary-General was authorized to take the necessary steps. The Observer Group was small, only about a hundred in number. Though supported by aerial observation, considering the the length of the border with Syria and the nature of the terrain, it was greatly handicapped in performing its assignment. Its report, denying that large-scale intervention existed, was not accepted as conclusive by the Lebanese government or by the United States.

The landing of U.S. Marines to support the Lebanese government led to a Council meeting at which a proposal to strengthen the Observer Group was vetoed by the Soviet representative. With the Security Council deadlocked, Secretary-General Hammarskjöld took the initiative, saying that in the circumstances it was "in keeping with the philosophy of the Charter" that he take action "to prevent a further deterioration of the situation." [19] As a result, the Observer Group was expanded to one hundred and ninety. Meanwhile, the question was transferred from the Security Council to the General Assembly, which adopted a resolution on August 21

18. Security Council Res. 128, June 11, 1958.
19. Security Council, *Official Records,* 837th meeting (July 22, 1958), paras. 12–14. On Hammarskjöld's role in the Lebanese operations, see Urquhart, pp. 261–92.

asking the Secretary-General to make such "practical arrangements" as would "adequately help in upholding the purposes and principles of the Charter" and thereby facilitate the early withdrawal of foreign troops.[20] By November the Observer Group had increased to 591, and had played a significant role in bringing about the withdrawal of United States forces and the establishment of stability in the area.

Success in the Middle East had created wide confidence in what the United Nations might accomplish through peace-keeping operations carried out under the general direction of the Secretary-General. Following the achievement of independence by the Republic of the Congo on June 30, 1960, the government was shortly faced with the collapse of its internal security arrangements and Belgian military intervention. It appealed to the United Nations for assistance. The Security Council, acting on the initiative of the Secretary-General, called upon Belgium to withdraw its forces and authorized the Secretary-General "to take the necessary steps, in consultation with the Government of the Republic of the Congo, to provide the Government with such military assistance as may be necessary, until, through the efforts of the Congolese Government with the technical assistance of the United Nations, the national security forces may be able, in the opinion of the Government, to meet fully their tasks." [21] The Secretary-General explained that in discharging his responsibilities he proposed to be guided by the principles that he had earlier formulated as governing the activities of UNEF.[22] These required that the operation be based upon consent—consent of the host state and consent of the contributing states; that it should be exclusively under the control of the United Nations and serve exclusively United Nations purposes; that it should not be used to influence the existing balance of forces; that it should not intervene in domestic affairs to influence in any way the internal political situation; and that it should use force only in self-defense.

20. General Assembly Res. 1237 (ES-III), Aug. 21, 1958.
21. Security Council Res. 143, July 13, 1960. (S/4387)
22. UN Doc. E/3943, Oct. 9, 1958.

It soon became apparent that these principles were not wholly adequate for the Congo situation since the assistance which the Security Council had decided to offer, given the condition of chaos that existed in the Congo, of necessity involved influencing the internal political situation. At the very beginning, Hammarskjöld was faced with the necessity of deciding the attitude he should adopt toward Tshombe and the Katanga secessionist movement. His refusal to give any support to the Leopoldville government in its efforts to reestablish its authority and his direct negotiations with Tshombe to achieve the right of the United Nations forces to enter Katanga inevitably strengthened the hands of the Tshombe regime which enjoyed outside support. With the collapse of the Central government and with Kasavubu and Lumumba competing for power, the closing of the Leopoldville radio station and the airport denied to Lumumba an advantage which he otherwise would have enjoyed. Though justified on the ground that it was necessary to avoid open violence, the UN action in fact weakened the position of Lumumba in the domestic struggle for power. It was only when the directives of ONUC were modified to permit the use of force, if necessary, to prevent civil war and to remove foreign mercenaries from the scene [23] that a result was achieved in terms of Congolese unity and the appearance at least of internal order and political stability that permitted the withdrawal of the Force with a valid claim to at least partial success. It could hardly be maintained, however, that the national security forces of the Republic were yet ready "to meet fully their tasks." [24]

Not only was ONUC the largest and most expensive of the UN peace-keeping operations up to that time—a force of 20,000 at its maximum strength and costing $120,000,000 a year—but it was also the most difficult to execute. It was particularly difficult to get member governments to agree on new directives for the Secretary-

23. Security Council Resolutions of Feb. 21, 1961 (S/4741) and Nov. 24, 1961 (S/5002).

24. The literature of the Congo operation is extensive. Specially recommended are Ernest W. Lefever, *Crisis in the Congo* (Washington: Brookings Institution, 1965); Catherine Hoskyns, *The Congo since Independence* (London: Oxford University Press, 1965); and Urquhart, pp. 389–598, which is specially valuable because of the author's access to Hammarskjöld's papers.

General as new situations and needs arose. In large measure this was due to the fact that ONUC became involved in internal struggles which had international implications because of the interests of outside powers in their outcome. As a consequence, the peace-keeping operation became entangled not only in domestic struggles which in principle it was supposed to keep clear of, but also in great power conflicts which it had been the initial purpose of ONUC to keep out of the Congo. A major casualty of this unfortunate development was the Secretary-General who, without adequate guidance from the political organs, found it necessary to take measures that could not possibly satisfy all the major interested parties.

A peace-keeping operation of still another kind—involving the use of military forces under the United Nations for temporary administrative purposes—was performed in connection with, and to facilitate, the transfer of West Irian, or West New Guinea, from The Netherlands to Indonesia. The United Nations had earlier contributed in a substantial manner to the creation in 1949 of the independent state of Indonesia out of territory that had formerly been part of the Dutch colonial empire.[25] The territory of West New Guinea was left under Dutch administration at the time as a result of failure to agree on its future disposition. Indonesia persisted in its claim to the territory, and brought increasing pressure to bear on The Netherlands to accept its claim, finally resorting to the mobilization and use of its armed forces. As a result of mediation by a representative of the Secretary-General, an agreement was reached on August 15, 1962, by which the United Nations would assume the administration of the territory temporarily, and then in a manner and at a time to be decided, turn the administration over to Indonesia. The UN agency was to be the United Nations Temporary Executive Authority (UNTEA), headed by a UN administrator and assisted by UN security forces. The agreement was approved by the General Assembly on September 21.[26] The

25. For an excellent account of the UN's part in this operation, see Alastair M. Taylor, *Indonesian Independence and the United Nations* (Ithaca, N.Y., Cornell University Press, 1960).

26. See UN Doc. A/5170 and Corr. 1 and Add. 1, and General Assembly Res. 1752 (XVII), Sept. 21, 1962.

necessary military units were provided by Pakistan. The transfer of administration to Indonesia took place on May 1, 1963, after seven months of UN administration. By the original agreement, Indonesia was under obligation to hold a plebiscite to determine the wishes of the population, but was free to decide the time and method. The role of the United Nations in this case was little more than that of giving assurance of orderliness and formal respect for Charter principles in the transfer of territory. Incidentally, it made the transfer easier for the Dutch to agree to.

The major controversy that erupted over the conduct of the Congo operation and its financing made it seem unlikely that any major peace-keeping operation would soon be undertaken. By 1964, however, the situation in Cyprus had become critical as the result of threatened intervention by Turkey on behalf of the Turkish minority whose position was being endangered by proposed changes in the constitution. The major powers had an interest in avoiding a major confrontation and were willing to have the United Nations undertake a peace-keeping operation provided their basic positions on authorization and financing were respected.

By its resolution of March 4, 1964, the Security Council recommended the establishment of a peace-keeping force by the Secretary-General "in consultation with the Governments of Cyprus, Greece, Turkey and the United Kingdom, in the interest of preserving international peace and security, to use its best efforts to prevent a recurrence of fighting and, as necessary, to contribute to the maintenance and restoration of law and order and a return to normal conditions." [27] The force was to be stationed for a period of three months; costs were to be met, and in a manner determined by them, by the governments contributing contingents and the government of Cyprus. The Secretary-General was authorized to accept voluntary contributions.

The situation was one of internal conflict, with a definitely international aspect resulting from the fact that the Constitution of Cyprus had been the subject of international agreement and guarantee, and that the two groups in conflict had the support of

27. Security Council Res. 186 (Doc. S/5575).

foreign powers—Greece and Turkey. Furthermore, the United Kingdom had special interests and responsibilities as the former colonial power and as the possessor of military base rights in the island. In fact, British forces had undertaken the responsibility of preserving peace between the two factions, and were present on the island in considerable numbers for that purpose, which explained their subsequent inclusion in the United Nations Force.

The Force was established by resolution of the Security Council and for a limited period of time, making it necessary that the Security Council take positive action to renew its mandate. This has repeatedly been done because of continued tension resulting from failure to achieve any settlement of the basic issues. Furthermore, as the result of the unwillingness of some states, including France and the Soviet Union, to accept the principle of compulsory assessment, the financing of the Cyprus force was placed on a voluntary basis. Recognizing that without a satisfactory resolution of the basic problems a situation would soon arise requiring the revival of United Nations intervention, the Council authorized the Secretary-General to appoint a mediator who would have the responsibility of assisting the parties to reach agreement upon a settlement of the issues dividing them. Thus it was recognized from the beginning that settlement of the basic issues responsible for producing conflict was essential if the work of the United Nations Force in bringing the fighting to an end was to have lasting value.[28]

BASIC PRINCIPLES OF PEACE-KEEPING

Peace-keeping operations have invariably been undertaken, not for the purpose of influencing the conduct of states by coercive methods, but rather to assist in the implementation of agreements already reached and incidental thereto, to perform such functions as observe, report, and assist in the settlement of minor differences

28. For more detailed discussions of the Cyprus operation, see James A. Stegenga, *The United Nations Force in Cyprus* (Columbus: Ohio State University Press, 1968); and James M. Boyd, "Cyprus: Episode in Peace-Keeping," *International Organization*, XX (1966), 1–17.

and perform local police functions, and in general to do those things that are thought to contribute to the ultimate goal of peaceful settlement or adjustment. In the case of ONUC, some confusion arose due to the fact that at certain stages in the life of the operation the use of military force seemed to be necessary in order to achieve its main purpose. It should be noted, however, that even in the Congo case, military force was not used against an established and recognized public authority.

The question of competence to authorize a peace-keeping force has been highly controversial. The United Nations Emergency Force was brought into being by a resolution of the General Assembly. Since the establishment of the Force had the approval of the Egyptian government, the Soviet Union never pushed its objection to General Assembly competence to the point of seriously obstructing the work of the Force. When, however, in 1960 the Security Council was unable to agree upon directives for the Congo force, and the question was brought before the General Assembly, the Soviet Union strongly challenged the Assembly's competence. This challenge was more vigorously stated in connection with the financing of peace-keeping operations. The Soviet Union, France, and other states took the position that the Security Council had the exclusive right to initiate peace-keeping operations because it only could decide on the use of organized military units. While this position has not been accepted by the United States and other members of the Organization, there is general recognition that the Security Council has the primary responsibility for initiating such operations and that appeal should be made to the General Assembly, if at all, only as a last resort and in exceptional cases.

Another basic principle is that peace-keeping operations rest on the consent of the parties concerned. The country in which peacekeeping forces are expected to be present and perform their functions must give its consent. The situation differs markedly from that envisaged under the terms of Article 42 of the Charter which authorizes the Security Council to take a decision requiring that armed forces enter the territory of a state for United Nations purposes without its specific consent. In the absence of agreements under Article 43 of the Charter, the Security Council does not have the authority to order the use of military forces of member states. The theory of peace-keeping operations is that the recommendation made by the Security Council is an invitation to member states to agree to and participate in an operation which the Security Council finds necessary and desirable. This applies equally to the entrance of forces into the territory of the host state and to the contribution of forces by member states. Of course the General Assembly has the power to recommend only, and consequently the need of consent is always implied.

The question of conditions that a host state may attach to its receiving a peace-keeping force and those that contributing states may attach to their voluntary contributions is one that has in practice presented some difficulties. In the organization of UNEF, Secretary-General Hammarskjöld insisted that in principle the choice of contingents was subject to the decision of the United Nations alone.[29] Nevertheless, he did agree that any objection which the host state might have to a particular member's contribution was a factor that must be taken into account, and in practice he did not insist on the inclusion of any unit to which strong objection was maintained. There have been instances where member states, in contributing units to peace-keeping forces, have attached conditions to their use. In 1956, for example, the Indian government attached conditions to the use of Indian units in the Middle East.[30] In view of the voluntary nature of such contributions, it must be assumed that a state has the right to withdraw its military unit if any condition which is attached to its use is violated. During the Congo operation a number of participating countries withdrew their units because they did not approve of the manner in which the operation was being conducted, notably the failure to give what they considered the proper assistance and protection to Lumumba. The question has been raised as to whether a force contributed for a United Nations peace-keeping operation can be used by the Security Council in the exercise of its powers under Article 42 for enforcement purposes. In light of the general principle of consent, it would seem that since units are contributed specifically for peace-

29. UN Doc. A/3943, Oct. 9, 1958.   30. Rosner, pp. 48–99.

keeping purposes, it is not within the authority of the Security Council to proceed on the assumption that they are available for coercive action.

Another aspect of the principle of consent relates to the right of the host state to demand the withdrawal of the force. Secretary-General Hammarskjöld attempted to achieve the agreement of the Egyptian government to a limitation upon its absolute right to demand withdrawal. By the terms of an *aide memoire* setting forth understandings between Hammarskjöld and the Egyptian government, each side undertook to act in good faith in exercising any right to demand withdrawal or to withdraw the force, taking into account whether the purpose of the United Nations operation had been achieved.[31] When, however, in 1967 President Nasser demanded the withdrawal of UNEF on the ground presumably that its presence interfered with necessary dispositions of U.A.R. forces vis-à-vis Israel, Secretary-General U Thant took the position, after consultation with his Advisory Committee, that he had no alternative but to accede to the demand.[32] A consequence of the admission of this right is not only that the operation may be terminated at any time before its purpose is fulfilled but also that the presence of the force cannot in fact be used as a leverage for getting the host state to agree to settlement of the issues which have produced the crisis. In establishing the second United Nations Emergency Force in the Middle East, following the resumption of hostilities in early October, 1973, the Security Council decided that "all matters which may affect the nature of the continued effective functioning of the Force will be referred to the Council for its decision." [33] That was interpreted by the United States representative as assuring an orderly agreed withdrawal of the Force, but only

31. UN Doc. A/3375, Nov. 20, 1956; and General Assembly Res. 1121 (XI), Nov. 24, 1956. See also the Secretary-General's "Summary Study" of UNEF experience. UN Doc. A/3943, Oct. 9, 1958, pp. 63–4.

32. Report of the Secretary-General on the Withdrawal of the United Nations Emergency Force to the Fifth Emergency Special Session of the General Assembly. UN Doc. A/6730 and Add. 3.

33. Security Council Res. 341 (1973) and UN Document B/11052/Rev. 1, October 27, 1943.

when the Council so decided. The Egyptian government declared that in the exercise of its sovereign rights in any matter concerning the functioning of the Force, it would "be guided by its acceptance of the United Nations resolutions." [34]

All the major peace-keeping operations up to the present time involving the use of organized military units have been placed under the direction and control of the Secretary-General acting under directives laid down by the Security Council or the General Assembly, in some cases in consultation with an advisory committee. There is of course no constitutional requirement that this should be the practice followed. The Security Council or General Assembly, in authorizing the operation, might provide that it should be under the direct control of a subcommittee, a designated government, an individual specially selected for the purpose, or some other agency. There have been two special reasons for selecting the Secretary-General for this purpose: the Charter specifically envisages the delegation of powers to the Secretary-General by the two organs; and the Secretary-General, by virtue of the staff available to him, the permanence of his position, and the knowledge and skill which he can be presumed to have, seems the obvious person to take on this responsibility. In its resolution of October 27, 1973, on the functioning of the second UNEF in the Middle East, the Security Council provided for closer and more detailed control of the actions of the Secretary-General than in previous instances, thereby reflecting the French and Soviet insistence on the exclusive responsibility of the Security Council and their unwillingness to give the Secretary-General discretionary powers of the kind Hammarskjöld had claimed and exercised, in the application of Council directives.

Another basic principle which has been demanded of every peace-keeping force is that it should adopt an attitude of neutrality and noninvolvement insofar as political conflicts between interested parties are concerned. This requirement is of course imposed upon the Secretariat in the performance of its functions although, as Secretary-General Hammarskjöld pointed out in his

34. *UN Monthly Chronicle*, X, no. 10 (November, 1973), pp. 64–65.

Oxford University lecture, this does not mean neutrality insofar as attitude toward the basic principles and purposes of the Charter is concerned. In the case of UNEF, Hammarskjöld took the position that the Force could not be used for the purpose of influencing in any way the balance of forces between the contesting parties in the Middle East, and consequently insisted that there must be a return to the *status quo ante*. In summarizing the principles that had guided the UNEF operation, the Secretary-General emphasized the requirement that the force should not be used in any way to influence the political situation and that it should refrain from interference in domestic affairs. In the Congo case, Hammarskjöld based his unwillingness to place the Force at the disposal of the Central government for putting down the Katanga independence movement on the ground that this would constitute an unjustifiable interference in the internal affairs of the Congo. It became obvious, however, that strict adherence to this principle constituted a considerable handicap in dealing with a condition of internal disorder, and that its strict application in fact might have a contrary effect from that desired.

Secretary-General Hammarskjöld attached great importance to the principle that the members of the peace-keeping force should not be allowed to use weapons except in self-defense. In the Congo situation, however, this principle could only be applied with an extremely liberal interpretation. In fact, initially it was a serious handicap to the effectiveness of the Force since it stood in the way of disarming members of the Force Publique, and thereby eliminating a detrimental element and preparing the way for a reorganization of the public security force. At a later time it was necessary to resort to forced interpretations of the principle to justify measures that seemed necessary in order to achieve what came to be recognized as an essential purpose of the operation. However, in the end, resolutions of the Security Council permitted the use of force for purposes other than self-defense by specifically authorizing that force might be used if necessary to prevent civil war and to apprehend foreign mercenaries.

As we have seen, one of the principles of peace-keeping operations has been that the force is not to be used to influence the final political settlement. The theory is that if fighting is brought to an end and guarantees are provided, tension will lessen and a situation will exist which will permit direct negotiations or the use of other means for achieving a settlement of basic issues. In practice, however, this has not commonly happened. In the Middle East, the peace-keeping operation has given no assurance of a final peace settlement. Even in the Congo, where some progress was made toward achieving a stable political situation while the Force was there, after its withdrawal there was a revival of political instability; and for a time Tshombe, who had headed the Katanga revolutionary independence movement, succeeded in establishing himself as Prime Minister of the Republic of the Congo, much to the dismay of other political groups in the Congo and of neighboring African states. In Cyprus, the Security Council recognized the need of pursuing efforts to achieve a political settlement at the same time that the Force was engaged in efforts to maintain order. The efforts of the United Nations Mediator, however, have been unsuccessful, and basic differences between the interested parties remain unresolved. Some would even conclude that peace-keeping operations have actually had the effect of making more difficult the settlement of basic conflicts in that they have removed the influence of the element of armed force which in many situations in the past has been a factor helping to overcome the reluctance of parties to make concessions.

The major problem facing peace-keeping operations up to the present time has been that of financing. Two basic principles have been asserted: (1) the costs of peace-keeping operations should be treated as expenses of the Organization to be borne by members as apportioned by the General Assembly; and (2) the Security Council has exclusive authority to authorize and apportion expenses. The first principle was followed with respect to the expenses of UNTSO until the early sixties. Until then the expenses were included in the regular budget and in the total expense apportioned annually by the General Assembly. The Secretary-General proposed, and the General Assembly initially agreed, that in the case of UNEF and ONUC, special accounts should be established but that these costs should be borne by members as apportioned by the Assembly. This position was challenged by some members. Two different arguments were advanced in support of this refusal to accept the principle of collective responsibility for financing. The Soviet position was that only the Security Council had the authority to determine how expenses should be allocated. France contended that since the operations were voluntary in character and dependent upon consent, financial contributions as well as military contributions should be voluntary. The General Assembly, failing to achieve a resolution of the problem itself, asked the International Court of Justice to rule on the question. The Court's opinion supported the principle of collective financial responsibility.[35] This, however, did not alter the attitudes of the major opponents of the principle. After the 1964 deadlock in the General Assembly over sanctions under Article 19 had been broken by the announcement of the United States delegation that it was not prepared further to insist on their application but reserved the right to withhold contributions in support of activities of which it did not approve, the General Assembly established the Special Committee on Peace-Keeping Operations to "undertake a comprehensive review of the whole question of peace-keeping operations in all their aspects, including ways of overcoming the present financial difficulties of the Organization." [36] To date, the Committee has not been able to come up with any generally acceptable answers to the questions of the authority to establish and the method of financing these operations.[37] As a consequence, financing has to be handled on an *ad hoc* basis. In establishing the second UNEF in the Middle East, the Security Council decided that the expenses for the six-month period for which the Force was authorized should be treated as part of the regular budget to be financed in accordance with the normal scale of assessments.[38]

35. Certain Expenses of the United Nations (Art. 17, par. 2 of the Charter), Advisory Opinion of 20 July, 1962, ICJ Reports 1962, p. 151.

36. General Assembly Res. 2006 (XIX), Feb. 18, 1965.

37. For the U.S. position, see UN Doc. A/8676, April 3, 1972; for USSR position, see UN Doc. A/8669, March 20, 1972.

38. Security Council Res. 341 (373) and UN Doc. S/11052/Rev. 1. For a more detailed discussion of the financing of peace-keeping operations, see Goodrich, Hambro, and Simons, pp. 157–65.

CONCLUSIONS

From experience up to the present it would seem unlikely that peace-keeping operations will be found feasible in the future except in those cases where there is agreement among the major powers—particularly the United States and the USSR—that such operations are in their interests or at least will not infringe upon any important interests that they may have. This means that, as one looks ahead, the conditions under which these operations are likely to be undertaken will be of a comparatively special nature. Much will depend upon the state of international relations at the time. This, however, does not exclude the possibility that such operations may be carried out under the auspices of regional organizations. Since they are not generally regarded as enforcement measures coming under the requirement of Article 53 that enforcement action under a regional organization be authorized by the Security Council, regional organizations are free to establish and conduct such operations without the need of Security Council action and without the possibility of a permanent member veto.

The likelihood that such operations will be conducted by the United Nations only if the major powers are in agreement leads to a second conclusion: that they will be undertaken only if authorized by the Security Council. There is, however, a possibility, which the United States government apparently wishes to keep open: that a situation may arise where it would be feasible for an operation to be undertaken on General Assembly initiative. This would necessitate financing on a voluntary basis which as experience to date shows is not very satisfactory.

While strong objection was made by the Soviet Union to the manner in which the Congo operation was directed by Secretary-General Hammarskjöld—and this criticism was used as a basis for attacking the Office of Secretary-General and demanding reorganization of it—subsequent events have indicated a recognition by all governments that when a peace-keeping operation is feasible, the most practical arrangement for its direction is to vest responsibility in the Secretary-General. Some members, particularly the Soviet Union and France, have shown a reluctance, however, to give to the Secretary-General the discretionary authority which was vested in Hammarskjöld in the conduct of the Congo operation, or at least which he chose to exercise. This reluctance is reflected in the insistence by these and other governments that the terms of the Secretary-General's authority be defined carefully, that the duration of the operation be carefully circumscribed, and that the principle of ultimate Security Council responsibility and control be carefully preserved. While there may be some willingness on the part of governments to accord the Secretary-General more freedom of decision in the future, this will depend no doubt upon the international political situation, the interests of the countries involved, and the extent to which the Secretary-General of the time is able to command confidence and trust.

One conclusion that can certainly be drawn from experience up to the present is that peace-keeping by itself does not provide any assurance that the task of peaceful settlement will be easier. And yet it must be recognized that peace-keeping is an important and essential first step. Unless this first step is taken, the opportunity for utilizing the methods of peaceful settlement and adjustment may not exist. And from still another point of view this first step is important. If it is not taken there is the ever-present danger that a local conflict will light the fuse of a major confrontation, with the terrifying possibility of appeal to the ultimate weapon.

CHAPTER EIGHT

THE PROTECTION OF HUMAN RIGHTS

ONE OF THE MAJOR CONCERNS OF THE UNITED NATIONS has been to promote and encourage "respect for human rights and for fundamental freedoms for all without distinction as to race, sex, language or religion." [1] This has distinguished it from the League of Nations. The Charter reflects a new approach to the protection of human liberty and freedom born of the experience of World War II and the years immediately preceding it when flagrant violations of human rights and the denial of the basic dignity of man were the hallmarks of regimes challenging and violating international peace and security.[2] This approach is a denial of the proposition that the way in which a state treats its nationals is of no concern to the outside world and therefore beyond the proper competence of international agencies.

HUMAN RIGHTS AND THE CHARTER

Under customary international law as it had developed and was practiced before the establishment of the League of Nations, ex-

1. Art. 1, par. 3 of the Charter.

2. For a good review of the United Nations activity during the first decade, see Robert E. Asher and others, *The United Nations and Promotion of the General Welfare* (Washington: Brookings Institution, 1957). For a twenty-year assessment, see Louis Henkin, "The United Nations and Human Rights," *International Organization,* XIX (1965), 504–17.

cept when some special provision had been made by international agreement, states were wholly free to determine the rights which their citizens enjoyed within their territories, and how those rights were to be protected. In some of the older democracies, the principle that the individual had certain legal rights which his government must respect was fully accepted, and a body of domestic law had been developed by constitutional enactment, by legislation, and by decisions of the courts and administrative agencies for giving effect to this principle. In many instances the constitutions of these states contained formal enumerations of certain rights enjoyed by the individual. An example was the Bill of Rights, the first ten amendments of the Constitution of the United States.

Nationals of one state within the territory of another were entitled to a minimum standard of treatment under customary international law. In case the foreign national was denied the internationally accepted minimum of justice, his government could intervene; and if it was sufficiently powerful it might succeed in getting his claim respected or at least submitted to an international claims commission where it would be decided whether he had been denied justice.[3] It was only, then, in the case of the national of one country present in the territory of another that international law recognized an international standard of treatment for the individual, and in this situation whether the individual was actually accorded that treatment depended on whether his state decided to take the matter up diplomatically and possessed the power to convince the other state that something should be done to give satisfaction.

At the end of World War I an important step was taken to provide international protection for certain individuals against their own governments. The limited application of the principle of self-determination in the drawing of new state boundaries radically reduced the number and size of national minorities in Europe, but it by no means eliminated them. This would have been impossible without large-scale population transfers. To improve the lot of the

3. See Edwin M. Borchard, *The Diplomatic Protection of Citizens Abroad* (New York: Banks Law Publishing Co., 1915).

national minorities that remained, a number of states were required to accept special minority regimes which guaranteed to individuals belonging to religious, linguistic, or cultural minorities certain political and civil rights. Furthermore, each minority treaty or declaration required that these provisions be made part of the fundamental law of the state. Finally, in case of alleged violation a procedure was provided by which appeal could be made to the League Council which was made responsible for seeing that rights conferred were respected.[4]

While the special minority regimes did purport to provide international protection for the members of certain minority groups which would have been left by customary international law completely at the mercy of the states in whose territory they found themselves, they did not prove to be very effective or satisfactory in practice. For one thing, they were basically discriminatory in that they applied only to states that had been defeated in the war, that had come into existence by the terms of the peace treaties, or that had acquired additional territory as the result thereof. Furthermore, the special protection for minorities as such had the effect of encouraging these groups to maintain their resistance to political integration and to remain discontented and rebellious minorities, lending encouragement to active irredentist movements in neighboring states. Finally, the procedures for assuring respect for minority rights were weak and ineffective, and by the late thirties any pretense of enforcing them had disappeared.

The excesses of the Hitler regime in Germany convinced many people that human rights and fundamental freedoms generally were matters with which the world must be concerned if international peace, security, and justice were to be achieved. President Roosevelt expressed this point of view in his annual message to Congress on January 6, 1941, when he said that ". . . in the future days, which we seek to make secure, we look forward to a world grounded upon four essential human freedoms . . . freedom of speech and expression . . . , freedom of every person to worship

4. See P. de Azcarate, *League of Nations and National Minorities: An Experiment* (Washington: Carnegie Endowment for International Peace, 1945).

God in his own way . . . , freedom from want . . . , and freedom from fear." [5] These freedoms were given general endorsement in the Declaration by United Nations of January 1, 1942, and thus became war aims of the anti-Axis coalition. [6]

In the preliminary discussions on the drafting of the United Nations Charter, little attention was given to the matter of human rights. This was not surprising since the major interest of responsible officials was in winning the war and in creating an international organization which would be effective in maintaining international peace and security once the war was won. At San Francisco, however, many official delegations, as well as representatives of private organizations, argued for the inclusion of detailed provisions regarding human rights. As a result of these pressures a number of amendments to the Dumbarton Oaks Proposals were adopted which had the common purpose of making specific the responsibilities and powers of the Organization with respect to human rights and fundamental freedoms, and providing the necessary machinery for discharging these responsibilities.

In the preamble to the Charter there is a reaffirmation of faith ". . . in fundamental human rights, in the dignity and worth of the human person, in the equal rights of men and women and of nations large and small." Article 1 proclaims as one of the purposes of the Organization the achievement of ". . . international cooperation . . . in promoting and encouraging respect for human rights and for fundamental freedoms for all without distinction as to race, sex, language, or religion." Article 55 provides that ". . . the United Nations shall promote . . . universal respect for, and observance of, human rights and fundamental freedoms for all without distinction as to race, sex, language, or religion," and by the terms of Article 56, ". . . all Members pledge themselves to take joint and separate action in cooperation with the Organization . . ." for the achievement of this purpose, along with others set forth in Article 55.

5. 77th Cong., 1st Sess., House Doc. No. 1 (1941).

6. Executive Agreement Series 236.

Under other Charter provisions the General Assembly is authorized to "initiate studies and make recommendations for the purpose of . . . assisting in the realization of human rights and fundamental freedoms for all without distinction as to race, sex, language, or religion." [7] The Economic and Social Council is authorized to "make recommendations for the purpose of promoting respect for, and observance of, human rights and fundamental freedoms for all" [8] and to establish a commission for the promotion of human rights to assist it in the performance of its functions.[9] Finally, one of the basic objectives of the trusteeship system is ". . . to encourage respect for human rights and for freedoms for all without distinction as to race, sex, language, or religion, and to encourage recognition of the interdependence of the peoples of the world." [10] It is to be noted, however, that nowhere in the Charter are "human rights and fundamental freedoms" enumerated. A proposal that a bill of rights be included was dropped in recognition of the lack of adequate time to draft its provisions.

The general philosophy of the authors of the Charter was well stated in the report of the Secretary of State to the President on the work of the San Francisco Conference. Commenting on the general significance of the human rights provisions, he observed,

> Finally, no sure foundation of lasting peace and security can be laid which does not rest on the voluntary association of free peoples. Only so far as the rights and dignity of all men are respected and protected, only so far as men have free access to information, assurance of free speech and free assembly, freedom from discrimination on grounds of race, sex, language, or religion and other fundamental rights and freedoms, will men insist upon the right to live at peace, to compose such differences as they may have by peaceful methods, and to be guided by reason and good will rather than driven by prejudice and resentment.[11]

7. Art. 13.   8. Art. 62.   9. Art. 68.   10. Art. 76.

11. *Report to the President on the Results of the San Francisco Conference by the Chairman of the United States Delegation, the Secretary of State,* Dept. of State Publ. 2349 (1945), p. 110.

THE UNIVERSAL DECLARATION OF HUMAN RIGHTS

While the San Francisco Conference did not undertake to define human rights and fundamental freedoms, it tacitly recognized that this must be one of the initial tasks of the United Nations. At its first session in February 1946, the Economic and Social Council established the Commission on Human Rights, and decided that its work should be directed towards submitting proposals and reports regarding:

(a) an international bill of rights;
(b) international declarations or conventions on civil liberties, the status of women, freedom of information, and similar matters;
(c) the protection of minorities;
(d) the prevention of discrimination on grounds of race, sex, language, or religion.[12]

When the Commission met in January and February of 1947, a difference of opinion soon developed over the exact nature of the end product which should be prepared. The United States favored a declaration setting forth goals and aspirations rather than legally binding commitments. This position was no doubt partly due to reluctance to embark upon the treaty-making process because of the need of Senate approval. The United Kingdom, on the other hand, was skeptical of the value of a declaration of general goals and preferred a treaty which would contain detailed and precise provisions and would legally bind all states accepting it. It was finally decided that both approaches should be adopted and that two major documents should be prepared: one, a declaration of general principles in the tradition of the French Declaration of the Rights of Man, and the other, a covenant containing binding obligations in the tradition of the English Bill of Rights.

In spite of obvious difficulties in getting general agreement on the definition of basic human rights and fundamental freedoms, the Commission was able to prepare a draft declaration of general

12. Economic and Social Council, *Official Records,* 1st Yr., 1st Sess. (1946), Annexes, p. 148.

principles within a comparatively short time. The task was facilitated in that the purpose of the document was to define goals to be achieved and not legal obligations to be respected. Representatives of states with different cultural backgrounds, political and legal systems, and ideologies found it much easier to agree on general principles and goals which left considerable latitude of interpretation and application than upon binding commitments with which they must harmonize their own national laws and practices. The Commission was able to finish its work by June 10, 1948. The draft was approved by the Economic and Social Council and adopted by the General Assembly without a negative vote on December 10 of that year.[13]

Since the Declaration was not a treaty and was not intended to impose legal obligations, it was not necessary to submit it to the members for ratification in accordance with their various constitutional procedures. The opening paragraph of the Declaration clearly states the nature of the document and the purposes it was intended to serve:

> The General Assembly,
>   Proclaims this Universal Declaration of Human Rights as a common standard of achievement for all peoples and all nations, to the end that every individual and every organ of society, keeping this Declaration constantly in mind, shall strive by teaching and education to promote respect for these rights and freedoms and by progressive measures, national and international, to secure their universal and effective recognition and observance, both among the peoples of Member States themselves and among the peoples of territories under their jurisdiction.

The Universal Declaration deals not only with civil and political rights but with social and economic rights as well. It asserts that ". . . all human beings are born free and equal in dignity and rights" and that everyone is entitled to "all the rights and freedoms set forth in the Declaration without distinction of any kind, such as race, colour, sex, language, religion, political or other opinion, na-

13. General Assembly Res. 217 (III), Dec. 10, 1948.

tional or social origin, property, birth or other status." [14] Further-more, it states that no distinction is to be based on the international status of the country or territory to which the person belongs, thus making it clear that the Declaration applies to all non-self-govern-ing territories.

The civil and political rights set forth in the Declaration are those that have been most widely recognized throughout the world, par-ticularly in the West. Among these rights are the following: the right to life, liberty, and security; the right to equal protection of the law; the right to a fair trial; the right to freedom of movement and residence within a country and to leave and return to it; the right to a nationality; the right to property; the right to freedom of thought, conscience, and religion; the right to freedom of opinion and expression; the right to freedom of peaceful assembly and as-sociation; and the right to participate in the government of his country.

The social and economic rights are of a more novel nature, though they find precedents in the more recent national constitu-tions. They include the right to social security, the right to work under just and favorable conditions, the right to equal pay for equal work, the right to rest and leisure, the right to a standard of living adequate for health and well-being, the right to education, and the right freely to participate in the cultural life of the commu-nity. Possibly the most novel provision of the Declaration is that which declares that ". . . everyone is entitled to a social and eco-nomic order in which the rights and freedoms set forth in this Declaration can be fully realized." [15]

After the Assembly had adopted the Universal Declaration, the President (Evatt of Australia) declared that it had "the authority of the body of opinion of the United Nations as a whole, and millions of men, women and children all over the world, many miles from Paris and New York, will turn for help, guidance and inspiration to this document." [16] Undoubtedly the adoption of this Declaration

14. Art. 2.   15. Art. 28.

16. Quoted in UN Department of Social Affairs, *The Impact of the Universal Declara-tion of Human Rights.* Doc. ST/50A/5/Rev. 1, June 29, 1953, p. 7.

without a dissenting vote was an impressive expression of a general consensus. While the Declaration did not technically have the character of a treaty creating legal obligations for members, it was bound to have a substantial influence on the subsequent discussions and decisions of the United Nations and to be invoked as setting standards that states should respect. It has been frequently referred to in resolutions of the United Nations organs, and its provisions have been many times invoked in United Nations discussions as defining the human rights and fundamental freedoms which member states are under obligation to respect.

HUMAN RIGHTS COVENANTS

Experience with the drafting of the Universal Declaration showed that it was easy to get nations to agree on a general declaration of human rights setting goals to be reached by various means and a standard of achievement by which the progress of states might be measured. It was, however, much more difficult to get states to agree to a treaty or treaties which would define these rights in legal language, impose upon the parties the obligation to conform, and provide means and procedures by which respect would be assured. Once the discussion started on the drafting of such a treaty, issues were raised which were not considered of particular importance so long as a declaration setting forth standards of achievement was being envisaged, but which became matters of deepest concern once the talk was of a legally binding treaty.

The first question to arise was whether there should be one or two treaties, or covenants as they came to be designated. The United States, the United Kingdom, and a number of other Western countries insisted that there should be a separate treaty for civil and political rights since these alone were capable of definition in legal terms and lent themselves to implementation by judicial procedures. These countries also pointed out that a treaty on economic and social rights would of necessity take the form of a commitment to legislative and administrative action and would therefore raise quite distinct problems of implementation. While strong objections were raised to separation, partly because of fear that the likelihood of a covenant on economic and social rights would be jeoparadized, the Assembly finally decided that there should be two covenants.

The attempt actually to define human rights and fundamental freedoms followed in general the pattern of the Universal Declaration, though exact definition in treaty language proved difficult because of differences of cultural background, legal systems, ideology, and economic, social, and political conditions. In addition, some special difficulties were encountered. One of these related to the inclusion in each covenant of a provision guaranteeing the right of self-determination. Although some members argued strongly that this was not an individual right, and in any case should not be restricted, as was proposed, to non-self-governing territories, the majority of members voted for its inclusion.[17]

There was strong disagreement with regard to the scope of application of the proposed covenants. Generally speaking, member states with federal forms of government desired the inclusion of a clause taking account of the limited powers of the central government. It was argued that while the central government under a federal system was able to commit the state with respect to matters which lay within the federal competence, all it could be expected to do with respect to matters falling within the competence of the political subdivisions was to bring the provisions of the agreements to the attention of the appropriate constitutional authorities. Member states with centralized forms of government objected, however, that it would be unfair to subject some states to more extensive obligations than others; in the end they were victorious in their in-

17. The principle of "self-determination of peoples," which is referred to in Art. 1, par. 2 of the Charter and which is the basis of "the right of self-determination" included in the Universal Declaration, had an interesting and illuminating history at San Francisco. The inclusion of the words "based on respect for the principle of equal rights and self-determination of peoples" was the result of a Soviet proposal which no one was willing to oppose, though suspicions existed as to its purpose. While there was some discussion of its meaning, there was no agreed interpretation that contributed to clarification. See Ruth B. Russell, *A History of the United Nations Charter* (Washington: Brookings Institution, 1958), pp. 810–13; and Leland M. Goodrich, Edvard Hambro, and Anne P. Simons, *Charter of the United Nations: Commentary and Documents* (3d rev. ed.; New York: Columbia University Press, 1969), pp. 30–4.

sistence that a clause be included providing that all provisions be extended to all subdivisions of federal states without exception.

A closely related question was that of the extension of the provisions of the covenants to non-self-governing territories. The members administering such territories argued that they should be allowed some discretion in determining whether the provisions of the covenants should be applied to these territories, but the view which finally prevailed allowed no exception to be made.

With respect to the implementation of the proposed covenants, a number of different views were expressed and proposals made. One view, held by the United States, the United Kingdom, and a number of other states, was that the implementation should be limited to the examination of complaints presented by states parties to the covenants. A second view, supported particularly by Asian and Latin American members, favored provision for petitions from individuals and nongovernmental organizations. The Soviet Union was against specific provisions for implementation of any kind. The majority of members, while believing that some provision for implementation was necessary, were unwilling to go beyond the use of inquiry and conciliation.

In December 1966 the General Assembly approved and opened to signature the Covenant on Civil and Political Rights and its Optional Protocol, and the Covenant on Economic, Social, and Cultural Rights.[18] These instruments translate into the language of legal obligation substantially the same range of rights that were enumerated in the Universal Declaration of Human Rights. In the case of the Covenant on Economic, Social, and Cultural Rights, measures of implementation are limited to the requirement that parties to the agreement make reports on progress in achieving observance of these rights. The Covenant on Civil and Political Rights provides for the establishment of an eighteen-member Human Rights Committee elected by the contracting parties at a meeting convened by the Secretary-General of the United Nations. This Committee is empowered to consider complaints directed against one party of the Covenant by another, provided that both parties

18. General Assembly Res. 2200A (XXI), Dec. 16, 1966.

have previously agreed to permit the Committee to review such complaints. It is limited, however, to exercising its good offices, and, with the consent of the parties if no agreement is reached, to instituting a conciliation procedure. The Optional Protocol to the Covenant on Civil and Political Rights provides for the submission of complaints from private citizens against states that have approved the Protocol.

The Covenants will not come into force until thirty-five ratifications have been deposited with the Secretariat. The Optional Protocol cannot come into force until the Covenant on Civil and Political Rights has been ratified by thirty-five states and ten ratifications to the Protocol have been deposited. As of October 12, 1973, nineteen states had ratified the Covenant on Economic, Social and Cultural Rights, the same number had ratified the Covenant on Civil and Political Rights, and nine had ratified the Optional Protocol. This dearth of ratifications suggests that the Covenants are not likely to become operative in the near future. Although United States policy has evolved, there continues to be some reluctance to submit human rights treaties to the Senate for approval. Recent years have witnessed a trend in the United Nations towards drafting conventions dealing with more limited subject areas, and these have attracted more ratifications than the more inclusive Covenants.

DECLARATIONS AND CONVENTIONS OF LIMITED SCOPE

Less ambitious but in some respects more promising than the drafting of a comprehensive covenant or covenants covering the whole field of human rights is the study of special topics and the drafting of appropriate proposals for dealing with them. A number of these special topics have thus been taken up by the United Nations with varying degrees of success.

A great deal of time and energy was devoted during the early years of the United Nations to the question of freedom of information. In one of its early resolutions the General Assembly characterized freedom of information as "a fundamental human right" and "the touchstone of all freedoms to which the United Nations is consecrated." [19] Efforts, however, to draft a convention on freedom of information which would be generally acceptable to members were unsuccessful. The specific issue on which agreement could not be reached was the extent to which this freedom should be subject to limitation in the interest of accuracy, fair play, and good international relations. The United States insisted on virtually unrestricted freedom of the press, which most other members were not willing to accept.[20]

One of the most publicized achievements of the United Nations in its early years was the drafting of the genocide convention and its submission to governments. In its first session in 1946 the General Assembly adopted a resolution [21] condemning genocide "as a crime under international law." In this resolution the Assembly declared genocide to be

> a denial of the right of existence of entire human groups, as homicide is the denial of the right to live of individual human beings; such denial of the right of existence shocks the conscience of mankind, results in great losses to humanity in the form of cultural and other contributions represented by these human groups, and is contrary to moral law and to the spirit and aims of the United Nations.

Subsequently, the General Assembly approved the Convention on the Prevention and Punishment of the Crime of Genocide, without a dissenting vote.[22] The Convention, after reaffirming the Assembly's declaration that genocide was a crime under international law, defined genocide as meaning

> any part of the following acts committed with intent to destroy, in whole or in part, a national, ethnical, racial or religious group, as such:
> a) killing members of the group;

19. General Assembly Res. 59 (I), Dec. 14, 1946.

20. See Carroll Binder, "Freedom of Information and the United Nations," *International Organization,* VI (1952), 210–26.

21. General Assembly Res. 96 (I), Dec. 11, 1946.

22. General Assembly Res. 266A (III), Dec. 9, 1948.

b) causing serious bodily or mental harm to members of the group;
c) deliberately inflicting on the group conditions of life calculated to bring about its physical destruction in whole or in part;
d) imposing measures intended to prevent births within the group;
e) forcibly transferring children of the group to another group.

It came into force on January 12, 1951. However, many ratifications were accompanied by reservations which raised questions regarding the exact nature of the commitments.

The United Nations has given a great deal of attention to the prevention of discrimination. At its first session in January–February 1947, the Commission on Human Rights created the Subcommission on Prevention of Discrimination and Protection of Minorities. Throughout the 1950s achievement was largely limited to the clarification of issues. With the admission of many African states to United Nations membership after 1960 these efforts developed new momentum and were directed more specifically against racial discrimination. In 1963 the General Assembly unanimously approved the United Nations Declaration on the Elimination of All Forms of Racial Discrimination.[23] Two years later it approved and opened to signature a convention on the same subject.[24] This convention provides for the initiation of a complaint procedure which is not dependent upon prior adherence to a special protocol, as in the case of the Covenant on Civil and Political Rights. Also, there is provision for initiation of complaints by individuals. The Convention entered into force on January 5, 1969, having received the required twenty-seven ratifications.

PROBLEMS OF COMPLIANCE

The drafting of declarations and conventions setting forth human rights to be respected has presented fewer difficulties than achiev-

23. General Assembly Res. 1904 (XVIII), Nov. 20, 1963.
24. General Assembly Res. 2106A (XX), Dec. 21, 1965.

ing compliance with human rights standards. The problem of compliance is complicated by the fact that there is not always agreement as to what the obligations of members are, and in the absence of such agreement there may be an initial denial on the part of the state whose compliance is in question of any obligation on its part to comply with a standard which it refuses to recognize. In the case of conventions defining specifically the obligations of states that ratify, this difficulty does not arise; but even in these cases, states are reluctant on grounds of sovereignty and fear of unfavorable consequences to accept procedures that go beyond negotiation and conciliation.

As we have seen, when the two Covenants were under consideration, some states were prepared to accept a procedure permitting individual petitions and their examination by a United Nations organ, but the majority were not prepared to go beyond allowing complaints by governments with provision for inquiry and conciliation, and this on an optional basis.

The Convention on the Elimination of All Forms of Racial Discrimination contains the strongest provisions for achieving compliance of any instrument adopted under United Nations auspices up to this time. It provides for the Committee on the Elimination of Racial Discrimination which receives biennial government reports on measures taken to implement the Convention and reports to the General Assembly. The Committee is charged with conciliating complaints by one contracting party against another. Under the terms of an optional clause, the Committee may receive petitions from individuals.

The matter of under what conditions individual petitions complaining of human rights violations are to be allowed and how they are to be treated has been much discussed and is highly controversial. Governments have quite generally objected on grounds of alleged violation of national sovereignty to any meaningful consideration of individual petitions by organs of the United Nations. In 1969, however, the Commission on Human Rights recommended a new and somewhat revolutionary course, which later was approved by ECOSOC.[25] Under this procedure, a working group of the Sub-

25. ECOSOC Res. 1503 (XLVIII), May 27, 1970.

Commission on Prevention of Discrimination and Protection of Minorities each year considers all petitions received and brings to the Sub-Commission's attention those "which appear to reveal a consistent pattern of gross and reliably attested violations of human rights and fundamental freedoms." The Sub-Commission then decides which cases warrant the attention of the Commission which may then undertake an investigation of the situation. Even this amount of attention by UN organs to individual petitions is strongly resisted by some members who apparently fear the consequences of this amount of outside investigation and publicity.

Similar objections have been raised to proposals for establishing a United Nations high commissioner. Even when the proposal was watered down from the original conception of an international ombudsman with broad powers of investigation and negotiation to a proposal for a high commissioner with the limited function of facilitating "the cooperative fulfillment" by members of their Charter obligations, resistance has been so strong that difficulty has been experienced in even bringing the matter to a vote. Even states that have been most insistent on strong measures for the implementation of the right against racial discrimination object to the commissioner proposal, possibly because they suspect that the broad approach to achieving compliance with human rights obligations will divert attention from the violation of the particular right that concerns them most directly. The problem of compliance presents itself in a particularly difficult form when an attempt is made to achieve respect for human rights standards which are claimed to have their basis in the Charter itself and the resolutions of United Nations organs. This problem has been presented in its most typical and dramatic form in efforts of the United Nations to achieve the elimination of racial discrimination in South Africa.

In this case there has been a refusal on the part of the Republic of South Africa to recognize any obligation on its part to discontinue policies of apartheid and any competence on the part of the United Nations to concern itself with these policies. In support of its position the Republic has consistently invoked the domestic jurisdiction principle of the Charter,[26] and has argued that in the ab-

26. Art. 2, par. 7.

sence of a specific treaty undertaking on its part not to adopt policies involving racial discrimination, any attempt by the United Nations to cause it to discontinue such policies constitutes an unjustified intervention in the domestic affairs of the Republic. The great majority of members of the United Nations have adopted the view that South Africa is violating its international obligations under the Charter and the resolutions of United Nations organs, and that the Organization has the competence to take appropriate measures to achieve South African compliance.

The United Nations has concerned itself with the racial policies of the South African government since 1946. In that year the Indian government requested the General Assembly to consider the alleged violations of the human rights of persons of Indian origin. The General Assembly never explicitly decided the question of competence, but at that time and subsequently it undertook to discuss the question and adopt resolutions urging settlement of the matter in accordance with Charter principles.

In 1952 the South African government's policy of apartheid was brought to the attention of the General Assembly, which set up a commission to study the situation and enunciate principles for the guidance of multiracial states. When the Commission reported that the apartheid legislation and regulations were incompatible with the provisions of the Charter and the Universal Declaration,[27] the Assembly took note of the report, asked the Commission to continue its study of the situation and to suggest measures of alleviation, and invited the South African government to cooperate with the Commission.[28] This invitation was refused.

Apartheid was discussed at succeeding sessions of the General Assembly and resolutions were adopted deploring the South African government's failure to observe its obligations under the Charter. After 1960, when a large number of African states became United Nations members, resolutions of the General Assembly and Security Council declared that the situation in South Africa disturbed international peace. In 1962 the Assembly requested member states to apply collective measures against South Africa

27. UN General Assembly, *Official Records,* 8th Sess., Suppl. 16 (Doc. A/2505).
28. General Assembly Res. 721 (VIII), Dec. 8, 1953.

and established the Special Committee on the Policy of Apartheid to keep the situation under review and report.[29] In 1963 the Security Council "solemnly called upon all states to cease forthwith the sale and shipment of arms of all types and military vehicles to South Africa." [30] The General Assembly has urged stronger and more extensive collective measures under Chapter VII, but important members have been reluctant to agree to such drastic steps. The United Nations has undertaken to provide assistance to South African refugees. Despite these efforts, the South African government has not substantially altered its policies, and has in fact extended its apartheid policies to South West Africa.

The General Assembly has been asked to consider cases where the Soviet Union has been accused of practising forced labor, wrongfully detaining prisoners of war, preventing Soviet brides from leaving the country, and imposing arbitrary personal restraints. In some instances resolutions adopted by the General Assembly have been followed in time by remedial action by the Soviet government. One cannot, however, establish with any certainty a cause-and-effect relationship.

CONCLUSIONS ON UNITED NATIONS EFFECTIVENESS

It is difficult to evaluate the work of the United Nations in promoting respect for human rights. Quite clearly the Organization has broken new ground in at least two important respects: (1) it has gone beyond the League and previous international law concepts in making respect for human rights, as distinguished from the rights of any particular group, a matter of general international concern; and (2) it has moved beyond the original Charter concept of promoting international cooperation for the protection of human rights to direct action for the protection of human rights in particular cases.

The Organization has a record of substantial success in its efforts to establish standards—by declaration and by international agreements—which are to guide states in matters of human rights. The

29. General Assembly Res. 1761, Nov. 6, 1962.
30. Security Council Res. (S/5386) of August 7, 1963.

Universal Declaration of Human Rights has had a significant influence on the development of standards that states are not only expected to treat as goals to be achieved but also as legal commitments to be respected. It is less clear whether the provisions of the Declaration have been widely respected or whether they have had a significant influence on the practice of those states that have been most backward in respecting human rights in the past. The reluctance of states generally—and particularly those with special internal security and development problems—to agree to respect universal standards is well demonstrated by the difficulties encountered in the drafting of the covenants and the unwillingness of states to ratify the covenants once drafted. Relatively more success has been achieved in the implementation of declarations and agreements dealing with particular topics, such as genocide and racial discrimination, though in these cases the gap between promise and performance—in any case, difficult to measure—is substantial.

The United Nations clearly performs a useful service in assembling and making available information regarding the status of human rights throughout the world. This information, though incomplete because of the unwillingness of some governments to cooperate, is valuable for governments seeking to improve their domestic legislation and administrative and judicial practices. Likewise, there can be no doubt that technical assistance to developing countries serves a useful purpose, as in many instances failure to give adequate protection to human rights is due, in part at least, to the inadequacy of administrative and judicial procedures, not to mention technical deficiencies in the statutory law.

Efforts to achieve compliance with human rights standards in cases of alleged violation have not been effective. Furthermore, it is doubtful that there is much that the United Nations can do, or should attempt to do, beyond proclaiming standards and seeking, by methods of moral and political persuasion, to influence the accused government to mend its ways. United Nations action is to some extent handicapped by the ambiguity that still exists in many minds with respect to the competence of the Organization to take direct measures to enforce compliance in particular cases. While the competence of the United Nations organs to take measures to achieve compliance has come to be generally accepted by members, there is not the same measure of agreement among members regarding the wisdom and likely effectiveness of many measures that have been proposed. Measures of economic pressure and vague threats of the use of force have had little effect in inducing the South African government to alter its policies. There is little evidence that members are willing to take stronger measures. Furthermore, those whose rights are being violated would in all likelihood be the first to suffer from stronger measures of economic coercion. Enforcement action on the premise that violation of human rights constitutes a threat to the peace is not likely to be acceptable to the members whose cooperation is necessary, and would in all likelihood be counterproductive.[31]

That the United Nations is concerned with human rights is a great advance in international thought and action. It is recognition that an international organization for peace must be concerned with the rights of individuals as well as the security of states. Our recent experience has demonstrated that a state that disregards the human rights of its people on a large scale is more likely to be a disturber of international peace than one that respects them. However, it must also be recognized that human rights are to a considerable degree the product of particular cultures, legal traditions, and political and economic ideologies and circumstances. Any international standards must be interpreted and applied, for the foreseeable future at least, to meet a wide variety of conditions. The acceptance of universal standards and willingness to apply them with close approach to conformity will come slowly, and as the result of education, persuasion, and the development of supporting economic, social, and political institutions. Certain flagrant abuses may call for special attention at a particular time, but the danger of vesting the responsibility for dealing with such abuses in the political organs of the United Nations is that the special interests of member states will determine which abuses will be overlooked and which will receive attention.

31. See Margaret Doxey, "International Sanctions: A Framework of Analysis with Special Reference to the U.N. and Southern Africa," *International Organization*, XXVI (1962), 527–50.

CHAPTER NINE

THE PASSING OF COLONIALISM

LESS THAN A HALF-CENTURY SEPARATES the year in which Rudyard Kipling wrote "The White Man's Burden" and the date of the signing of the Charter of the United Nations, and yet the attitudes expressed with respect to colonies seem to be centuries apart. Kipling gave expression to sentiments of racial superiority and paternalistic altruism and asserted the special God-given responsibility of the white peoples to govern and educate the colored peoples of Asia and Africa. The Charter emphasized the equality of peoples and their equal claims to self-determination and full economic, social, and political development within a world organization in which all peoples participate. Recognizing that many peoples in the world were not in control of their own destinies and were still at primitive levels of development, the Charter asserted the special responsibility of the United Nations to see that proper assistance was given in order that the natives of dependent and underdeveloped territories might experience some of the advantages of more developed societies.

IMPERIALISM AND THE LEAGUE MANDATE SYSTEM

Modern imperialism—the control by the economically and politically more advanced states over areas inhabited by peoples of a different culture—reached its height in the closing years of the nineteenth century. It was in fact to meet the indictment of imperialism, as formulated by Hobson [1] and other writers, that proposals were made at the time of the drafting of the League Covenant to place certain colonial territories under an international mandate system.[2] As the result of President Wilson's insistence, and in the face of strong opposition from some of the would-be beneficiaries from an old-style division of the colonial spoils, certain territories which were ceded by the defeated Central Powers to the victorious Principal Allied and Associated Powers were placed under the League mandate system, to provide international guarantees that these areas would be administered in the interest of the native peoples and the world community. It was also believed that these guarantees would contribute to the alleviation of international tensions and the avoidance of future international conflict.

Under the mandate system, territories were placed under the administration of more advanced states, generally the states that would have annexed them outright if former practices had been followed. While the mandatory power was made responsible for administering the territory, it was required to do this subject to certain international obligations imposed by the Covenant and the mandate agreement. These obligations, varying with the category into which the mandate fell,[3] were (1) to assist the territory to achieve full independence (Class A), (2) to guarantee to the native peoples certain minimum rights and to protect them against specific abuses and evils (Classes A, B, and C), and (3) to secure equal opportunities for the trade and commerce of all nations (Classes A and B). The League Council was made responsible for supervising the administration of mandated territories. However, it was a polit-

1. J. A. Hobson, *Imperialism, A Study* (London: Allen and Unwin, 1902).

2. Notably by General Jan Smuts of the Union of South Africa in his *League of Nations: A Practical Suggestion* (New York: The Nations Press, 1919).

3. Class A: Palestine (U.K.), Syria and Lebanon (France), and Iraq (U.K.); Class B: Tanganyika (U.K.), Togoland (U.K.), Togoland (France), Cameroons (U.K.), Cameroons (France), and Ruanda/Urundi (Belgium); Class C: Western Samoa (New Zealand), Nauru (U.K., New Zealand and Australia), New Guinea (Australia), North Pacific Islands (Japan), and Southwest Africa (Union of South Africa).

ical body whose decisions were often determined by purely political considerations, and it lacked any effective power to enforce compliance with its decisions.[4]

While failing to live up to the expectations of its more idealistic proponents, the League mandate system did achieve good results both in improving the quality of administration of dependent territories and in changing prevailing attitudes and expectations regarding the treatment of dependent peoples. There is evidence that standards of colonial administration generally were favorably affected by League standards. Certainly the League mandate system gave encouragement and support to those who, more conscious of the evils of colonialism than of its benefits, were working for its termination and for the realization by colonial peoples of the benefits of self-government.

WORLD WAR II AND THE CONCEPT OF TRUSTEESHIP

With the outbreak of World War II, the colonial problem was presented in a more urgent context. The unexpected ease with which Japan conquered Western colonial possessions in Asia and the Pacific area, in contrast to the resistance of the Philippine people to whom independence had been promised, and the need of the Allies for the cooperation of Asian peoples if Japanese military aggression was to be defeated, convinced many, in the United States especially, that the age of colonialism was past, and that new assurances must be given to the dependent peoples of Asia. In particular it was felt that they should be given firm assurance that within measurable time they would have the opportunities and advantages of self-government. This feeling was particularly strong in the United States government where, from the beginning of the war, responsible officials, from the President down, were convinced that colonialism was doomed and that at the conclusion of

4. On the working of the League mandate system, see Quincy Wright, *Mandates under the League of Nations* (Chicago: University of Chicago Press, 1930).

the war some comprehensive system of international trusteeship must be established.[5]

A major obstacle to the development of an agreed Allied position during the war was the reluctance of Prime Minister Churchill to accept any position which implied a weakening of the British Empire. His attitude was dramatically expressed when he said that he had not ". . . become the King's First Minister in order to preside over the liquidation of the British Empire." [6] In the Atlantic Charter, Roosevelt and Churchill had asserted ". . . the right of all peoples to choose the form of government under which they will live." This was interpreted by Churchill, however, as not applying to colonial peoples, though Roosevelt never accepted this view.

During the war a great deal of time and thought was given in the Department of State to the preparation of proposals for an expanded system of trusteeship which would apply to all colonial areas. However, the proposals that the United States submitted to the other Dumbarton Oaks conferees in the summer of 1944 contained nothing on trusteeship due to disagreement between the Department of State and the War and Navy Departments over the application of the trusteeship principle to Japanese-owned or Japanese-mandated islands in the Pacific. This was one of the gaps left to be filled by later negotiations.

At the Yalta conference in February 1945, Churchill, Roosevelt, and Stalin agreed that the five nations that were to have permanent seats on the Security Council should consult to draft Charter proposals relating to the establishment of a trusteeship system. It was also agreed that trusteeship would ". . . only apply to (a) existing mandates of the League of Nations; (b) territories detached from the enemy as the result of the present War; (c) any other territory which might voluntarily be placed under trusteeship." [7]

At San Francisco, though the United States had earlier been the

---

5. See Ruth B. Russell, *A History of the United Nations Charter* (Washington: Brookings Institution,1958), chap. IV. See, for example, Cordell Hull, *The Memoirs of Cordell Hull* (New York: Macmillan, 1948), 1234–38.

6. *The London Times*, Nov. 11, 1942.

7. Department of State, *Foreign Relations of the United States: The Conferences at Malta and Yalta, 1945.* Publ. 6199 (1955), p. 977.

advocate of a comprehensive declaration of principles applicable to all colonial territories, this approach seems to have been overlooked in its proposals; it was the United Kingdom and Australia that took the lead in proposing what subsequently became Chapter XI of the Charter. The original United Kingdom proposal, however, was that it should be an annex to the Charter.[8]

With respect to trusteeship, the United States proposals, particularly those providing for a Trusteeship Council with substantial powers, were generally accepted. Nevertheless, the strong initiative which the United States had earlier taken was considerably dulled by the concern which the United States delegation showed for the protection of American strategic interests in the Pacific area. Instead of appearing as the uninhibited leader of the attack on old-style colonialism, the United States found itself in the embarrassing position of having to defend one of the traditional interests of colonial powers—national security—against proposals intended to give greater recognition and protection to the special interests of native peoples. The debates at San Francisco and the provisions of the Charter as finally written made it clear that colonialism as it had been practiced in the nineteenth century and the first decade of the twentieth was in retreat. It was not so apparent, however, that this retreat would become a precipitous and disorderly rout. Rather, an orderly and supervised transition from dependence to independence was envisaged.

THE CHARTER AND COLONIAL PEOPLES

The Charter [9] went considerably further than the Covenant in providing the legal basis and the practical means for making international accountability for the administration of colonies effective. In the first place, it defined the purposes of the United Nations and

8. See Russell, pp. 808–43; and Geoffrey L. Goodwin, *Britain and the United Nations* (New York: Manhattan Publishing Co., 1957), pp. 352–53.

9. For a good analysis of the Charter system and the first ten years of its operation, see Robert E Asher and others, *The United Nations and Promotion of the General Welfare* (Washington: Brookings Institution, 1957), Part IV (by Emil J. Sady).

the responsibilities of its principal organs in such broad and generous terms as to bring all aspects of the administration of dependent
territories within its sphere of concern and to provide the basis for
appropriate action by these organs. The broad powers of discussion and recommendation given to the General Assembly provided
the legal basis for that organ's playing an active and wide-ranging
role in applying the principle of international accountability and
in achieving the ultimate termination of the colonial relationship.

One of the Charter's major advances over earlier international
arrangements was the Declaration Regarding Non-Self-Governing
Territories contained in Chapter XI. According to Article 73,

> Members of the United Nations which have or assume respon-
> sibilities for the administration of territories whose peoples
> have not yet attained a full measure of self-government recog-
> nize the principle that the interests of the inhabitants of these
> territories are paramount, and accept as a sacred trust the
> obligation to promote to the utmost, within the system of inter-
> national peace and security established by the present Charter,
> the well-being of the inhabitants of these territories.

In the discharge of these responsibilities, members accepted the
obligation (1) to ensure "the political, economic, social and educational advancement" of these peoples, "their just treatment, and
their protection against abuses"; (2) "to develop self-government"
and assist in the progressive development of free political institutions; (3) "to further international peace and security"; (4) "to promote constructive measures of development," to encourage research, and to cooperate with each other and with specialized
international bodies in the practical achievement of the above social, economic, and scientific purposes, and (5)

> to transmit regularly to the Secretary-General for informa-
> tion purposes, subject to such limitation as security and consti-
> tutional considerations may require, statistical and other infor-
> mation of a technical nature relating to economic, social, and
> educational conditions in the territories for which they are re-
> spectively responsible other than [territories under trustee-
> ship].[10]

10. Paragraph e. of Art. 73.

It is particularly to be noted that the obligation which members assumed with respect to the non-self-governing territories they administered was "to develop self-government." It was explained, however, by the United Kingdom representative at the Conference that independence was one form of self-government though not necessarily the only one. It is also to be noted that the obligation under paragraph (e) to transmit information "of a technical nature" did not extend to information relating to political conditions. Finally, Article 73 did not contain any provision expressly giving to any organ of the United Nations any supervisory power or function.

The trusteeship provisions contained in Chapters XII and XIII of the Charter, together with the provisions of the trusteeship agreements, went considerably beyond the Declaration in defining the obligations of members and in providing machinery and procedures of international supervision. However, these provisions were made applicable only to those areas, falling within any of three enumerated categories, that were placed under trusteeship by agreements concluded between the "states directly concerned." The three categories were:

(a) territories then held under mandate;
(b) territories detached from enemy states as a result of the Second World War; and
(c) territories voluntarily placed under the system by states responsible for their administration.[11]

The basic objectives of the trusteeship system were stated to be (1) the furtherance of international peace and security, (2) the promotion of the political, economic, social, and educational advancement of the inhabitants and "their progressive development towards self-government or independence," (3) the encouragement of respect for human rights and fundamental freedoms and of recognition of the interdependence of peoples, and (4) the assurance of equal treatment in social, economic, commercial, and legal matters for all members and their nationals. The duties of administer-

11. Art. 77.

ing states, as well as the extent of their authority, were spelled out in considerable detail in the trust agreements.

A trusteeship agreement might designate a particular area or areas as strategic. For areas designated as strategic, the functions of the United Nations were to be exercised by the Security Council instead of the General Assembly. The Charter provided, however, that the basic objectives of the trusteeship system should apply to strategic areas so designated, and that the Security Council, in discharging its responsibilities, should avail itself of the assistance of the Trusteeship Council when performing functions relating to political, economic, social, and educational matters.[12]

As indicated above, the Charter provided that supervisory functions of the United Nations with respect to trust territories other than strategic areas were to be performed by the General Assembly, assisted by the Trusteeship Council, an organ to be composed of an equal number of administering and nonadministering states and operating under its authority.[13] This represented a marked contrast to the League mandate system where this authority was vested in the Council acting with the advice and assistance of the Permanent Mandates Commission, composed of persons chosen for their individual competence. Thus, ultimate authority under the trusteeship system was vested in the representative organ instead of the organ of limited membership. The Charter defined this authority more liberally than the Covenant. For example, the General Assembly and, under its authority, the Trusteeship Council, might "consider reports submitted by the administering authority, provide for periodic visits to the respective trust territories," and "take these and other actions in conformity with the terms of the trusteeship agreements." [14]

12. Art. 83.

13. Since only two trust territories remain and the Charter provides that permanent members of the Security Council shall be permanent members of the Trusteeship Council, this requirement can no longer be satisfied by the election of nonadministering members by the General Assembly, as provided in Art. 86, par. 3.

14. Art. 87.

THE TRUSTEESHIP SYSTEM IN OPERATION

In the years since its establishment, the United Nations trusteeship system has largely completed its task. In comparison with what the early planners in the Department of State envisaged, it has been a modest and relatively short-lived operation. Any hopes that the system might be applied voluntarily to dependent areas other than the former mandated territories proved unfounded.

Eleven territories in all were placed under trusteeship. Ten of these were former mandated territories and one (Somaliland) was detached from Italy under the terms of the Italian peace treaty and placed under trusteeship by an Assembly resolution [15] which the parties to the Italian peace treaty had agreed in advance to accept. The territories thus placed under trusteeship were

TERRITORY	ADMINISTERING AUTHORITY	FORMER STATUS
Cameroons (British)	United Kingdom	League Mandate (B)
Togoland (British)	United Kingdom	League Mandate (B)
Tanganyika	United Kingdom	League Mandate (B)
Cameroons (French)	France	League Mandate (B)
Togoland (French)	France	League Mandate (B)
Ruanda-Urundi	Belgium	League Mandate (C)
Nauru	Australia	League Mandate (B)
New Guinea	Australia	League Mandate (C)

15. General Assembly Res. 289 (IVA), Nov. 21, 1949.

TERRITORY	ADMINISTER-ING AUTHORITY	FORMER STATUS
Western Samoa	New Zealand	League Mandate (C)
North Pacific Islands	United States	League Mandate (C) (administered by Japan)
Somaliland	Italy	Italian colony

Except for the Class A mandated territories which had either achieved independence or at the time the Charter was written were considered ready for it, South West Africa is the only former mandated territory that was not placed under trusteeship. The Union (now Republic) of South Africa refused to be moved from its position that the territory should be integrated into the Union and that in so doing it was violating no international obligation. Though the legal right of the South African government not to place the territory under trusteeship was admitted by most of the other members and by the International Court in its advisory opinion,[16] the General Assembly, supported by the Court's opinion, insisted that South Africa was under international responsibilities in the administration of the territory and that the Assembly, as the successor to the League Council, was responsible for seeing that these responsibilities were discharged. South Africa, however, showed no willingness to accept this view or to cooperate with the General Assembly in its efforts to exercise its supervisory function through a special committee on South West Africa.

In October 1966, several months after the Court, by a narrow majority, had refused to rule on the merits of a suit brought by Liberia and Ethiopia alleging South Africa's violation of the mandate agreement,[17] the General Assembly revoked the South Afri-

16. ICJ *Reports,* 1950, p. 19.

17. South West Africa, Second Phase, Judgment, ICJ *Reports,* 1966, p. 6. For critique of judgment, see Richard A. Falk, "The South West Africa Case: An Appraisal" *International Organization,* XXI (1967), 1–23.

can government's mandate over the territory.[18] It subsequently established a United Nations Council to administer the territory and proclaimed "Namibia" to be its name. In spite of the efforts of the General Assembly and the Security Council to implement the Assembly's decision, the Republic of South Africa continues to remain in effective control of the territory and refuses to give any heed to the efforts of the United Nations to make it an independent state.[19] Though the United Nations and South Africa agree on the goal of "self-determination and independence" for the peoples of the territory, they differ on the manner of implementation. The United Nations insists that the territory must be granted independence as a unified entity within its present borders; South Africa insists on the fragmentation of the territory, with native self-government in certain designated areas and the continuance of South African administration in others.

The emphasis upon positive constructive action, both in the general purposes of trusteeship and in the specific commitments assumed by administering authorities, helped to speed up the economic, social, and political development of trust territories, and by the example set, the trusteeship system has accelerated this development in all non-self-governing territories.

The procedures developed under the trusteeship system for giving interested parties the opportunity to present complaints and for establishing the facts regarding the administration of trust territories have been a considerable improvement over League procedures and have provided the basis for more effective international supervision. The annual reports, prepared by the administering authorities and their examination by the Trusteeship Council, have been the essence of the system of international supervision.

The right of petition has been widely accorded and exercised with the result that a major problem facing the Trusteeship Council has been the screening of petitions to prevent abuse and misuse

18. General Assembly Res. 2145 (XXI), Oct. 27, 1966.

19. To assist it in determining the legal consequences of South Africa's continued occupation and administration of the territory, the Security Council on July 29, 1970 requested an opinion from the International Court of Justice. For opinion, given June 21, 1971, see Advisory Opinion, ICJ *Reports*, 1971, p. 16.

of the Council's time. Petitions have been presented not only to the General Assembly and the Trusteeship Council but also to the visiting missions, and not only in writing but also orally. A major departure from League practice has been to allow the petition to come to the United Nations organ directly without the requirement that it be first submitted to the administering authority.

The greatest improvement in trusteeship arrangements for hearing grievances and establishing the facts has been the provision for visiting missions, making it possible for the General Assembly and the Trusteeship Council to get firsthand information. The visiting missions have provided the Assembly and Council with an invaluable means of independent intelligence.

Vesting responsibility for the performance of United Nations functions in all trust territories, except strategic areas, in the General Assembly, assisted by the Trusteeship Council, was intended to strengthen the Organization's authority, as indeed it has. The General Assembly, composed as it is of a majority of states with anti-imperialistic leanings, has proven to be a vigorous defender of the rights of dependent peoples and an alert critic of the conduct of administering states. Any hope that may have been entertained of keeping the Assembly under restraint by having initial responsibility assumed by the Trusteeship Council, and by giving that organ the status of a principal organ of the United Nations, has not been realized. Since the Council is a political organ of limited membership, unrepresentative of the total membership of the Organization, and with no convincing claim to independent expert status, members who desire the United Nations to exert strong pressure on the administering authorities to speed up the development of trust territories or show more consideration for the rights and interests of the native peoples have naturally preferred to utilize the Assembly where their numbers are more likely to assure a favorable result.

At the present time only two of the territories originally placed under trusteeship—New Guinea and the Pacific Islands—are still so administered. This striking achievement of the trusteeship system, in comparison with the League mandate system, has been due to a combination of factors. These include the greater willingness of administering authorities to terminate their responsibilities for reasons independent of the United Nations, and the stronger pressures that it has been possible to mobilize through the General Assembly in contrast to the limited use that could be made of the League Council. The Charter contained no provisions regarding the termination of trusteeship arrangements, nor did it anticipate a time when the United Nations had largely discharged its responsibilities. One can read into the Charter provisions an implicit hope, if not expectation, that the trusteeship system would provide the means by which colonies would progressively be brought under its terms and through it achieve ultimate self-government or independence by an orderly and carefully monitored process of evolutionary development. If this was the expectation, it soon became apparent that it would not be realized since colonial powers showed no willingness to voluntarily place their colonies under trusteeship, and within the United Nations the majority of members showed impatience with any delays in granting self-government or independence on grounds of lack of preparation. Furthermore, administering states demonstrated none of the nineteenth-century desire to shoulder the burdens of tutelage, and were quite prepared to withdraw from their responsibilities provided this could be done with a certain amount of dignity and show of independence. A special concern of the United Nations organs has been to see that the "freely expressed wishes of the people" should be allowed to determine their future, and that these "wishes" should be expressed in an approved manner.[20]

THE GENERAL ASSEMBLY, THE DECLARATION, AND SELF-DETERMINATION

The basis of the United Nations' responsibilities and authority in dealing with colonies outside the trusteeship system was to be

20. See Leland M. Goodrich, Edvard Hambro, and Anne P. Simons, *Charter of the United Nations: Commentary and Documents* (3d rev. ed.; New York: Columbia University Press, 1969), pp. 464–543, for a fuller discussion of the working of the Trusteeship system.

found in other parts of the Charter. Until 1960 the Declaration on Non-Self-Governing Territories—Chapter XI of the Charter—was the main basis of UN action. From 1960 on the emphasis shifted to the principle of self-determination, that seemingly innocuous principle introduced into the Charter at San Francisco by the Soviet Union without any agreement at that time as to its exact meaning.

Though the Declaration defines the duties of members administering non-self-governing territories, it does not expressly provide for any form of supervision or control by organs of the United Nations. Administering states are required to transmit certain kinds of information to the Secretariat regularly "for information purposes," but there is no suggestion in the Declaration that this information is to be used in any way as the basis for international supervision.

The issue was raised at the first session of the General Assembly in 1946. It was strongly argued that the General Assembly had no authority under the Charter to consider this information, to set up special machinery for its study, or to make any recommendations to members regarding the discharge of their responsibilities under the Declaration.[21] Such action, it was asserted, would violate the domestic jurisdiction principle of the Charter and in any case would be unwise. In support of the General Assembly's competence, it was pointed out that under Article 10 of the Charter the General Assembly "may discuss any questions or any matters within the scope of the present Charter" and may make recommendations to members.

After a heated debate the Assembly finally adopted a resolution [22] which requested the Secretary-General to summarize, analyze, and classify the information submitted under Article 73(e) and to report to the General Assembly. It also set up an ad hoc committee to examine the Secretary-General's report and make recommendations to the Assembly regarding the procedures to be followed. In 1949 the Assembly established the Special Committee

21. See Goodrich, Hambro, and Simons, pp. 456–58.
22. General Assembly Res. 66 (1), Dec. 14, 1946.

on Information from Non-Self-Governing Territories on a three-year basis to perform the functions of the ad hoc committee. This committee was renewed in 1952, and on renewal three years later "special" was dropped from its title. As in the case of the Trusteeship Council, the composition of the Committee was based on the principle of parity between administering and nonadministering states.

From the beginning the General Assembly was concerned with determining which territories were non-self-governing. The Charter did not specify who was to make this determination, nor did it indicate in any detail the considerations that were to be taken into account in determining whether the people of a particular territory had "attained a full measure of self-government." In its first session the General Assembly adopted a resolution listing as non-self-governing territories the seventy-four territories concerning which eight members had transmitted information. Thus the Assembly initially accepted determination by the administering states. Subsequently, however, the Assembly took the view that, while the administering state might make the initial determination, once that state had determined a territory to be non-self-governing by accepting the obligation to transmit information, it could not by itself decide that the territory had become fully self-governing, and cease to transmit information. It claimed this right in a number of instances.[23] In 1960 the Assembly decided that certain territories under Portuguese administration were non-self-governing and that Portugal was obligated to report on them, even though Portugal had consistently maintained that they were overseas provinces.[24]

Prior to 1960 the debates of the General Assembly, both on factors to be taken into account in determining whether full self-government had been achieved, and on the question whether particular territories had achieved it, emphasized the complexity of the problem and the limitations of Assembly action. They also reflected the attitudes of Western developed states who were inclined

23. Greenland, Indonesia, Puerto Rico, Surinam and the Dutch Antilles, Gold Coast, Tunis, and Morocco.

24. General Assembly Res. 1542 (XV), Dec. 15, 1960.

to stress the basic responsibility of the administering state for determining the readiness of a colony for self-government or independence and who, in some instances for strategic reasons, were not prepared to bring excessive pressure to bear on the administering state. If an administering state took the position that a particular territory was self-governing and ceased to transmit information, there was an inclination on the part of influential members to accept this, particularly since there was little that the Assembly could do except exercise moral suasion. The Assembly and its subsidiary organs had limited means of establishing the facts since they did not have the authority to send visiting missions into the territory. The majority of the General Assembly were inclined to recognize that the effectiveness of the United Nations was dependent on the voluntary cooperation of the administering states, which could only be gained by the adoption of a reasonable and conciliatory attitude on the Assembly's part.

Prior to 1960 the efforts of the General Assembly were mainly to strengthen the system of international accountability under Chapter XI, both by expanding and making more precise the duties of administering states and by increasing the scope and effectiveness of General Assembly supervision. Thus, one of the issues with which the Assembly was very much concerned was the kind of information to be transmitted under Article 73(e). The administering state, while obligated to assist the people of the non-self-governing territory "in the progressive development of their free political institutions," was not required to transmit information relating to political development. Some administering states transmitted information about political development on a voluntary basis. The Assembly encouraged all administering states to do so.

Prior to 1960, while it was widely accepted that the General Assembly might consider the information transmitted by the administering states and make recommendations to members with regard to matters covered by Chapter XI, it was also generally agreed that the Assembly should not direct its criticisms or recommendations to a particular administering state, as it was entitled to do under the trusteeship system. While recommendations assumed a fairly specific form, they were general in the sense that they were directed to all similarly situated. The Assembly adopted the practice of devoting its attention each year to some major aspect of colonial administration. Its resolutions reflected this functional specialization.

Beginning in 1960 the influx of a large number of new states with recent colonial backgrounds caused the United Nations' efforts with regard to colonialism to undergo a sharp transformation. These efforts were directed along two different lines which were shortly to merge into one. One aim was to strengthen the control experienced under Chapter XI by further defining the territories for which information must be submitted and the conditions under which reporting might cease. The General Assembly had at its previous session established a special committee to recommend principles that should guide members in determining whether an obligation to report under Article 73(e) of the Charter existed.[25] With one modification, the Committee's report was accepted by the General Assembly in 1960.[26] Two of the principles that were adopted were of special significance: (1) that *"prima facie* there is an obligation to transmit information in respect to a territory which is geographically separate and is distinct ethnically and/or culturally from the country administering it"; and (2) that a "Non-Self-Governing Territory can be said to have reached a full-measure of self-government by (a) Emergence as a sovereign independent state; (b) Free association with an independent state; or (c) Integration with an independent state." The first of these principles was to provide the basis for the position, vigorously advanced from 1960 on, that Portugal's claim that her overseas territories were part of metropolitan Portugal and therefore not to be treated as non-self-governing territories was without foundation.

The second line of attack was to shift the Charter basis of the effort to eliminate colonialism from Chapter XI (Declaration on Non-Self-Governing Territories) to "the principle of equal rights and self-determination of peoples." [27] Whereas earlier United Na-

25. General Assembly Res. 1467 (XIV), Dec. 12, 1959.

26. General Assembly Res. 1541 (XV), Dec. 15, 1960, adopted by a vote of 69 to 2 (Portugal and South Africa), with 21 abstentions.

27. Art. 1, par. 2.

tions efforts had been to assure that administering states were promoting the welfare and progressive development of their colonial territories with a view to ultimate independence or self-government, the new members of the United Nations launched a campaign designed to eradicate colonialism as rapidly as possible and without regard to the degree of preparation for independence. The initiative was taken by the Soviet Union at the fifteenth session of the General Assembly when Chairman Khrushchev, increasingly dissatisfied with the course of United Nations action in the Congo and desiring to place his country in the role of friend of the Third World, introduced a proposal for the complete and final elimination of colonialism "in all its forms and manifestations." [28] The adoption by the General Assembly in December 1960 of an alternative draft sponsored by Asian and African members, and less objectionable to the colonial powers than the Soviet proposal, marked the beginning of the new phase in United Nations activities in this field.[29] According to the Declaration, colonialism is contrary to the Charter. All peoples have a right to self-determination, and inadequate preparation does not constitute a valid reason for delaying independence. The Declaration called for immediate steps to transfer power to peoples not yet independent.

In 1961 the Committee of Twenty-Four,—formally entitled the Special Committee on the Situation with Regard to the Implementation of the Declaration on the Granting of Independence to Colonial Countries and Peoples—was established.[30] In 1963 the Committee was given the responsibilities of the Committee on Information from Non-Self-Governing Territories, which was dissolved.[31] Whereas in the composition of the Committee on Information the principle of equality between administering and nonadministering states had been respected, the membership of the Committee of Twenty-Four was initially composed to reflect

28. Doc. A/4501, Sept. 23, 1960, and Doc. A/4502 and Corr.

29. Declaration on the Granting of Independence to Colonial Countries and Peoples, General Assembly Res. 1514 (XV), Dec. 14, 1960.

30. General Assembly Res. 1654 (XVI), Nov. 27, 1961.

31. General Assembly Res. 1970 (XVIII), Dec. 16, 1963.

the membership of the United Nations as a whole, which after 1960 contained a majority of Afro-Asian states. Furthermore, the General Assembly resolution establishing the Special Committee directed it "to carry out its task by employment of all means which it will have at its disposal within the framework of the procedures and modalities which it shall adopt for the proper discharge of its functions." Relying on this open-ended grant of authority, the Special Committee has not hesitated to assert its right to use powers, techniques, and procedures going beyond those used by the Committee on Information. It has encountered less than full cooperation on the part of administering states.[32]

The Committee of Twenty-Four has not hesitated to define which territories it considers to be non-self-governing. It has examined conditions existing in these territories on the basis of information available to its members and has not hesitated to make recommendations to administering authorities concerning the political development of these areas. In performing its functions, the Committee has been free in the choice of methods. The Committee accepts petitions and grants interviews to individuals from non-self-governing territories, including representatives of rebel groups. It organizes fact-finding missions which have attempted to visit colonial areas with little success, and its subcommittees have sought to enter into discussions with colonial powers. The Committee produces a continuous stream of recommendations and reports, often directed at specific colonial governments in reference to specific conditions in particular territories. Unlike the Committee on Information, there is clearly no reluctance to pinpoint the shortcomings of particular colonial powers in its resolutions and to urge the acceptance of very specific policies.

The tone of debates in the Committee of Twenty-Four and in the General Assembly since 1960 has often been bitter. The majority has not been satisfied with conciliatory, moderately phrased resolutions. The new nations have also sought to gain the assistance of the Security Council in an attempt to secure mandatory sanctions to

32. With the withdrawal of the United States and the United Kingdom in January 1971, the Committee no longer had an administering state as a member.

enforce some of its decolonization proposals. In the case of Southern Rhodesia, the Security Council has used its powers under Article 41 of the Charter to order mandatory economic and political sanctions, in effect to enable the people to secure the enjoyment of their rights under the Charter and the 1960 Declaration.[33] The Council has thus far refused to order mandatory sanctions against Portugal for its failure to give independence to Angola and Mozambique, or against the Republic of South Africa for refusing to accept the Assembly's decisions on South West Africa. Nor has the Security Council been willing to accede to General Assembly requests that military measures be used if necessary to gain compliance with the 1960 Declaration in these areas. Furthermore, recommendations of the Assembly addressed to members and calling upon them to take collective measures to achieve compliance with the 1960 Declaration by Portugal and the Republic of South Africa have had little effect, not alone due to the failure of the major Western powers to cooperate.

One should not conclude that the pressures mounted by the new majority in the General Assembly have had no effects. Some of the member states with colonial possessions have come to realize that their actions can produce loud outcries in the United Nations organs which could prove embarrassing to them. Probably no administering state would admit that its policies have been decisively affected by this United Nations prodding. Yet there is reason to believe that to some extent the speed with which colonies have been transformed into self-governing units in recent years has resulted from United Nations pressure. Perhaps the greatest changes, however, have occurred in the realm of attitudes. Since 1960, in particular, the new nations in the United Nations have succeeded in establishing the generally accepted principle that colonialism must be rapidly terminated. This, in effect, has amounted to a redefinition of the purposes and assumptions of the United Nations Charter, which envisioned a more deliberate and orderly development toward independence or self-government than is now acceptable.

33. Security Council Res. 253 (1968), May 29, 1968, and Res. 277 (1970), March 18, 1970.

CONCLUSIONS

The change that has taken place in the generally prevailing attitudes toward colonialism and its future is one of the significant phenomena of our time. Before World War II there was widespread criticism of colonialism and support for the principle of trusteeship but, generally speaking, colonial powers were still hopeful that by adopting more enlightened policies they could continue to maintain their special positions and responsibilities in their colonies for an extended period of time. While the mandate system had been accepted on a limited basis, it had involved no real commitment to ultimate self-government or independence for any territory other than those under Class A mandates.

World War II and the years following witnessed a remarkable change. A large number of colonies soon became independent and were admitted as United Nations members. The remaining colonial powers were put on the defensive. Except for Portuguese territories in Africa, Southern Rhodesia,[34] and South West Africa, most remaining dependencies are small, scattered islands, many with limited resources. Yet self-government and even independence are being urged for these territories.

The United Nations has been an important factor in the process of translating dependence into independence or self-government,[35] and it can continue to play a constructive role in dealing with remaining colonial problems. During the first ten years of the United Nations, issues involving the future of dependent peoples became enmeshed in the strategies and rivalries of the cold war. The support of the Soviet Union and the other Communist countries for the demands of Asian and African peoples for independence weakened the willingness of Western colonial powers to ac-

34. The United Nations treats Southern Rhodesia as a non-self-governing territory and refused to recognize the Smith government's declaration of independence for "Rhodesia."

35. For assessments of the United Nations' role, see Harold K. Jacobson, "The United Nations and Colonialism: A Tentative Appraisal," *International Organization,* XVI (1962), 37–56; and Rupert Emerson, "Colonialism, Political Development, and the U.N.," *International Organization,* XIX (1965), 484–503.

cept United Nations supervision or grant native demands. Beginning in the middle fifties, the colonial powers increasingly came to recognize that the end of colonial rule was inevitable, and indeed that it was in their interest to speed the process and get as much benefit as possible from seeming to act voluntarily. The major breakthrough came in 1960 with the granting of independence to French African colonies and the adoption by the Assembly of the 1960 Declaration. Since 1960 the influx of new members, only recently themselves colonies, has increased the pressure for independence, even under conditions that were earlier considered premature.

The problems that remain are of a particularly difficult nature, involving as they do challenges to the competence of the United Nations to act, allegations of racial discrimination, and the future status of miniscule insular territories. In the matter of the Portuguese African territories, the United Nations is faced with a challenge to its competence based on the claim that the territories in question are integral parts of the Portuguese state and are not to be treated as non-self-governing territories. So long as Portugal maintains this attitude, the question facing the United Nations is how can the Portuguese government be brought to see that its interests can best be served by pursuing the policy followed by other Western European powers. The problems of South West Africa and Rhodesia have a common element: the insistence of a white minority on the right to rule and determine the future of a territory inhabited by a black majority, without according to the black inhabitants any meaningful participation. Again the question arises of means at the disposal of the United Nations for persuading the white regimes that it is in their interest to comply with United Nations standards.

For the miniscule colonial territories that remain—mostly insular—the issue is of a different kind. What status can be accorded to these territories which will satisfy the basic needs of the populations, while avoiding the heavy burdens and responsibilities that full independence and membership in the United Nations would involve? The retention of special relations with the colonial power, a form of limited membership in international organizations, and the rendering of special services by the United Nations and the specialized agencies are among the possible alternatives.[36]

It must be recognized that the achievement of the goal of independence or self-government by colonial peoples is not sufficient in itself. The United Nations has new and in some respects more difficult tasks to perform in helping to create those conditions—political, economic, social, and educational—which are the necessary foundations of stable and responsible government. After a colonial people has achieved independence, the task remains of helping the new state to acquire the political, social, and economic strength that will permit it to survive and prosper. As the process of freeing people from colonial rule is hastened and brought to fruition without regard to the readiness of the people for self-government, the need of such assistance becomes all the greater. This is one of the challenges which the United Nations and its related agencies are called upon to face in their programs of development assistance to new and developing countries.

36. For discussion of the problem, see above, pp. 49–51.

CHAPTER TEN

PROMOTING ECONOMIC AND
SOCIAL WELL-BEING

UNLIKE THE AUTHORS OF THE LEAGUE COVENANT those responsible for drafting the Charter recognized from the beginning the importance of establishing sound economic and social foundations for a world of peace and security. In his report on the work of the San Francisco Conference, the U.S. Secretary of State stressed that:

> The battle of peace has to be fought on two fronts. The first is the security front where victory spells freedom from fear. The second is the economic and social front where victory means freedom from want. Only victory on both fronts can assure the world of an enduring peace.[1]

To those who had lived through the years preceding the war and witnessed the political consequences of economic collapse—extreme nationalist and authoritarian regimes in German and Japan, the impotence of Western democracies, and a world in flames—it was clear that a world secure in peace required the reasonable satisfaction of economic and social needs.

In 1945 the atmosphere of public opinion and government policy in the principal democracies was extremely favorable to interna-

---

1. *Charter of the United Nations. Report to the President on the Results of the San Francisco Conference by the Chairman of the United States Delegation, the Secretary of State,* Dept. of State Publ. 2349 (Wasington, 1945), p. 109.

tional cooperation for economic and social well-being. The war had been preceded by a world-wide depression which had required the active intervention of governments. Cooperation on an unprecedented scale between allied countries had been necessary to meet their needs for munitions, raw materials, food, and shipping. The war's disruptive effects on national economies and the destruction which it had wrought convinced peoples and governments that wartime cooperation could not be suddenly ended, as had happened after World War I. The ground work for postwar cooperation was laid in Article VIII of the 1942 Lend-Lease Agreement between the United States and the United Kingdom.[2] The need of a cooperative approach to postwar economic problems was stressed by Under-Secretary of State Welles in a speech delivered at the University of Toronto in February 1943, in which he advocated conferences and consultations with a view to reaching agreement on policies and institutional arrangements for promoting the common economic welfare of the nations united in the war.[3] Clearly, such cooperation in dealing with pressing economic problems was viewed in Washington as preparing the way for the permanent political cooperation for peace and security.

The pattern of postwar cooperation in dealing with economic and social problems was only in part determined by the San Francisco Conference. At the time the Charter was being put into final form, specialized intergovernmental agencies for dealing with postwar economic and social problems were already in operation or in the process of being established under the pressure of current or widely anticipated needs. The International Labour Organisation, established at the end of World War I to further social justice by improving the conditions of labor, was actively functioning, though the circumstances of the war had forced the temporary transfer of its headquarters from Geneva to Montreal. To assist in the work of relief and rehabilitation in liberated areas, the United Nations Relief and Rehabilitation Administration had been established in

2. See Ruth B Russell, *A History of the United Nations Charter* (Washington: Brookings Institution, 1958), pp. 47–50, 59–74.

3. Department of State, *Bulletin*, VIII (1943), 179.

1943 and was already at work when the San Francisco Conference met. Also, in the same year, the United Nations Conference on Food and Agriculture had met at Hot Springs, Virginia, and had taken the first step toward the establishment of the United Nations Food and Agriculture Organization. Its purposes were to raise nutritional levels, to improve the efficiency of agricultural production, and to better the conditions of rural populations. In July 1944, at Bretton Woods, the Articles of Agreement of the International Monetary Fund and of the International Bank for Reconstruction and Development were signed after extensive preliminary negotiations between the United States and the United Kingdom. These agencies were established to assist in stabilizing national currencies and to provide financial aid in economic reconstruction and development. Later that same year another United Nations conference, meeting in Chicago, drafted the constitution of an international organization to assist in the development of safe and efficient international civil aviation (the International Civil Aviation Organization). Plans were well under way at the time of the San Francisco Conference for the establishment of an international organization to further educational, scientific, and cultural cooperation, though the conference which drafted the Constitution of the United Nations Educational, Scientific and Cultural Organization did not meet until November 1, 1945, over four months after the Charter of the United Nations was signed.

With these various agencies already in existence or in process of being established, with national governments committed to them and to the piecemeal functional approach which they represented, and with powerful pressure groups in many instances insisting on the autonomy of agencies in which they were specially interested, those engaged in writing the Charter at San Francisco were not free to determine the future pattern of international organization for economic and social cooperation on the basis of what was ideally desirable. They had to accommodate their thinking and adapt their conclusions to institutional developments already well advanced, and these dictated a decentralized system, with great variety of structures, powers, and procedures, and with the general international organization playing an important role, but not a controlling one. Furthermore, they had before them a proposal which was based on the functional approach and provided in some detail for a decentralized system of organization.[4]

UNITED NATIONS RESPONSIBILITIES AND MACHINERY

While the authors of the Charter recognized that intergovernmental cooperation in the economic and social fields would not be the monopoly of the United Nations, they were nevertheless in agreement that the new organization should have important and comprehensive responsibilities. In principle, the scope of the United Nations' work was to be as broad as the area of international concern. Lest the words of the Dumbarton Oaks Proposals permit a too narrow interpretation of the Organization's responsibilities, delegations at San Francisco, under pressure from private groups, insisted on a more explicit and detailed description of the United Nations' responsibilities.[5] While it was assumed that the specific actions to be taken by the Organization might vary depending upon what had already been done, what agencies were already in existence or functioning, and what specific type of activity seemed most appropriate to the given situation, there was no inclination to accept any qualification in principle of its broad responsibility for promoting international cooperation in economic, social, cultural, educational, health, and related fields.

The Charter not only defines the scope of responsibility in broad terms but also commits the Organization and its members to some fairly specific objectives and principles of policy. It declares that the United Nations should promote "higher standards of living, full

4. The provisions of the Dumbarton Oaks Proposals on economic and social cooperation followed closely the initial United States proposals. On them, see Russell, pp. 303–29.

5. In place of "solutions of international economic, social and other humanitarian problems", Art. 55 of the Charter substitutes "solutions of international economic, social, health and related problems; and international cultural and educational cooperation."

employment, and conditions of economic and social progress and development." [6] Thus, the Organization was not to play a passive role with respect to matters which laissez-faire economic doctrine might consider outside the realm of direct state responsibility. Rather, it took as guiding principles of international economic and social policy the basic premises of the New Deal in the United States and of social democracy in other advanced countries. While the Charter did not attempt to prescribe the specific policies by which its social and economic goals were to be achieved, it did make it clear that members of the United Nations were to "take joint and separate action in cooperation with the Organization" to achieve the purposes set forth in the Charter.[7] This should at least be interpreted as requiring that members show good faith and seriousness of purpose.

While the Charter placed primary responsibility for the maintenance of international peace and security on the Security Council, it was equally explicit in making the General Assembly the central organ for discharging the Organization's responsibilities in the economic and social field,[8] with the Economic and Social Council and the Secretariat acting under its authority. Thus it was recognized that in an area where all states were concerned and where the cooperation of all was necessary for success, it was fitting and proper that the General Assembly should have the major role. It was in dealing with questions in the area of economic and social cooperation that the Assembly could most fittingly be thought to serve as a "town meeting of the world."

To understand and to evaluate fairly the work of the United Nations in the economic and social field, it is first necessary to recognize the nature and limits of what the General Assembly and the Economic and Social Council can do. Neither the Assembly nor the Council has the power to make decisions, with respect to matters of substance within the economic and social field, that are binding upon member states or upon the citizens of those states. The powers of legislation and taxation are exclusively the prerogatives

6. Art. 55a.   7. Art. 56.   8. Art. 60.

of the governments of the member states. The Assembly can initiate studies, hold discussions, make recommendations, set up programs, and call upon members to give them their support. It can establish subsidiary organs to perform its functions, and it can direct the activities of these organs and of the Economic and Social Council and the Secretariat. It can authorize expenditures for administrative purposes and apportion these expenditures among members. All the specific powers which the Charter confers upon the Assembly fall into one or more of these categories.[9]

The authors of the Charter saw the need of a quasi-executive organ performing functions in the economic and social field which the Assembly, because of its size, would be poorly equipped to carry out. Under the League Covenant, the Council, primarily a political organ, had important responsibilities in connection with the initiation of proposals in the economic and social field and the implementing of decisions. There was, however, growing sentiment toward the end of the League's active existence that this arrangement was not satisfactory, and the Bruce Committee proposed the establishment of a special committee to take over the Council's responsibilities in this area.[10] At San Francisco it was decided to create a separate council to perform the quasi-executive functions which the League Council had performed. Thus, the Economic and Social Council became one of the principal organs of the United Nations, though acting "under the authority of the General Assembly." [11]

The Economic and Social Council was initially composed of eighteen members elected by the General Assembly for three-year terms. Membership was increased to twenty-seven in 1966 as the result of pressures by new Asian and African members for wider geographic representation.[12] In 1971 the Assembly approved a

9. See Arts. 10, 13, 17, 19, 58, and 59.

10. League of Nations, *The Development of International Cooperation in Economic and Social Affairs*, Report of the Special Committee, Doc. A. 23 (1939).

11. Art. 60 of the Charter.

12. General Assembly Res. 1991 (XVIII), Dec. 17, 1963.

Charter amendment which, brought into force by the necessary ratifications, doubled the size of the Council.[13] The Assembly declared the increase desirable to provide broad representation of the United Nations membership and to make the Council a more effective organ. Until 1960 the Council's membership was predominantly of Western and developed nations. Since then the composition of the Council has steadily changed. Currently thirty-seven of the Council's fifty-four members are developing countries, seventeen are developed countries, of which five are Eastern European Socialist states.

The Council's powers on paper are extensive. It may make studies and reports; make recommendations to the General Assembly and to the specialized agencies; prepare draft conventions for submission to the Assembly; call international conferences with respect to matters within its competence; conclude agreements with intergovernmental agencies, defining their relations to the United Nations, subject to approval by the Assembly; coordinate the activities of the specialized agencies through consultations and recommendations; and perform such other functions as fall within its competence in connection with carrying out the recommendations of the Assembly.[14] But while these powers appear adequate to permit the Council to assume an important role in United Nations activity, in practice the Council has been overshadowed by the Assembly. This has in large measure been due to its composition. Until the increase in the size of the Council, the older and more developed states had representation out of proportion to their actual numbers in the Organization. This made the Council a more cautious and conservative body than the Assembly, particularly in dealing with questions of economic development, which have come to be a major concern of the majority of members. Consequently, those states interested in having the United Nations take positive action on this issue have found it to their advantage to appeal from the Council to the Assembly and to reopen and fully discuss questions which the Council has already considered.

13. General Assembly Res. 2847 (XXVI), Dec. 20, 1971. On September 24, 1973, the amendment entered into force.

14. See Arts. 62, 63, 64–66 of the Charter.

The enlargement of the Council in 1973, by making it more representative of the total membership, eliminated one reason for downgrading the Council's role in the Organization. By itself, however, it does not assure that the Council will be restored to the position that the framers of the Charter sought to give it. For a substantial revitalization of the Council to take place, other remedial steps are needed, including a clearer definition in practice of its primary responsibility, a more rational division of labor between Assembly and Council, and an improvement in the quality of member representation. Back of these needs is the necessity that governments of member states take the Council more seriously and seek to make it an effective organ in promoting economic and social cooperation.[15]

To give the Council—composed of representatives of governments—the expert assistance it would need, the Charter provides for "commissions in economic and social fields and for the promotion of human rights, and such other commissions as may be required for the performance of its functions." [16] Acting under this provision, the Council has established a number of functional commissions such as the Population Commission and the Commission on Narcotic Drugs. Following League practice, the Dumbarton Oaks Proposals envisaged that the commissions should be composed of experts chosen on the basis of personal qualification. At San Francisco this requirement was dropped; the view has come to prevail that these commissions should be composed of member states whose governments in turn appoint the individuals who serve.[17] These individuals may or may not be experts in their fields, and in most cases they act under government instructions. The reasoning in support of this practice is twofold: that so-called independent experts always have national biases, and eventual agreement among governments is facilitated if the positions of member governments are taken into account at all levels of discussion. One

15. For fuller discussion of the problem, see Walter R. Sharp, *The United Nations Economic and Social Council* (New York: Columbia University Press, 1969), pp. 203–78.

16. Art. 68.

17. For a critical view, see A. Loveday, "An Unfortunate Decision," *International Organization,* I (1947), 279–90.

result has been that a heavy responsibility has been placed on the Secretariat, though this load has been somewhat lessened by the practice of setting up ad hoc committees of experts.

In addition to the functional commissions, the Economic and Social Council has established five regional economic commissions to assist it. The creation of these commissions was not foreseen at the San Francisco Conference. The General Assembly, in its first session, urged the establishment of regional economic commissions for Europe, and for Asia, and for the Far East "in order to give effective aid to the countries devastated by war." [18] This the Council did on March 28, 1947. Later, in 1948 the Council established the Economic Commission for Latin America, and in 1958, the Economic Commission for Africa. Finally, in 1973, the Council established the United Nations Economic Commission for Western Asia to consist of UN members who had utilized the services of the United Nations Economic and Social Office at Beirut. These commissions undertake research, advise the Council on problems of a regional nature, and make direct recommendations to member governments, governments admitted in an advisory capacity, and specialized agencies on matters falling within their competence. They are composed of countries within the areas and of other countries with special interests. These commissions have proved to be among the most successful of the United Nations' organs in promoting constructive cooperation in the economic field.[19] Being close to the problems of their respective areas, they have been responsive to them and have on the whole dealt with them to the satisfaction of both the countries of the region and outside states. Furthermore, they have stimulated the spirit of self-help in meeting regional problems. With economic and social development a principal concern of the United Nations, the regional commissions for Asia and the Far East, Latin America, and Africa have come to

18. General Assembly Res. 46 (1), Dec. 11, 1946.

19. See Sharp, pp. 17–20. For studies of particular commissions, see David Wightman, *Economic Cooperation in Europe: A Study of the United Nations Economic Commission for Europe* (New York: Stevens, 1956); and *Toward Economic Cooperation in Asia: The United Nations Economic Commission for Asia and the Far East* (New Haven: Yale University Press, 1963).

play important roles in the development and carrying out of programs for this purpose.

With the expansion of United Nations membership, mounting pressure has been exerted to reorient the work of established United Nations organs and to create new ones designed to maximize the influence of developing countries, all with the common purpose of contributing to their economic and social development. On the other hand, the developed and more highly industrialized countries, while accepting the objectives of the developing countries and seeking to make existing programs more effective, have been reluctant to give full support to proposals which tend to take out of their hands decisions with regard to programs to which they are expected to give financial and other needed support.

Pressure from the less-developed states was primarily responsible for the establishment in 1964 of the United Nations Conference on Trade and Development (UNCTAD) as an autonomous organ of the General Assembly.[20] UNCTAD consists of a Conference meeting once every three years, the Trade and Development Board of 55 members meeting every two years, a number of committees and subgroups of varying sizes, and a secretariat located in Geneva. Less-developed states have preferred this agency to the General Agreement on Tariffs and Trade as a forum in which to discuss their special trade needs and to bring pressure on advanced states to adopt trade policies which will contribute to the economic development of underdeveloped countries. UNCTAD also provides a preferred means of coordinating policies and activities in the development field. As a result, its establishment has further complicated the efforts of those wishing to strengthen the role of the Council in the coordination of United Nations activities in the economic and social fields.

Responding to similar pressures from the developing countries, the General Assembly has established the United Nations Industrial Development Organization (UNIDO) as an autonomous organ to promote and accelerate industrial development in less-

20. General Assembly Res. 1955 (XIX), Dec. 30, 1964. On UNCTAD, see Richard N. Gardner, "The United Nations Conference on Trade and Development," *International Organization*, XXII (1968), 99–130; and Sharp, pp. 217–29.

developed countries.[21] UNIDO follows the example of UNCTAD in having its own separate conference, executive body, secretariat and headquarters. In this respect it resembles a specialized agency, but it differs in having been created by and in being responsible to the General Assembly. Its activities to date suggest that UNIDO will seek to provide developing states with a wide range of services and technical assistance designed to assist them in developing industrial projects and to encourage developed countries to provide the needed financial and other assistance. Its establishment was another example of the success of the developing countries in bypassing ECOSOC.

After many years of pressure, the less-developed states succeeded in establishing the United Nations Capital Development Fund (UNCDF) in 1966.[22] Economically advanced states in general have opposed the establishment of such a fund, preferring to rely instead on assistance available through the Special Fund, the World Bank and related institutions, and agencies of a regional character. Less-developed states look upon UNCDF as a way to get financial assistance on more liberal terms than the developed nations are willing to agree to. However, since UNCDF relies on voluntary contributions for the funds to be used in making grants, its success is bound to depend upon the willingness of the developed countries to make the funds available. Thus far they have not shown a willingness to do so. Up to June 1972 total pledges amounted to less than six million dollars of which less than half had been paid, mostly in nonconvertible currencies.

INTERGOVERNMENTAL ORGANIZATIONS RELATED TO THE UNITED NATIONS

A major part of the work of international cooperation in the economic and social field has been carried out by intergovernmental organizations other than the United Nations. These organizations

21. General Assembly Res. 2089 (XX), Dec. 20, 1965. See Sharp, pp. 229–37.
22. General Assembly Res. 2186 (XXI), Dec. 13, 1966.

can be classified in various ways. Some are temporary in character, as was the United Nations Relief and Rehabilitation Administration (UNRRA), set up during the war to meet what was then viewed as a passing need of great urgency. Others, much more numerous, are viewed as permanent, and meet the continuing needs of an increasingly interrelated world society. Some are limited in membership, though global in their concerns, such as the Organization for Economic Cooperation and Development (OECD), which is composed of developed countries and has as its purposes the coordination of the policies of its members with respect to trade, economic stability, and aid to developing countries. Others are universal in membership—at least in principle—and are concerned with problems worldwide in scope. Some are definitely regional in their membership and concerns, such as the European Community and the economic agencies of the Organization of American States (OAS), while others are global. And, finally, some are independent of the United Nations in origin and in their operations as, for example, the regional organizations and many global organizations with limited technical functions.[23] Others are global in nature, "having wide international responsibilities," [24] and have been brought into relation with the United Nations as "specialized agencies." [25] These agencies and the United Nations constitute the United Nations family; any understanding of the work of the Organization in the economic and social fields requires that attention be given to all parts of this highly complex system.

The intergovernmental organizations with "wide international responsibilities" that have been "brought into relationship" with the United Nations are fourteen in number (see Table 2).[26] They

23. The International Bureau of Weights and Measures and the International Union for the Protection of Industrial Property are examples.

24. Art. 57 of the Charter.

25. The International Atomic Energy Agency is technically in a class by itself due in part to its special relation to the Security Council. It is related to the United Nations but not referred to as a specialized agency.

26. GATT is sometimes included in the list, though it can better be thought of as the fragment of a planned specialized agency, the International Trade Organizatiom, which it was not possible to activate.

Table 2. Intergovernmental Organizations Related to the United Nations

Agencies	Date of Establishment	Headquarters	Membership (as of 12/31/70)	Principal Organs
International Labour Organisation (ILO)	1919	Geneva	121	Conference, governing body, office
Food and Agriculture Organization of the United Nations (FAO)	1945	Rome	119 + 2 associate	Conference, council, secretariat
United Nations Educational, Scientific, and Cultural Organization (UNESCO)	1946	Paris	125 + 3 associate	General conference, executive board, secretariat
International Civil Aviation Organization (ICAO)	1947	Montreal	120	Assembly, council, air navigation commission, secretariat
International Bank for Reconstruction and Development (World Bank)	1945	Washington	115	Board of governors, executive directors, president
International Finance Corporation (IFC)	1956	Washington	95	Board of governors, directors, president
International Development Association (IDA)	1960	Washington	107	Board of governors, directors, president

Organization	Year	Location	Members	Structure
International Monetary Fund (IMF)	1945	Washington	117	Board of governors, executive directors, managing director
World Health Organization (WHO)	1948	Geneva	128 + 3 associate	Assembly, executive board, secretariat
Universal Postal Union (UPU)	1875	Bern	143	Congress, executive council and bureau
International Telecommunications Union (ITU)	1934	Geneva	139	Conference, administrative council, general secretariat, international frequency registration board, and 3 consultative committees
World Meteorological Organization (WMO)	1950	Geneva	122 + 11 territories	Congress, executive committee, secretariat
Inter-Governmental Maritime Consultative Organization (IMCO)	1958	London	72	Assembly, council, maritime safety committee, secretariat
International Atomic Energy Agency (IAEA)	1957	Vienna	102	General conference, board of governors, secretariat
General Agreement on Tariffs and Trade (GATT)	1948	Geneva	78 + 15 limited	Secretariat

have certain features in common: Each is concerned with problems that fall within an important field of international economic and social cooperation. The Preparatory Commission, in its 1945 report, envisaged these fields as relief and rehabilitation, monetary cooperation and investment, trade policies, food and agricultural policies, labor standards and welfare, educational and cultural cooperation, health, and certain aspects of transport and communication.[27] With the exception of trade policies, these fields are presently occupied by established specialized agencies. In addition, a largely unforeseen set of problems resulting from the release of atomic energy is the special responsibility of an agency (International Atomic Energy Agency) with all the significant characteristics of a specialized agency but without that official designation. A second common feature of the specialized agencies is their autonomy. Each has its own constitution, its own membership, its own constitutional structure with principal organs paralleling in function those of the United Nations, and an independent competence to determine its own programs and financial arrangements.[28] Also, each agency is a part of the United Nations system, engaged in furthering purposes set forth in the Charter. The United Nations has responsibility for achieving coordination of its policies and activities and those of the specialized agencies. The legal relationship of each specialized agency to the United Nations is determined in part by the terms of the Charter but in greater detail by a special agreement between the agency and the United Nations.[29]

The highly decentralized arrangements of the United Nations system for the promotion of economic and social cooperation contrast rather sharply with what was at least the theory of the League of Nations that all cooperation in this field should be under the control and direction of the Council and the Assembly. The

27. Report of the Preparatory Commission (PC/20, Dec. 23, 1945), p. 35.

28. For texts of constitutions, see Amos J. Peaslee, *International Government Organizations Constitutional Documents* (2 vols., rev. 2d ed. The Hague: Nijhoff, 1961).

29. On terms of agreements, see Leland M. Goodrich, Edvard Hambro, and Anne P. Simons, *Charter of the United Nations: Commentary and Documents* (3rd rev. ed.; New York: Columbia University Press, 1969), pp. 421–25.

League system, however, developed centrifugal tendencies of its own due in part to the desire to involve the United States in cooperation in the economic and social matters without requiring its participation in political activities. At the time the Charter was written, this special reason for a decentralized functional approach did not exist. Rather, as we have seen, the principal reason for following this course was that governments had largely committed themselves to it by institutional arrangements already made or in process of being made.

There are also reasons of a more theoretical nature that can be advanced in support of the UN system. By permitting each agency to have its own separate membership, it allows those states desiring to establish and cooperate for a particular purpose to do so without being held back by unwilling states. Thus, the World Bank and its related financial institutions and the Monetary Fund could be set up and function with only a part of the members of the United Nations participating and with some states, such as Switzerland and the Federal German Republic, participating without being members of the United Nations.

Another advantage of the specialized agency arrangement is that the organizational structure and operating procedures of each agency can be adapted to the practical needs of cooperation in the field in question. Thus, in the organization dealing with labor problems (ILO), it has seemed desirable to provide for direct representation of private organizations (employer and employee organizations) as well as member governments. In the organizations dealing with investment and monetary matters (the Bank and its associated agencies, and the Fund), it was necessary to give added weight to the votes of those states making the larger contributions to the financial resources of the agencies in order to assure their participation. In the agency dealing with atomic energy matters (IAEA), it was found necessary to make special provision for membership in the executive organ of those states with the most highly developed atomic technology. On the other hand, in agencies where there are no special national interests to be taken into account, as in the case of UNESCO, it has not been necessary to make special structural or procedural arrangements of this kind.

Another and closely related advantage of the specialized agency setup is that, where the subject matter permits or effective cooperation requires, some significant steps can be taken toward subordinating the member states to a supranational authority. The continuing strength of the concept of national sovereignty makes this impossible where important national interests are at stake or where the effectiveness of cooperation for common purposes does not make it appear necessary. However, in some fields, the nature of the problems or the strength of forces supporting cooperation make this possible, and the decentralized functional approach of the United Nations system permits advantage to be taken of the opportunity. Thus, under the ILO Constitution, members are obligated to submit to their constitutional authorities labor conventions adopted by the Conference by a special majority vote and, furthermore, they are required, even if they do not ratify a given convention, to report on their practice. Under the Constitution of the World Health Organization the Assembly may adopt certain technical regulations by a majority vote, and members are bound by them unless they expressly indicate their desire not to be.

Though the United Nations approach to the organization of economic and social cooperation has its advantages and was indeed imposed on the authors of the Charter by developments already underway, it has in practice come in for serious criticism. For one thing, it is an approach which permits and encourages what many would view as an excessive proliferation of international agencies, each with its own expanding network of organs, commissions, committees, and working groups. The specialized agency setup provides bureaucrats and special interest groups in member states with favorable opportunities to press for more committees and more meetings to consider matters in which they are particularly interested. Furthermore, the existence of a large number of autonomous agencies, many working to promote the same general purposes under constitutions that do not sharply define the outer limits of their activities, is highly conducive to competitive empire-building. Each agency consists of staff members and member representatives who not only are interested in promoting the general purposes of the United Nations, but also have a special interest in improving the relative position of their particular agency, with respect both to the scope of the program and the amount of money spent. This competitive process does not necessarily result in all being done that needs to be done, in things being done most effectively and economically, or in the right priorities being established and followed. Furthermore, the cost has been considerable, though the hundreds of millions of dollars being spent under the regular budgets of the United Nations and the specialized agencies is miniscule in comparison with amounts currently being spent by governments for much less socially desirable purposes.[30]

To remedy these deficiencies in the system the United Nations was given the function of coordinating policies and activities. However, the powers given to the United Nations—to the General Assembly and the Economic and Social Council—have been inadequate to the task, with the result that the defects have only to a small degree been corrected. Coordination remains a major unattained objective, chiefly due to the fact that in a system of international cooperation such as the United Nations, the major responsibility for coordination must rest on member governments; unless they do their work, the responsible organs can do little. This is particularly true, of course, when the organs responsible for coordination—the Assembly and the Economic and Social Council—do not have effective control over the programs and budgets of the specialized agencies. It is significant that the most successful coordination has been achieved under special programs such as the United Nations Development Programme, which provides financial leverage in dealing with the specialized agencies.[31]

HOW THE UNITED NATIONS SEEKS TO ACHIEVE ITS GOALS

Since the United Nations is not equipped with the normal powers of national governments, it is forced to rely primarily on methods

30. For details on cost of United Nations system through 1969, see Inis L. Claude, Jr., *Swords into Plowshares* (4th ed.; New York: Random House, 1971), Appendix V.

31. For further discussion, see Sharp, especially chaps. 6-8; Walter M. Kotschnig, "The United Nations as an Instrument of Economic and Social Development," *International Organization*, XXII (1968), 16–43; and Mahdi Elmandjra, *The United Nations System: An Analysis* (London: Faber and Faber, 1973).

of information, persuasion, and voluntary cooperation to achieve its purposes. Having to deal directly with national governments, its methods are directed toward influencing the policies and acitivities of these governments. Only exceptionally is it able to undertake operations permitting it to deal directly with the individuals who are in need of assistance or guidance or whose conduct needs to be controlled, and then only with the consent of the governments directly concerned. We cannot, then, expect the United Nations to use the methods with which we are familiar when problems are being handled by state authorities, nor can we fairly use the same standards in judging the United Nations' performance that we use in judging the work of national or local governments.

Generally speaking, the methods available to the United Nations and to the specialized agencies for achieving economic and social objectives are (1) the preparation and publication of information on, and analytic studies of, economic and social problems, (2) the illumination of issues, the presentation of different points of view, the narrowing of areas of disagreement, and the development of areas of consensus, (3) the use of international conventions and other forms of written international agreements, and of resolutions, recommendations, and declarations to establish standards and "ordering principles" for the guidance of governments in their legislative and administrative acts and in their cooperative activities, and (4) the development of operational activities and programs to be carried out independently or in cooperation with the programs of national governments.[32]

The statistical, informational, and analytical work of the United Nations has been of outstanding importance. It has benefitted greatly from the pioneer work done by the League of Nations. By virtue of the nearly universal character of its membership and the willingness and even eagerness, in most instances, of member governments to cooperate, the United Nations has been able to extend the geographic coverage of reliable statistical data, and extend reliable statistical coverage to new substantive areas. Before statis-

32. For more extended discussion, see Asher and others, *The United Nations and Promotion of the General Welfare* (Washington: Brookings Institution, 1957), pp. 108-49; and Kotschnig.

tical data can provide useful guidance in the formulation of policy or the solution of international problems, they must be analyzed, various hypotheses must be advanced and tested, and sound conclusions must be drawn. The work of the United Nations and the specialized agencies in this respect has been of great value. Most of this work has been done by the experts in the United Nations Secretariat and the secretariats of the specialized agencies. However, the United Nations has also drawn on outside experts, either as consultants or as members of ad hoc committees, for assistance in preparing analyses and reports. The results of these studies are usually made public and are generally available to governments and scholars. They thus can serve as a common aid to governments in formulating policy, and do undoubtedly have an important, though quantitatively unmeasurable, influence on government policies. Among the more important surveys annually prepared and published by the United Nations are the *World Economic Report* and the *Report on the World Social Situation*.

An important part of the UN activity takes the form of discussions and debates in its various organs and in the specialized agencies. These serve the useful purpose of drawing attention to important questions, giving governments the opportunity to present their views, helping to clarify issues, and assisting in developing wider agreement on critical issues. However, their importance and their contribution to the actual achievement of useful results may be overemphasized. Certainly their constructive value cannot be measured by the amount of space that has to be given to them in United Nations publications.

The opportunities afforded for public debate are very wide indeed. Under the Charter the General Assembly can discuss and make recommendations with respect to any matter within the scope of the Charter. While it is true that the Assembly and the Economic and Social Council, like the other organs of the United Nations, are subject to the limitation that they cannot intervene in any matter essentially within the domestic jurisdiction of a state, discussion as such is not regarded as intervention under the Charter. Consequently, any member can request the General Assembly to consider any question it pleases and, so long as procedural requirements are adhered to, it can be assured at least of a debate on whether the item should be included in the agenda. Furthermore, the general debate at the beginning of each session gives every member government the opportunity to raise those issues which are of particular concern to itself and to make public observations upon them.

Generally, though not always, the purpose of discussion in the General Assembly and the Economic and Social Council is to come to some conclusion. This conclusion is commonly registered in the form of a resolution which, insofar as it deals with substantive matters, is a recommendation addressed to members, to other organs, or to the specialized agencies. Though such a resolution may be adopted by the necessary majority, it does not as a rule impose upon members any legal obligation to take action. Consequently, the possibility of adopting substantive decisions by a majority vote—thought by many to be a great advance at the time that the Charter was written—does not eliminate the desirability, in fact the necessity, of achieving a more substantial consensus, particularly on the part of states whose active cooperation is required for the implementation of the resolution, if any concrete result is to be achieved. Thus, for instance, the General Assembly may adopt a resolution calling upon members to make funds available to under-developed countries for financing non-self-liquidating projects such as public roads and school buildings. If, however, the major developed countries, do not give their support to the resolution, it is likely to prove of little avail since their financial assistance is necessary for carrying out such a program.

Though the United Nations political organs do not in principle have the power to create new legal obligations for members, the General Assembly and the Economic and Social Council, acting under its authority, may prepare draft conventions and submit them for ratification, or organize international conferences for that purpose. The same may be done by the specialized agencies. The United Nations has found this a useful method of dealing with problems which lend themselves particularly to the legal approach. Thus, the United Nations General Assembly or ECOSOC approved and submitted to members and other states for ratification a convention on genocide, the constitution of the World Health Organization, and the Single Convention on Narcotic Drugs. Of the specialized agencies, the ILO has made the most frequent use of the convention technique. Under its constitution, the ILO Conference may adopt conventions by a two-thirds vote and submit them to member states for their approval, each member being obligated to bring the convention to the attention of the appropriate constitutional authorities. Since World War II, however, this method has been less commonly used, in part because the possibilities of fruitful use have been less apparent than formerly and also because the special problems of underdeveloped territories have commanded increasing attention.

Finally, the United Nations seeks to achieve its economic and social purposes by initiating and carrying out, with the consent and cooperation of states concerned, programs which may involve extensive field operations. These programs may take a variety of forms. The United Nations, acting alone or in cooperation with the specialized agencies, may provide technical assistance to countries that are in particular need of the services of experts for purposes of internal modernization and development. From the beginning the United Nations has had a modest technical assistance program financed under its regular budget. In 1949 the General Assembly adopted the Expanded Program of Technical Assistance which provided for cooperation between the United Nations and the specialized agencies in carrying out a more ambitious program financed by voluntary grants.[33] In 1958 the General Assembly set up the Special Fund for financing preinvestment projects, to be administered and financed in a similar manner.[34] At its twentieth session in 1965 the Assembly combined these two programs into the United Nations Development Programme.[35]

The success of technical and preinvestment assistance emphasized the need for financial assistance to permit developing countries to undertake substantial development projects. From the

33. General Assembly Res. 304 (IV), Nov. 16, 1949.
34. General Assembly Res. 1240 (XIII), Oct. 14, 1958.
35. General Assembly Res. 2029 (XX), Nov. 22, 1965.

beginning the Bank had provided loans on bankers' terms, but these were not adequate to finance development projects that were not self-liquidating or required for their financing specially generous terms of repayment. To meet the increasingly urgent demands for financial assistance, which would permit the developing countries to improve the living conditions of their people, the International Development Association was established as an affiliate of the Bank, with authority to make loans on more liberal terms. These modest steps did not satisfy the demands of the developing countries, who became more influential and insistent in their demands from 1960 on. As the result of their voting power, the General Assembly in 1966 finally took the long-debated step of establishing the United Nations Capital Development Fund to supplement existing resources of developing countries by grants or by loans free of interest or at low interest rates. The Fund, however, has been hamstrung by lack of funds, due to the failure of the developed nations to contribute to it.

The widening economic gap that has existed between the developed countries of the West and the developing countries—particularly the new states of Asia and Africa—during the years since the war has led to increasing emphasis being placed within the United Nations on programs of assistance to developing countries. In 1952 ECOSOC recommended that the overriding objective in UN economic and social programs should be the development of underdeveloped areas.[36] The desirability of giving priority to underdeveloped countries was stressed in the program appraisal requested by the General Assembly and ECOSOC [37] and in resolutions adopted by these organs on the basis of the appraisal. In 1961, on the suggestion of President Kennedy, the General Assembly designated the 1960s "the United Nations Development Decade," [38] and called upon states to pursue policies which would contribute to maximum development. During the last decade, the General Assembly and ECOSOC have given particular attention to

36. ECOSOC Res. 451A (XIV), July 28, 1952.

37. *Five-Year Perspective,* 1959–1964. UN Doc. E/3347/ rev. 1, June 20, 1960.

38. General Assembly Res. 1710 (XVI), Dec. 19, 1961.

making the United Nations effort more effective, not only by persuading member governments to increase their contributions but also, and in a sense more importantly, by achieving better coordination, planning, and evaluation of the work undertaken by the United Nations and the various cooperating agencies.[39] The decade ended, however, with general recognition of the inadequacy of the United Nations effort, the need of larger member contributions, and a major restructuring of the mechanism of development assistance and the improvement of its operating procedures.[40]

At the beginning of its twenty-fifth session the General Assembly proclaimed the Second United Nations Development Decade and adopted an "International Development Strategy" for the years 1971 to 1980.[41] In its resolution the Assembly fixed as a goal "an average annual rate of growth in the gross product of the developing countries as a whole" of six percent. The resolution spells out in considerable detail the policy measures that member governments must adopt and carry out if this goal is to be achieved. These include appropriate trade policies on the part of developed countries favoring the exports of developing countries (the special concern of the United Nations Conference on Trade and Development), increased financial assistance by developed to developing countries (with one percent of gross national product a target to be met by 1972), increase of the science and technology capacity of developing countries, improvement of their human resources, and expansion and diversification of their production. The strategy thus outlined is impressive in conception and recognizes the dimensions of the task to be undertaken. The experience of the past decade does not, however, justify confidence that the goal will be fully achieved. In its first biennial review of progress under the new strategy, the Council recognized serious failures to meet the goals set.[42]

39. See, for example, General Assembly Res. 2188 (XXI), Dec. 13, 1966.

40. See *Partners in Development: Report of the Commission on Economic Development* (New York: Praeger, 1969); and United Nations, *A Study of the Capacity of the United Nations Development System* (2 vols.; Geneva, 1969).

41. General Assembly Res. 2626 (XXV), Oct. 24, 1970.

42. *UN Monthly Chronicle.* (August–September, 1973), pp. 78–81.

AN ASSESSMENT AND A LOOK AHEAD

The authors of the Charter were right in believing that an organization for the maintenance of international peace and security
should also be concerned with the solution of economic and social
problems. This conclusion was firmly grounded in the experience
of the interwar period when the failure of governments to make
the necessary adjustments in their trade and financial relations following the dislocations of World War I produced widespread unemployment and social discontent, a major cause of World War II.
What the authors of the Charter did not foresee was what the principal focus of United Nations activity in the economic and social
field would be. The experience of the interwar period suggested
that unemployment and social discontent in the more highly industrialized countries constituted the principal evil to be guarded
against. Consequently, the Charter places emphasis on "higher
standards of living, full employment, and conditions of economic
and social progress and development" as objectives of United Nations action. While the word "development" appears, it is used, in a
different context than at a later time, to emphasize the need of
fully prosperous and dynamic economies in all countries to prevent
those conditions arising again which had so recently been the cause
of so much human suffering.

But when we look to the record of the United Nations for the
past twenty-five years we see that it has been primarily concerned
with the economic conditions of the underdeveloped and backward
areas of the world. These were to a large extent non-self-governing
territories at the time the Charter was written. To justify this concern on the ground that neglect would lead to major world conflict
seems difficult. Rather, we must find the justification primarily in a
changed attitude on the part of the advanced industrial nations
towards the less-developed countries, an attitude already apparent
in the Charter provisions regarding non-self-governing territories,
and in the growing political influence within the Organization of
the less-developed countries of the world.

The United Nations and its related agencies can, as a matter of
fact, claim only limited credit for the reconstruction of the world's

economic and financial system after the dislocations caused by the war, and for placing it on a sufficiently sound and stable basis to permit a quarter of a century to pass without a serious economic depression accompanied by large-scale unemployment and social disorder. While the United Nations Relief and Reconstruction Agency (UNRRA) made a major contribution to the relief of suffering and the care of refugees in war-torn countries, the job of reconstruction was largely done outside the United Nations. In the defeated enemy countries the occupation policies of the Western Allies contributed substantially to economic recovery. For the United Kingdom and Western Europe the Marshall Plan contributed decisively to restoring war-battered economies. The massive United States loan to Britain in 1947 did for the stabilization of the pound sterling—so important to currency stabilization generally— what the International Monetary Fund was without the means to do, though initially established for this purpose.[43] Furthermore, the United States lend-lease policy during the war gave assurance that major countries emerging from the conflict in weakened conditions would not be saddled with debt payments endangering their international payments position and the stability of their currencies.

In the field of trade policy, the United Nations has made a limited contribution compared with original expectations. The International Monetary Fund did little initially to establish currency stability as the basis for expanded trade, though after the initial job of reconstruction was completed it came to play a major role in maintaining an orderly system. The attempt to establish the International Trade Organization on the basis of the Habana Charter failed. What was salvaged—the General Agreement on Tariffs and Trade (GATT)—has provided a useful framework for reducing tariff barriers, eliminating certain forms of trade restrictions, and achieving stability of tariff rates.[44] The decisive initiative in moving

43. See Richard N. Gardner, *Sterling-Dollar Diplomacy: Anglo-American Collaboration in the Reconstruction of Multilateral Trade* (Oxford: Clarendon Press, 1956).

44. See Gerard Curzon, *Multilateral Commercial Diplomacy: An Examination of the Impact of the General Agreement on Tariffs and Trade on National Commercial Policies and Techniques* (London: Michael Joseph, 1965).

for freer trade was taken by Secretary of State Hull before the war, and GATT was in effect the general application of the reciprocal trade agreement idea. Some of the more spectacular developments in the trade policy field have in fact taken place outside the United Nations system in such regional arrangements as The Organization of European Economic Cooperation (OEEC) and the European Economic Community.

Without underestimating the value of highly technical work done by the United Nations and the specialized agencies in a wide variety of fields, one can justifiably say that assistance to developing countries in their economic, social and political development is the activity that has constituted the Organization's major achievement. While the condition of underdevelopment of certain areas was recognized from the beginning and the need of giving some attention to remedying it was recognized, the dimensions of the problem and, in effect, its importance and urgency were not seen until the unexpectedly rapid liquidation of colonialism and the resulting creation of new independent states added greatly to the number of underdeveloped countries needing assistance and to the political pressures in the United Nations for programs of assistance. In a real sense, as a result of these parallel developments the United Nations has been asked to assume responsibilities formerly discharged by colonial powers—responsibilities which, in the view of the defenders of colonialism, the colonial power had not had the time nor been given the opportunity to fulfill and which, in the view of the opponents of colonialism, the colonial power by the very nature of the relationship was incapable of fulfilling.

The assistance given by the United Nations and the related agencies to the developing countries has covered a wide spectrum. Membership, alone, in the United Nations and the agencies has been of special value to the new states in giving diplomatic, administrative, and technical experience to their people, and the opportunity to make known their needs and learn from the experience of others. But in addition, United Nations and specialized agency programs have provided them with a wide range of specific aids: technical assistance, preinvestment assistance, grants, and loans on a wide variety of terms adapted to particular needs and circumstances. To be sure, the United Nations and the agencies are not alone in providing this assistance. In fact, of the total financial assistance rendered, the much greater part comes from other sources, especially from individual countries under bilateral arrangements.[45] Also, substantial amounts are provided under regional and limited-party arrangements such as the European Economic Community's program and the Colombo Plan. Advocates of multilateral aid, such as is provided under United Nations and specialized agency programs, claim special virtues for it which give it an importance out of proportion to its absolute amount. In comparison with aid under bilateral arrangements, the terms of which are often largely dicatated by the donor country, the United Nations and the agencies give the recipient countries the opportunity to participate as equals in determining the terms under which assistance is to be rendered; they give assurance that aid will not be made an instrument for advancing the interests of a particular country, thus giving the operation a neocolonial character; they assure the widest participation of countries in providing trained personnel, resources, and equipment; and in general they provide maximum assurance that the aid will be given in the interest of the receiving state.

While the case for the superiority of United Nations and specialized agency aid may be valid, it does not necessarily follow that all aid should take this form, least of all that it actually will. The ready availability of aid from other sources or the special relationship of a developed to a developing country may result in a preference for aid under bilateral arrangements, even from the point of view of the recipient country. Furthermore, there are limits to the capacity of the United Nations system to render such aid, a capacity that can be increased but which as of now is limited. The development of this capacity requires greater willingness on the part of governments to support and contribute to United Nations programs, and

45. According to the Report of the Pearson Commission (*Partners in Economic Development*, p. 209), bilateral aid accounted for "almost 90 percent of the official development assistance" in 1967.

improvements in organizational structure and operational procedures of such programs.[46] There is some evidence of a growing
awareness on the part of countries making the major contributions
under bilateral arrangements that their interests may best be
served by providing assistance under United Nations and specialized agency arrangements. Important steps have been taken to
improve the structure and operational procedures of UN programs. A substantial number of the recommendations contained in
Sir Robert Jackson's "Capacity Study" have been put into effect.[47]
Of equal, if not greater significance, is the growing recognition that
attention should be shifted from the abstractions and generalities
of economic growth "to the immediate, concrete, and critical needs
of human beings." [48]

46. Two important reports, cited above in footnote 40 have recently been published, assessing the record and prospects of developmental aid and the capacity of
the United Nations system.

47. General Assembly Res. 2688, Dec. 11, 1970. See "Issues Before The 25th General Assembly," *International Conciliation*, 579 (September 1970), 186–93; and "Issues Before the 26th General Assembly," *International Conciliation*, 584 (September
1971), pp. 153–59.

48. See Barbara Ward, "A People's Strategy of Development," *Vista* (October 1973),
pp. 15–21.

CHAPTER ELEVEN

MEETING THE DEMANDS OF
MODERN TECHNOLOGY

CLEARLY THE MOST PUBLICIZED and significant activity of the
United Nations during 1972 was the Stockholm Conference on the
Human Environment which produced agreement on a Declaration
on The Human Environment, an Action Plan, and new institutional
arrangements, all subsequently approved with minor change by the
General Assembly. The significance of this activity lay only in part in
its success, measured by the degree of consensus achieved, which
marked a happy contrast to failures on many other issues in recent
years. To a greater extent its significance derived from the fact that
the Organization had been called upon to deal with questions which
until recently had not been matters of international concern. Even
governments of member states had not for long been giving their
attention to the consequences of man's misuse of his environment
and the possibility of using available means to limit, if not undo, the
damage that has been done.

The concern of the United Nations with problems created by
modern technological developments or susceptible to treatment by
methods made available by that technology is not of course a new
one. It goes back to the first year of the Organization when its
members were asked to consider ways and means of controlling the
use of nuclear energy. However, it was only in the decade of the
sixties that the importance of using the achievements of science
and technology for furthering United Nations objectives came to

be fully recognized. In 1960, stimulated by a survey of "Current Trends in Scientific Research," the General Assembly initiated serious consideration of the possibility of using the achievements of modern science for furthering UN purposes, "especially for accelerating the economic and social progress of the less developed countries." [1]

In the years that followed, the transfer of technology from advanced to developing countries, the peaceful use of outer space, the uses of the sea and its resources for the peaceful purposes of mankind, and the protection of the human environment against the abuses incident to modern economic development have come to occupy an ever increasing part of the UN's attention.

THE CHARTER AND MODERN TECHNOLOGY

Admittedly, scientific and technological development have had an important influence on international relations and the development of international institutions during the course of the past hundred years. The public international unions of the nineteenth and early twentieth centuries, such as the Universal Postal Union and the International Telegraphic Union were responses to significant technological developments.[2] Technological developments, by creating the possibility of greater national self-sufficiency, made possible the World War I of four odd years, in contrast to one of a few months which was the maximum many had thought possible, and by increasing capacity for destruction produced a war of such unprecedented suffering and destructiveness as to make the League of Nations appear a practical necessity, even to hardened statesmen.

We cannot know what would have been the effects of knowledge of and experience with the destructive force of atomic fission on the architects of the United Nations if the San Francisco Conference had met after instead of before the bomb was exploded. In

1. General Assembly Res. 1512 (XV), Dec. 12, 1960.

2. See Paul S. Reinsch, *Public International Unions* (2d ed.; Boston: World Peace Foundation, 1916).

any case we know that the Charter that was drafted and agreed to was based to a large extent on the lessons drawn from past experience, and that technological developments, whether for peaceful or war purposes, had effects not greatly different in degree or in kind from what they had had a quarter of a century earlier. The need of improved cooperation at the administrative level to provide better services in the fields of transportation and communication, and of a "general international organization to save succeeding generations from the scourge of war" was fully recognized, but institutional arrangements and thinking regarding the role of the nation state followed traditional patterns. It was not until the atomic bomb had been exploded that people in responsible positions began to question the adequacy of traditional approaches to meet the challenges of the new technology—to cope with its problems and to make the best use of its gifts in making the earth livable.

The Charter gives no specific recognition to the importance of technology in shaping the problems of the postwar world or in providing important assistance in meeting those problems. It places responsibility on the Organization for promoting "solutions of internatonal economic, social, health, and related problems; and international cultural and educational cooperation," [3] and empowers the General Assembly and, acting under its authority, the Economic and Social Council, to initiate studies and make recommendations for promoting international cooperation in these fields.[4] Specific responsibility for dealing with problems in particular areas is recognized as belonging to specialized intergovernmental organizations to be established or already in existence, functioning under the loose guidance of the General Assembly and ECOSOC. It is significant that these organizations, insofar as they were directly concerned with problems affected by modern technology, were structured to function along traditional lines. The functions to be performed by these organizations were essentially those of development and exchange of information, and the development of standards and technical agreements necessary to the effective func-

3. Art. 55.   4. Arts. 13 and 62.

tioning of national services. The primary locus of decision-making remained within the member states, and the primary criterion for action was the national interest.[5] Thus the International Civil Aviation Organization was set up primarily to provide for the safe and orderly development of international civil aviation. The World Health Organization was established to achieve "the highest possible level of health," primarily by promoting research, providing information, developing standards, and giving technical assistance to governments. The World Meteorological Organization was erected to improve meteorological services by gathering better information and making this information more widely available. The United Nations Educational, Scientific, and Cultural Organization was established to provide "collaboration among nations through education, science and culture" as the necessary basis for peace and security, but its activities in the science field were to be primarily in the increase and diffusion of knowledge and not in the application of scientific knowledge to the solution of the problems of society.

IMPACT OF TECHNOLOGICAL DEVELOPMENT ON POSTWAR INTERNATIONAL RELATIONS

Modern technological developments have had significant effects on the power relations of states, on the concerns of governments in their domestic policies and their relations with each other, and on the means that are available for furthering—as well as damaging—the common interests of people. And yet, little change has thus far occurred in the institutional arrangements, the procedures followed, and the location of primary responsibility and authority for dealing with the problems that modern technology has created or for the solution of which it has provided additional aids.[6]

5. See Eugene B. Skolnikoff, *The International Imperatives of Technology* (University of California, Institute of International Studies, Research Series No. 16), pp. 2–3.

6. Ibid.; and Eugene B. Skolnikoff, "Science and Technology: The Implications for International Institutions" (with comments by Harold K. Jacobson and Franklin A. Long), *International Organization*, XXV (1971), 759–89.

The technological development that was most revolutionary and far-reaching in its effects was the production and practical application of the atomic bomb which demonstrated the effectiveness of a new weapon of mass destruction and suggested possibilities not only of further developments for war purposes but also of a new and relatively unlimited source of energy for peaceful uses. Though there was wide recognition of the dangers of leaving the development and use of atomic energy under the control of national governments, efforts to avoid these dangers by creating some form of effective international control came to naught. National rivalries and suspicions proved too strong. The result has been a dangerous competition between states for advantage; and since this rivalry is very costly and requires a highly developed technology and an extensive industrial base, the competition has necessarily been limited to a small number of states. In fact only the United States and the Soviet Union have been able to go the course; and their ability alone to develop and support the advanced technology necessary to the testing and production of atomic weapons and their methods of delivery provides the chief basis for their ranking as superpowers. The fact that only these two countries have had the capability required to support this advanced technology explains also why the postwar world has been bipolar. The current emergence of rival centers of economic power and political influence may modify—but does not eliminate—this basic bipolar relation based on advanced technology.

Since the technology involved in the development of atomic energy for war and peacetime uses is largely interchangeable, it has not been possible to explore and develop plans for its peaceful use as a valuable new source of energy for meeting human needs, without, at the same time, considering the possibilities of diversion to nonpeaceful purposes. Consequently, for reasons of world peace and security, as viewed from the special perspective of the two superpowers, it has not been considered desirable that the technology for the development and use of atomic energy should be too widely possessed, except under very strict safeguards. Consequently there has developed a very high degree of dependence of states in the use of atomic energy for peaceful purposes upon those who have already achieved the advanced technological capability.

As is obviously true of the technology involved in the development of atomic energy, modern technology in general is expensive, requires a base of highly developed scientific knowledge and research, and is not something that nations can easily acquire in a short period of time by a process of osmosis or planned transference. The resources that are needed, both in personnel and in capital, are substantial and the lead-time required for achieving the desired capability is long. As a consequence, one of the significant effects of modern technology is to widen the gap not only between developed and developing countries but also between developed countries as well.[7] Since in non-Communist countries private enterprises have played a major role in the development of technology in the production and distribution of goods, private companies, more particularly multinational corporations, have come to play an increasing role in the transfer of the benefits of modern technology, if not the technology itself, from country to country. This is one important reason why the full understanding of the international political process today requires consideration of the role of nongovernmental actors such as the multinational corporation.[8]

Modern technology has opened up new areas of concern that national governments must deal with in their relations with each other. That was the immediate and continuing consequence of the explosion of the atomic bomb, as we have seen. The success of the Soviets in putting a man in orbit led to the rapid development of technology for the exploration and use of outer space with the result that national governments found it desirable to seek agreement on such matters as the permissible uses of outer space, the possibility of acquiring sovereignty over celestial bodies, the re-

7. See Jean-Jacques Servan-Schreiber, *The American Challenge* (New York: Atheneum, 1968).

8. See Robert O. Keohane and Joseph S. Nye, Jr. (eds.), "Transnational Relations and World Politics," *International Organization*, XXV (1971), 329–748, esp. articles by Edward L. Morse and Louis T. Wells, pp. 374–98 and 448–65, respectively.

sponsibility for damages resulting from outer-space activities, and the possibility of joint enterprises. An aspect of outer-space technology that has been of special concern to governments has been the possibility it offers through the use of satellites greatly to expand the extent and speed of communications, and more particularly to extend broadcasts across national lines, thus fracturing the tight control which many governments seek to maintain over what their people see and hear.

Another example of new areas of concern opened by modern technology is the uses of the sea. The success of modern technology in penetrating the secrets of the sea and in making available for exploitation and use the resources above, on, and below the seabed for increasing distances from shore and ever-greater depths, has made it a matter of pressing urgency to determine the extent of national control and the nature of the regime under which resources beyond national control are to be exploited. Furthermore, the possibility of more successfully concealing military installations and weapons of an offensive and defensive nature under the surface of the sea than on land has given the seabed and superjacent water an important place in efforts to regulate national armaments.

Only within relatively recent times have we come to recognize that as the result of our success in harnessing the forces of nature and applying modern technology to the production of goods to meet the ever-increasing demands of higher consumption standards, we are actually endangering our environment and risking the very survival of the human race. As Maurice Strong has written, "[modern man's] mastery of science and technology gives him unprecedented power, but his living world is threatened as at no time since his planetary home first gave him warmth and shelter." [9] Protecting the human environment while at the same time encouraging the use of materials and techniques which will contribute to greater human well-being is obviously a complicated matter. Meeting the food needs of the present population of the world, leaving out of account likely substantial increases, will require the increased use of chemical fertilizers which in turn may have a dele-

9. Maurice F. Strong, "The United Nations and the Environment," *International Organization*, XXVI (1972), 169.

terious effect on the environment by causing the eutrophication of lakes and streams. Prohibiting the use of DDT because of its fatal effects on many forms of wildlife, including birds and fish, makes more difficult the elimination of diseases such as malaria and the prevention of the destruction of crops and forests by insects. Restrictions placed on offshore drilling for oil and the construction of pipelines through the Arctic tundra may be justified as protection against damage to the environment but, nevertheless, also will delay and make more costly the utilization of needed sources of energy. As a result of such conflicts, national governments and international organizations in dealing with environmental problems often, and in fact usually, are subject to conflicting pressures from groups whose interests are opposed and are difficult to reconcile. Modern technology has contributed to creating the problems, but it also makes available methods which are indispensable to their solution.

Environmental protection is first and foremost the responsibility of each national government, and there can be no question that much can still be done by national governments acting alone or in cooperation with their immediate neighbors without the need of international cooperation on a global or even a broad regional scale. However, one consequence of modern technology has been to greatly broaden the area of legitimate concern and to widen the scope of cooperation needed for effective action.[10] If, for example, efforts at weather control should be successful, the consequences of control in one country would not be limited to that country, and might be quite different for different countries. Also, the failure of one country to regulate the discharge of pollution into its rivers and streams flowing into the open ocean or to regulate the discharge of waste by its ships at sea would have consequences for all bordering on or making use of the high seas. Modern technology, as one of its most important effects, has increased the interdependence of states, though admittedly it has also increased their ability to act independently.

10. See Skolnikoff, *International Imperatives;* and David A. Kay and Eugene B. Skolnikoff (eds.), "International Institutions and the Environmental Crisis," *International Organization*, XXVI (1972), 167–478.

PEACEFUL USES OF ATOMIC ENERGY

Modern technology struck the United Nations with a powerful impact in its first year of existence. As we have seen, the General Assembly in its first session was called upon to consider the question of international control of atomic energy. The initiative was taken by the United States which, though responsible for its successful use for war purposes, was deeply alarmed over the future consequences of its act. Efforts to achieve agreement on a plan of international control which would assure the use of atomic power for peaceful purposes only were unsuccessful.

In 1953 President Eisenhower, in an address to the General Assembly, gave UN consideration of the problem a new and constructive direction by proposing that the governments principally involved should explore the possibility of establishing an international atomic agency, "under the aegis of the United Nations," to be made responsible for the "impounding, storage and protection" of fissionable material contributed by members, and for devising "methods whereby the fissionable material would be allocated to serve the peaceful pursuits of mankind." [11] After long and involved negotiations, the Statute of the International Atomic Energy Agency was signed at UN Headquarters on October 26, 1957, and entered into force on July 29 of the following year.[12]

The Agency was slow in getting under way in the performance of its functions, due to the reluctance of governments to accept its strict safeguards. The conclusion of the Treaty on the Non-Proliferation of Nuclear Weapons [13] served as a powerful support to the work of the Agency, as it was given a central responsibility in assuring that nuclear materials transferred to a nonnuclear state were used exclusively for peaceful purposes.

As a second follow-up to General Eisenhower's speech, the Gen-

11. U.S. Department of State, *American Foreign Policy, 1950–1955,* Publ. 6446 (Washington: Government Printing Office, 1957), II, 2803–04.

12. On negotiations, see Bernhard G. Bechhoefer, "Negotiating the Statute of the International Atomic Energy Agency," *International Organization,* XIII (1959), 38–59. For text of Statute, see *Yearbook of the United Nations, 1957,* pp. 417–24.

13. General Assembly Res. 2373 (XXIII), June 12, 1968.

eral Assembly in 1954 decided that an "international technical conference of governments" should be held, under UN auspices, to explore means of developing the peaceful uses of atomic energy through international cooperation,[14] and an Advisory Committee was created to advise the Secretary-General on the details of the conference, including the preparation of the agenda. The 1955 Conference was followed by later conferences in 1958, 1964, and 1972. These conferences have been valuable in making available, through scientific papers and discussions, knowledge regarding the range of possible peaceful uses of atomic energy. In addition, the General Assembly has adopted measures to achieve better understanding of the perils involved in the use of atomic energy. In 1955 the Assembly established a scientific committee to assemble and make available information on the short- and long-term effects upon man and his environment of ionizing radiation.[15] This United Nations Scientific Committee on the Effects of Atomic Radiation has not only provided indispensable information for governments and others on the permissible limits of radiation but has also been instrumental in mobilizing support for the prohibition of the testing of nuclear weapons.

SCIENCE AND TECHNOLOGY IN DEVELOPMENT PROGRAMS

As we have seen, assisting the economic and social development of underdeveloped countries has become the first priority of United Nations activity in the economic and social field. In spite of what has been done under UN and other multilateral and bilateral programs, the relative condition of the underdeveloped (developing) countries has not improved. In the words of the Pearson Report, "[t]he widening gap between the developed and developing countries has become a central issue of out time."[16] An important aspect of this widening gap has been the limited development of

14. General Assembly Res. 810 (IX), Dec. 4, 1954.

15. General Assembly Res. 913 (X), Dec. 3, 1955.

16. *Partners in Development, Report of the Commission on International Development* (New York: Praeger, 1969), p. 3.

technology in low-income countries. Rough estimates of the Pearson Commission were to the effect that while expenditures for research and development in Latin America were 0.2 percent of the GNP, in Asia, between 0.1 and 0.5 percent, and in Africa, negligible, in the Soviet Union, the United States, and Europe the figures were 4.2, 3.2, and 1 to 2 percent, respectively. "As the ability to analyze scientific, technical, and managerial problems and propose new solutions has grown in industrial countries, low-income countries have become increasingly dependent on a technology conceived and produced outside their borders and without reference to their special needs." [17]

From the beginning the United Nations, in its consideration of ways and means of assisting in the economic and social development of countries with low standards of living, has placed emphasis on making available to these countries the benefits of the technology possessed by the more advanced countries. Under the UN's regular technical assistance program and the Expanded Program of Technical Assistance adopted in 1949, technical experts were made available on terms worked out between the receiving country and the United Nations, and fellowships and other assistance were made available for the training of native personnel. With the establishment of the Special Fund in 1958, provision was made for the financing of preinvestment projects. A substantial part of this aid has been devoted to research and training programs, enabling receiving countries to develop the kind of technology appropriate to their particular circumstances and adapted to meet their special needs.

In addition to providing technical assistance to developing countries, the United Nations has also attempted to mobilize the scientific and technological resources of the advanced countries to a greater extent in the service of general development. In 1963 the Economic and Social Council held an international conference of governments to explore the application of science and technology for the benefit of the less-developed areas.[18] The purpose of the Conference, held in Geneva, was to explore the possibilities of ac-

17. *Partners in Development,* p. 66.
18. ECOSOC Res. 834 (XXXII), August 3, 1961.

celerating development by better utilization of human, raw material, and energy resources; the development and use of advanced industrial technologies; utilization of the advanced agricultural techniques; the training of scientists, teachers, engineers and technicians; the organization of scientific research; and improvements in public health. Following the Conference, and on the basis of the Secretary General's report on its work, the Economic and Social Council established the Advisory Committee on the Application of Science and Technology to Development to review and advise on programs and activities and the possible application of the latest scientific and technological advances.[19] The General Assembly followed up by requesting the Advisory Committee to examine "the possibility of establishing a programme on international cooperation in science and technology for economic and social development." [20]

Since its establishment, the Advisory Committee has been active in preparing recommendations on a wide range of topics related to development. These have included the World Plan of Action, the relation of science and technology to industrial development, computer technology and development, the protein crisis in the developing countries, and the role of science and technology in reducing the impact of natural disasters. The Committee's recommendations have been favorably received by member governments. The importance of science and technology in work programs of the United Nations and related organizations is recognized in the statement of the International Development Strategy for the Second United Nations Development Decade [21] which contains a section devoted explicitly to science and technology.

PEACEFUL USES OF OUTER SPACE

It was not mere coincidence that the UN's interest in outer space coincided in time with the negotiation of a treaty for Antarctica, for

19. ECOSOC Res. 990A (XXXVI), August 1, 1963.
20. General Assembly Res. 1944 (XVIII), Dec. 11, 1963.
21. General Assembly Res. 2626 (XXV), Oct. 24, 1970.

both had their initial inspiration in the cooperative experience of the International Geophysical Year (IGY), 1957–1958. Vast and desolate space and a rigorous environment are characteristic of both regions.[22] The attack upon the scientific problems of Antarctica came as part of the IGY program, and led directly to the conclusion on December 1, 1959 of the Antarctica Treaty, providing for the demilitarization of Antarctica, the freezing of the status of territorial claims, a ban on nuclear explosions and the dumping of radioactive wastes, and the encouragement of scientific investigation and cooperation.[23]

In somewhat similar fashion, it was cooperation among physical scientists on a worldwide basis in the IGY program, made possible by the objective, universal quality of science and the previous cooperative experience of the world's leading scientists, which facilitated and encouraged the use of UN machinery for dealing with the problems of outer space.[24] Clearly an important, if not essential, stimulant to government action was the successful launching of Sputnik by the Soviet Union in 1957 and the proof which this offered that the exploration and use of outer space was a practical reality.

The problems presented by this opening up of outer space to exploration and use had much in common with those resulting from the harnessing of atomic energy. Both developments presented the possibility of harmful as well as beneficial uses. Both were the product of scientific research of a high order and the development and use of a highly sophisticated technology. Though atomic energy was harnessed in wartime, initially for war purposes, and outer space was opened up in time of peace, the international situation was such that a real danger existed in both cases that the new technology would be used to achieve strategic advantage and, if the

22. Hugh Odishaw, "International Cooperation in Space Science," in Lincoln Bloomfield (ed.), *Outer Space* (Englewood Cliffs, N.J.: Prentice-Hall, 1962), pp. 106–07.

23. See Philip C. Jessup and Howard J. Taubenfeld, *Controls for Outer Space and the Antarctic Analogy* (New York: Columbia University Press, 1959); and Howard J. Taubenfeld, "A Treaty for Antarctica," *International Conciliation*, No. 531 (January 1961).

24. See Odishaw.

occasion arose, for destructive purposes. Admittedly the danger was greater in the case of atomic energy since its use for non-peaceful purposes had already been tested; with regard to outer space, this was not the case: the strategic advantage to be gained by its use was uncertain.

However, the launching of Sputnik in October 1957 was a cause of alarm to many members of the United Nations; immediately following the event, the General Assembly adopted a disarmament resolution which included a paragraph urging the states concerned, and particularly the members of the Sub-Committee of the Disarmament Commission, to give priority to reaching an agreement providing for "the joint study of an inspection system designed to ensure that the sending of objects through outer space shall be exclusively for peaceful and scientific purposes." [25] The 1958 Assembly had before it two requests for the consideration of the peaceful uses of outer space: one from the Soviet Union and the other from the United States. It decided to establish an ad hoc committee to report to the next session on the activities and resources of the United Nations, the specialized agencies, and other international bodies relating to the peaceful uses of outer space and the kind of activity the United Nations might appropriately undertake.[26] In 1959 the Assembly established a Committee on the Peaceful Uses of Outer Space to review the area of international cooperation and to study practical and feasible means for giving effect to appropriate programs, including assistance for continuation of research in outer space carried on within the framework of IGY, organization of the mutual exchange and dissemination of information on outer-space research, and encouragement to national programs of research, and to study the nature of legal problems which may arise from the exploration of outer space.[27]

The Committee, with Secretariat assistance, has through its reports and recommendations been the proposer and initiator of United Nations actions. The General Assembly has provided guid-

25. General Assembly Res. 1148 (XII), Nov. 14, 1957.
26. General Assembly Res. 1348 (XIII), Dec. 13, 1958.
27. General Assembly Res. 1472 (XIV), Dec. 12, 1959.

ance and pressure, and has developed general principles, agreements, and programs for giving effect to the Committee's recommendations. The specialized agencies with interests in outer space have given their assistance, and in the discharge of their own responsibilities have performed valuable services. An example of the latter is the establishment by the World Meteorological Organization of the World Weather Watch.

The achievements of the United Nations have fallen into two principal categories, corresponding to the two major functions of the Committee: (1) the development of general principles and legal rules governing activities in outer space, and (2) the encouragement of international cooperation in the organization and conduct of research, the collection and distribution of information, and the implementation of operational programs. Under the first heading, the General Assembly by unanimous vote proclaimed the principles which should guide states in the exploration and use of outer space.[28] These principles were then elaborated and put into treaty form by the Committee's Legal Sub-Committee. The resultant Treaty on Principles Governing the Activities of States in the Exploration and Use of Outer Space, including the Moon and Other Celestial Bodies, was approved by the General Assembly,[29] opened for signature and ratification, and has entered into force. By a similar procedure, an Agreement on the Rescue of Astronauts, the Return of Astronauts and the Return of Objects in Outer Space [30] and a Convention on International Liability for Damage Caused by Space Objects were drafted, approved by the General Assembly,[31] and opened for signature and ratification. Achievements under the second heading include the holding of the International Conference on the Exploration and Peaceful Uses of Outer Space (Vienna, August 1968), the encouragement of cooperative programs such as the World Weather Watch and the World Magnetic Survey, the registration of space launchings, the sponsoring of

28. General Assembly Res. 1962 (XVIII), Dec. 13, 1963.
29. General Assembly Res. 2222 (XXI), Dec. 19, 1966.
30. General Assembly Res. 2345 (XXII), Dec. 19, 1967.
31. General Assembly Res. 2777 (XXVI), Nov. 29, 1971.

rocket launching sites, and encouragement of the use of satellites for communications purposes.

Even more than in the case of atomic energy, outer-space technology is extremely complex, highly sophisticated, and very expensive. As a result, only states with highly developed technologies and the capacity and willingness to spend large amounts of money can hope to achieve leadership roles. Within the United Nations, as well as outside, the United States and the Soviet Union have been the principal actors in outer-space activities; what has been accomplished has been due in large measure to their finding a common interest in cooperation. The announcement of President Nixon and General Secretary Brezhnev on May 29, 1972 of their agreement to make suitable arrangements to permit the docking of American and Soviet spacecraft and stations [32] was therefore encouraging not only with respect to detente in U.S.–Soviet relations but also as an indication that United Nations activity in the field of outer space will continue to be productive.

USES OF THE SEA AND THE SEA BED

Up to the end of World War II, interest in the sea was largely restricted to the extent of the territorial sea for general purposes of national jurisdiction, the existence of a wider band for special jurisdictional purposes such as the enforcement of customs regulations and the protection of fisheries, and the free use of the open seas. The traditional limit of the territorial sea was three miles, but many governments were laying claim to greater widths, and even the minimalists were making more extended claims for special purposes. The growing realization at the end of World War II of the long-range need for new resources of petroleum and other minerals led to interest in the exploitation of the mineral wealth of the seabed—which developing technology made practical—and to the proclamation by President Truman in September 1945 asserting

32. *New York Times,* May 30, 1972.

the jurisdiction of the United States over the resources of the continental shelf.[33]

This new principle was generally accepted. It presented a difficulty for many countries, however, who though facing the open ocean, had no continental shelf in the geological sense. When the question of the development and codification of the law of the sea was taken up by the International Law Commission, that body was faced with national claims to territorial waters up to 200 miles in width. To a certain extent these extreme claims compensated for the absence of a geological continental shelf.[34] The Commission and the 1958 Law of the Sea Conference, called to consider the Commission's proposals, finally agreed to a compromise by which the continental shelf was defined as referring "to the seabed and subsoil of the submarine areas adjacent to the coast but outside the area of the territorial sea, to a depth of 200 metres or, beyond the limit, to where the depth of the superjacent waters admits of the exploitation of the natural resources of the said areas." [35] While the Law of the Sea Conference was able to reach agreement on a definition of a state's continental shelf and its right to exploit the resources of that area, it was unable to reach agreement on the width of a state's territorial waters for purposes of general jurisdiction. A second conference held in 1960 was equally unsuccessful.

In August 1967 the question of the uses of the sea was again brought into prominence by the request of Malta that the General Assembly consider a proposal regarding a "Declaration and Treaty" reserving the seabed and the ocean floor exclusively for peaceful purposes and the use of their resources in the interest of mankind. In support of the proposal, Malta pointed out that recent developments in science and technology had made the exploitation of these resources a practical possibility within the next decade. These resources were considerable, consisting of petroleum, natu-

33. See Louis Henkin, *Law for the Sea's Mineral Resources* (ISHA Monograph No. 1, 1968), pp. 13–14.

34. For example, Chile, Peru, and Educador.

35. Art. 1 of the Convention on the Continental Shelf (U.S. Dept. of State, *Treaties and Other International Acts Series*, No. 5578).

ral gas, sulfur, manganese nodules, and other minerals. There was the danger that these resources would be developed by countries with more advanced technology exclusively for their own use. There was the further danger that the ocean floor would be utilized for military purposes.

The General Assembly followed a practice which had become standard when dealing with questions of great technical and political complexity. It created in 1967 an ad hoc committee to provide information and make recommendations, and in 1968 it established a Committee on the Peaceful Uses of the Sea-Bed and the Ocean Floor beyond the Limits of National Jurisdiction.[36] The Committee was instructed to study and report on (1) the elaboration of "the legal principles and norms which would promote international cooperation in the exploration and use of the sea-bed and the ocean floor, and the subsoil thereof, beyond the limits of national jurisdiction," and assure the exploitation of their resources for the common benefit of mankind, (2) ways and means of promoting the exploration and use of these resources, (3) exploration and research that has been carried out, (4) measures of cooperation to prevent marine pollution, and (5) the possible reservation of the seabed and ocean floor exclusively for peaceful purposes. The General Assembly also requested the Secretary-General to make a study of appropriate international machinery for the use of the Committee which in turn was to report to the General Assembly.[37]

The Committee's assignment has turned out to be a highly complex one, involving a large number of important but interrelated issues, divergent and conflicting national interests, and uncertainty regarding the practical importance of the areas and resources in question because of lack of present knowledge regarding the extent of these resources and the future capacity of a developing technology to exploit them. Under such circumstances there is a tendency for governments to be cautious and, insofar as possible to keep their options open by not limiting unduly their future freedom of action. Furthermore, many governments, faced with con-

36. General Assembly Res. 2467A (XXIII), Dec. 21, 1968.
37. General Assembly Res. 2467C (XXIII), Dec. 21, 1968.

flicting pressures of domestic interest groups and the divergent interests of different branches of government, find themselves in the position where it is extremely difficult to bargain or compromise. This has been true, for example, of the United States.[38]

While the item submitted by Malta called for the consideration of the regime of the seabed and the ocean floor "beyond the limits of national jurisdiction," it has become clear that most governments find it difficult to consider this without reference to the extent of territorial waters and the extent of the continental shelf. Two conferences have failed to produce agreement on the first matter. The 1958 agreement on the extent of the continental shelf has proven to be unsatisfactory because technology has developed to the point where resources on the ocean floor to the depths of three to four thousand meters can be exploited.[39] Clearly, modern technology makes wholly inadequate the 1958 definition since it would permit states with the highest developed technology to take over large areas of the high seas for exclusive exploitation. Maritime nations and naval powers naturally have an interest in keeping territorial waters narrowly defined; [40] and while a generous definition of the continental shelf would not in principle interfere with the right of free passage, there is the fear that it might prove the entering wedge for other claims. The developing countries find it difficult to determine their position on the regime for the ocean floor and the seabed without knowing the extent of national jurisdiction. If states bordering on the open seas are to have extensive jurisdiction over the seabed and ocean floor as the result of liberal definitions of territorial waters and adjacent areas in which they enjoy exclusive rights of exploitation, then for the little that is left it is not too important whether there are real assurances that exploitation will be for the benefit, in part at least, of the developing countries. If, on the other hand, the areas of exclusive exploitation are narrowly

38. See Ann L. Hollick, "Seabeds Make Strange Politics," *Foreign Policy* (Winter 1972–1973), pp. 148–70.

39. Evan Luard, "Who Gets What on the Seabed?" *Foreign Policy* (Winter 1972–1973), p. 137.

40. The United States and the United Kingdom have insisted on the three-mile limit but have been willing to consider a modest extension.

defined, then the nature of the regime and the assurances given become matters of great importance. Since a bird in the hand is worth two in the bush, some of the developing countries are inclined to opt for wide zones of exclusive exploitation instead of taking their chances on such distribution of benefits as might be achieved through an international regime.

It has become obvious that in order to provide answers to the many interrelated questions raised by the uses-of-the-sea issue, a further development and clarification of the rules of international law and agreement upon appropriate institutional arrangements is necessary. To achieve this result, wide international agreement such as can be conceivably achieved through a general international conference is necessary. The Sea Bed Committee and the General Assembly have made considerable progress in clarifying the issues and developing areas of agreement, but it still remains an open question whether the Conference on the Law of the Sea, due to hold its first substantive session in Caracas, Venezuela, June 20–August 29, 1974, will be able to produce the necessary agreements.

Apart from this exploratory and preparatory work, however, the United Nations has achieved substantial results. It has brought to the forefront of public attention a question which will have increasing importance with the ever-growing consumption of our natural resources and the further development of a technology permitting the exploitation of the hitherto hidden resources of the sea. It has achieved wide agreement on a Declaration of Principles Governing the Sea-Bed and the Ocean Floor, and the Subsoil Thereof, Beyond the Limits of National Jurisdiction.[41] It has assisted in the drafting of, and sponsored a treaty prohibiting the emplacement of nuclear weapons and other weapons of mass destruction on the seabed and ocean floor.[42] Substantial progress in the control of marine pollution by oil has been achieved through the activities of the United Nations and the Inter-Governmental Maritime Consultative Organization (IMCO).

41. General Assembly Res. 2749 (XXV), Dec. 17, 1970.
42. General Assembly Res. 2660 (XXV), Dec. 7, 1970.

PROTECTION OF THE HUMAN ENVIRONMENT

Until comparatively recently, technology has principally served modern industrial society by making possible the increased and cheaper production of goods, greater speed in travel and communication, and in general by relieving mankind of the necessity of engaging in some of the more exhausting forms of human labor. It has contributed to the consumption of natural resources on an ever-increasing scale, thereby creating problems of scarcity, though at the same time it has made possible the use of substitute materials, sometimes relieving one scarcity to create another. Modern industrial society has not, until comparatively recently, paid much attention to the effect of all this on the human environment. It is coming to be recognized, however, that technology must be controlled and used to a greater extent to provide an environment which permits mankind to live and work in comfort and security.

While the need of concerted action to protect the human environment had been recognized in many quarters, and a number of intergovernmental organizations—more particularly the World Health Organization, the Food and Agricultural Organization, and UNESCO—had given serious consideration to the matter, it was not until 1968 that serious attention was given in the United Nations to the problems involved. The initiative then was taken by the Swedish government in a proposal to the Economic and Social Council that an international conference on the problems of human environment be convened. Acting on a recommendation of the Council to this effect, the General Assembly decided to convene in 1972 a United Nations Conference on the Human Environment.[43] The following year the General Assembly defined the main purpose of the conference: "to serve as a practical means to encourage, and to provide guide lines for, action by governments and international organizations designed to protect and improve the human environment and to remedy and prevent its impairment, by means of international cooperation, bearing in mind the particular importance of enabling developing countries to forestall the occurrence of such developments." [44]

43. General Assembly Res. 2398 (XXIII), Dec. 3, 1968.
44. General Assembly Res. 2581 (XXIV), Dec. 15, 1969.

The Assembly entrusted the Secretary-General with overall responsibility for organizing and preparing for the Conference, established a preparatory committee to advise the Secretary-General, and requested that he set up a small conference secretariat and appoint a conference secretary-general. The Assembly accepted the Swedish government's offer to host the Conference. Subsequently, Maurice F. Strong of Canada was appointed Secretary-General of the Conference.

The subsequent success of the conference was due in very large measure to the skill with which Strong and his staff carried out the advance preparations. As the result of keeping the objectives of the Conference within realistic limits, making the fullest use of expert knowledge and opinion, and conducting extensive consultations and discussions with governments, it was possible to present to the Conference draft agreements which could be accepted without radical change. The major difficulty that Strong had to surmount was the suspicion prevalent in many of the developing countries that the developed countries were seeking to protect the human environment by limiting the economic growth of the underdeveloped countries. By giving special attention to this suspicion, and by convincingly pointing out to the representatives of developing countries that this suspicion was not well founded and that they would achieve positive advantages from effective environmental protection, he was able to command their support at the Conference.[45]

Over 1200 representatives from 113 countries participated in the meetings at Stockholm over a twelve-day period. The major achievements of the Conference were a Declaration on the Human Environment setting forth general principles to "inspire and guide the peoples of the world in the preservation and enhancement of the human environment," a series (109) of recommendations of measures to be taken as a coordinated attack on the pressing problems of the environment, and recommended measures to be taken to assure continuing international action. Specifically the Confer-

45. On the environment development issue, see "Environment and Development," *International Conciliation* (January 1972).

ence recommended to the General Assembly that it create a Governing Council for Environmental Programmes, a voluntary Environment Fund to finance the programs, and a small high-level secretariat needed by a secretary-general to serve the Governing Council, administer the Fund, and coordinate the activities of the United Nation agencies concerned with the environment.

The declarations and proposals of the Conference were for the most part approved by the General Assembly in its 1972 session, and permanent machinery was established to carry them out. Nairobi, Kenya, was chosen as the location of the Secretariat, and Maurice Strong became the first Secretary-General; $100 million was authorized for programs over a five-year period. The UN's initial consideration of problems of the human environment thus resulted in substantial achievements, more than reasonably could have been expected considering the complexity of the problems, the inadequacy of our knowledge, and the variety and strength of interests to be harmonized.

The future of concerted action for environmental protection remains uncertain, but there can be no doubt of its necessity. The sudden emergence of the energy crisis emphasizes the interrelation of environmental protection not only to the economic development of the underdeveloped areas but also to the maintenance of economic stability and full employment. The nations of the world are squarely faced with the necessity of harmonizing the demands of economic well-being and prosperity with the basic requirements of a reasonably safe and pleasant natural environment and, in the long run, of human survival. Obviously, the United Nations and its family of specialized agencies have an important role to play, as national and regional action must be supplemented and supported by global cooperation.

CHAPTER TWELVE

LOOKING AHEAD

P‍ROPHECY IS A TRICKY BUSINESS, and it is particularly so when account must be taken of the innumerable variables that will determine the future of the United Nations. For the unadulterated pessimist the task, of course, is easy, since premising as he does the inherent inadequacy of such an organization and the inevitability of self-centered policies on the part of national states, he foresees nothing but ultimate failure and collapse. For the complete optimist the task is easy also, since he is convinced that an organization whose purposes are generally recognized to be good must in the end prevail. For one who seeks to evaluate future prospects in the light of the motives and influences that actually determine human behavior and the conduct of governments in a world of the future—the essential features of which are at best a matter of informed speculation—the task is indeed a difficult one. It can only be undertaken with great caution and a full awareness of the tentative and conditional nature of its conclusions.

However, one is not without some solid supports in undertaking this task. If we are concerned with the developments of the next decade or two—which is probably about the limit of the time period in which we can foresee developments with any degree of clarity—we can get some assistance from recent and current trends in the activities of the Organization. Unless there is some change in the world situation of a catastrophic nature, such as a major economic depression or another world war, we can probably assume that current trends will not completely run their course or be superseded by new and fundamentally different tendencies. Also, we can find some basis for prophecy in the likely state of the world political and economic system as indicated by current trends in the relative importance of constituent states and the growing network of interdependencies. The way governments will react to these changes—particularly in their use of the United Nations and its specialized agencies, and in their policies within it—can also to some extent be foreseen; this provides a basis for judging the importance of the United Nations in the years ahead. Finally, we have in the work of scholars on the process of political integration some basis for judging whether the United Nations will be able to generate for itself an expanding role in managing the interdependencies of nations and resolving their conflicts.

CURRENT TRENDS

If we look at the recent and current trends in the activity of the United Nations we find little that justifies great optimism that the Organization is going soon to assume the important and central role in international relations that the words of the Charter would suggest. If we think in terms of Hammarskjöld's two concepts, "The Organization as a static conference machinery" and "The Organization—as a dynamic instrument of governments," [1] it must be admitted that in recent years, and since Hammarskjöld's death, there has been little movement toward the second objective. The emphasis has clearly been on the independence and sovereignty of member states and the role of the Organization in promoting voluntary cooperation between states. While the Asian and African states have shown a desire to have greater respect shown for the decisions of the General Assembly on questions of racial equality, self-determination, and economic development with which they are particularly concerned, there is little evidence that other members are willing to accord these decisions respect solely on the

1. Introduction to the Annual Report—16 June 1960–15 June 1961 (General Assembly *Official Records,* 16th sess., Suppl. 1A), pp. 1.

basis of their having been adopted by the required number of votes.

The United Nations is clearly moving in the direction of universality of membership. The resolution of the question of Chinese representation by the acceptance of the People's Republic of China, and the Quadripartite Declaration of November 9, 1972, followed by the admission of the two Germanies to membership, constitute two major steps toward universality.[2] There remain, of course, the two divided countries of Vietnam and Korea, the remaining dependencies whose future status remains to be determined, and Switzerland which continues to see in nonmembership a status more consistent with its national interests than membership. The trend is definite, and one can anticipate substantial universality of membership by the end of another decade or two, irrespective of any strengthening of the UN's role in dealing with the substance of world affairs.

While there has been some measure of return to the originally conceived relationship between the Security Council and the General Assembly in dealing with questions of peace and security, it still remains true that the role of the United Nations in this area, originally considered its most important responsibility, continues to be a minor one. For many years the explanation was to be found in the cold war, which prevented the Security Council from taking timely decisions and encouraged the use of the General Assembly for cold war purposes instead of for achieving a general agreement. Since the relations between the United States and the Soviet Union have entered into a phase of detente and increasing cooperation, there has not been a corresponding increase in the effectiveness of the Organization in matters of peace and security as might have been expected. Rather, the cooperation has taken place outside the United Nations in negotiations and agreements limited to the parties directly concerned. This has been due in large measure to the explosive increase in UN membership and changes in the composition and procedures of UN organs, making them less attractive to the major powers as forums for discussion and instruments for cooperation.

2. See General Assembly Res. 2925 (XXVII), Nov. 27, 1972.

In recent years the United Nations has been increasingly concerned with questions in the fields of human rights and economic and social cooperation that are the special concern of the new members, predominantly Asian and African. These new members, supported as interests may dictate by Latin American members and the Socialist states of Eastern Europe, have given their support strongly and continuously to programs for assisting less advanced countries in their economic and social development, to measures for eliminating racial discrimination in the southern part of Africa, and to whatever steps may be needed to put an end to the remnants of colonialism.[3] While phenomenal progress has been made in recent years in the liquidation of colonialism, the persistence of certain pockets of resistance and the inappropriateness of full independence in other cases make it reasonably certain that the United Nations will continue to be concerned with questions in this area for some years to come. Similarly, the current concern of the Organization with the elimination of racial discrimination is likely to continue. The Afro-Asian majority is not likely to be, nor should it be, discouraged by the slow progress that has been made. Finally, the wide recognition that has been given to the need of lessening the economic and social gap between developing and developed countries, and the wide support given to programs with that end in view, combined with the limited progress that has been made in closing the gap, makes it almost certain that this will continue to be the central concern of the United Nations and its specialized agencies in the economic and social field.

THE CHANGING WORLD ENVIRONMENT

The United Nations functions in a world environment which is constantly in a state of change. To be effective in performing its functions it must, in its composition, reflect that environment and in its institutional arrangements give reasonable opportunity for the dominant interests and forces to express themselves and to

3. See David A. Kay, *The New Nations in the United Nations 1960–1967* (New York: Columbia University Press, 1970).

work out accommodations and cooperative undertakings that are generally acceptable. While the Organization may in practice have rigidities, as illustrated by Charter provisions with regard to membership, composition of organs, and voting procedure that prevent or make difficult adaptation to changes in the world system, it is reasonable to expect that these changes will influence the development of the United Nations and indicate the direction of its activity in important respects.

In the years since the Charter was written, important changes in the world political and economic system have taken place and continue to do so. Responsible governments are finally in the process of completing the task of making the peace which the United Nations was to have the responsibility for maintaining. The 1971–1972 quadripartite and bipartite agreements on Berlin and Germany complete the task of making peace in Europe and provide the basis for greatly improved relations between East and West.

Until the middle fifties and even later the activities of the United Nations were to a large extent influenced, if not dominated, by the cold war conflict, with the United States and the Soviet Union the major parties. It not only influenced the concerns and decisions of the United Nations, particularly in the peace and security field, but also resulted in much international cooperation which otherwise might have been channelled through the Organization being carried on outside the United Nations, as illustrated by collective self-defense arrangements and much of the work of economic reconstruction.

With the emergence of new leadership in the Soviet Union following the death of Stalin, the cooling off of anti-Communist hysteria in the United States, the achievement of something approaching nuclear parity between the two countries, and the fuller recognition on both sides of the consequences of nuclear conflict, there has been a growing detente between East and West—the United States and the Soviet Union in particular—and a recognition of common interests justifying an increased measure of cooperation, particularly in measures to reduce the likelihood of armed conflict. It is not clear as yet that this trend will result in any overall strengthening of the United Nations or any increase in its effectiveness in maintaining peace and security. In the negotiations on the regulation of armaments, there has been a distinct preference on the part of the major powers to keep talks on a restricted basis and to limit the role of the United Nations largely to General Assembly approval of agreements already reached. It is significant, for example, that notwithstanding the Charter provision placing on the Security Council the responsibility for formulating plans for the regulation of armaments, since 1948 the Council has not been used at all for this purpose.

Another significant trend of recent years has been the emergence of new relationships between the more advanced states. While the positions of the United States and the Soviet Union as the dominant military powers, in large measure due to their superiority in atomic and thermonuclear weapons, has not been challenged, other states have greatly improved their relative positions, particularly in economic strength. Also, it must be recognized that the atomic superiority possessed by the two superpowers loses much of its significance when they themselves recognize that the likely consequence of atomic warfare is complete self-destruction. On the assumption that the nuclear arsenals of the two superpowers are unusable, their superiority to second-order powers becomes less impressive, particularly when one takes into account that in a world of nuclear stalemate and at worst limited conventional wars, economic strength takes on an added importance in international relations.

If due weight is given to the economic components of national power, it must be recognized that recent years have witnessed important changes. Japan has emerged as a major economic and financial power, with the capability to support a strong military establishment if it should make that choice. In Europe, Western Germany has done likewise. Its future role, however, is even more uncertain than Japan's because of its dual position as a member of the European Community on the one hand, and its special relationship to the German People's Republic (East Germany) on the other. The European Community has become a center of great economic strength and vitality, in contrast to the early dependence of the exhausted countries of Western Europe on U.S. aid and support. Whether or not this Community develops in time into a political union, speaking with one voice in its foreign relations and ranking with the United States and the Soviet Union in power and influence, the fact that France, the Federal Republic, and the United Kingdom are thus associated in a common evolving enterprise is bound to have considerable significance for the United Nations.

The past decade and a half has witnessed the near doubling of the number of independent states and the emergence to self-consciousness of that most populous and neglected part of the world—Africa and Asia. The states of these two continents and Latin America have joined in demanding that they be allowed a greater share of the world's prosperity and well-being. The South-North confrontation has tended to move into the forefront of public notice as East-West tensions have receded. While it may be exaggerating to say that the South-North confrontation poses the same threat to peace and security as did the East-West, it is nevertheless true that the growing and unrelieved dissatisfaction of the less developed countries with their lot in comparison with that of the older and more developed nations is bound to be a continuing cause of concern. The acceptance and entrance of the Chinese People's Republic into active participation in the global system and the United Nations assures the smaller countries of support at the level of major power relations. Although there has been general recognition of the justice of the demands of developing nations, in spite of what has been done to date to satisfy them, the gap widens instead of narrowing, and the certainty increases that the problems of this relationship will continue to be central concerns of the international community in the years ahead.

More fundamental than the changes in the power relations of government, the emergence of new political alignments, and the growing economic disparities between states has been the marked increase, in recent years, of the interdependencies between the states and peoples of the world. Some of the reasons for this trend are improved means of transportation and communication, technological developments that widen the areas of human concern, the growing recognition of the need to conserve natural resources, and the sudden awareness of the threats to the human environment as the result of pollution. In the economic sphere this interdependence has recently been evidenced by the monetary crisis, trade imbalances, and the energy crisis, and the growing influence of the multinational corporation. All of these raise questions of international concern that cannot be adequately handled by national governments acting alone. Recognition of this fact, and the certainty of continued efforts to find solutions through international agreements and institutional arrangements, give assurance that in the years ahead these interdependencies will lead to further development of international organization in some form or other.

THE POLICIES OF MEMBER STATES

The future of the United Nations—its nature, its role in dealing with the wide range of matters of international concern, the nature of its activity, and the effectiveness of its actions—will in the final analysis be determined by the policies and actions of its members, more particularly the major powers. This is because of the relationship which the Charter establishes, and which the members have insisted on maintaining. This relationship is not likely to be changed without the agreement of its more important members. While there is some possibility that in technical matters the Organization or a related agency may successfully generate support for new tasks and by a process of accretion develop a wider competence and greater authority, as the neofunctionalists have suggested, there is no certainty that this will happen—far from it—and little likelihood that this will lead to anything approaching political integration whether in the form of a confederation or a federal union.[4]

It can be assumed that the policies of the major governments will

4. For discussion of regional integration which, it is agreed, presents fewer obstacles than global, see Leon N. Lindberg and Stuart A. Scheingold (eds.), *Regional Integration: Theory and Research* (Cambridge: Harvard University Press, 1971); and Roger D. Hansen, "European Integration: Forward March, Parade Rest, or Dismissed?" *International Organization*, XXVII (1973), 225–54.

be most influential in the future of the UN. The attitudes of the United States and the Soviet Union will be decisive at least so far as concrete results in the peace and security field are concerned. This was true at San Francisco in the making of the Charter, and it has been largely true in the activities of the Organization since then.

While the United States government continues to proclaim the importance of the United Nations' role in world affairs and to profess its desire to make it a stronger and more effective organization,[5] it is quite clear that the government, as well as the American people, have lost much of their earlier enthusiasm for the Organization. This has been due to a number of causes that are likely not to be of passing importance: the financial crisis, disillusionment over peace-keeping, dominance of the General Assembly by members whose votes outrun their contributions, and the adoption of resolutions without thought to their implementation.[6] It must also be recognized that the Nixon administration's approach to establishing peace makes little use of the United Nations, relying principally on the adjustment of major power relations. However, the United States and the Soviet Union, in their efforts to accommodate their respective policies and interests, may find it useful to make use of the United Nations as a means of defusing a major crisis, as illustrated by their initiative and cooperation in the establishment by the Security Council of the second United Nations Emergency Force in the Middle East following the threat of Soviet military intervention in support of Egypt. The Nixon administration does recognize that the Organization has played, and should continue to play, a significant role in dealing with problems in the economic, social and technical fields.[7] This can be regarded as the principal U.S. interest in the Organization in the years immediately ahead, with the possibility that with a change of administration there will be a greater

---

5. See *United States Foreign Policy, 1972, A Report of the Secretary of State* (Dept. of State Publ. 8699), pp. 101–2; and address by Secretary of State Kissinger before the General Assembly, Sept. 24, 1973. The *New York Times*, Sept. 25, 1973.

6. For further discussion of reasons of U.S. dissatisfaction see Hollis W. Barber, "The United States vs. the United Nations," *International Organization*, XXVII (1973), 139–63.

7. *United States Foreign Policy 1972*, pp. 102–4.

interest in making use of it in the field of peace and security.[8]

The Soviet Union is unlikely to depart to any great degree from the position that it has consistently held that the Organization is composed of sovereign states and that the Charter provisions are to be interpreted strictly to preserve the principles of independence of states, nonintervention, and peaceful coexistence.[9] It accepts enthusiastically the Nixon policy of seeking to organize peace through bilateral negotiations between the major powers and shares to a larger degree some of the U.S. concerns over the undue influence of small states in the United Nations. However, it is willing to exploit the special interests of the Asian and African states in the elimination of colonialism and racial discrimination without, however, going so far as to recognize that the Organization has effective governmental authority outside of Security Council decisions which are, of course, subject to the veto. There is, therefore, little likelihood that the Soviet Union will take any initiative to strengthen the role of the United Nations in the peace and security field. Though the Soviet Union has shown increasing willingness to participate in United Nations consideration of economic, social, and technological matters, it has not taken initiatives in these areas, and its participation has not gone beyond the requirements of national interest narrowly defined or contrary to its basic ideological commitments. It is true that of late Moscow has shown great interest in developing trade and financial relations with the West, due primarily to food shortages and the Soviet economy's need for better access to and use of Western technology and managerial skills. This interest, however, is expressed primarily in bilateral negotiations and agreements, and not in negotiations leading to agreement on improved international standards and the establishment of new institutions or strengthening of existing ones for dealing with economic and social problems.

The policies of the major western European countries are likely

8. For a careful and dispassionate analysis of the U.S. experience and future role in the United Nations, see Ernest Haas, *Tangle of Hopes* (Englewood Cliffs, N.J.: Prentice-Hall, 1969).

9. See Alexander Dallin, *The Soviet Union and the United Nations: An Inquiry into Soviet Motives and Objectives* (New York: Praeger, 1962).

to be deeply influenced by their membership in the European Community. The United Kingdom, which in the past has followed a policy roughly parallel to that of the United States, in spite of its disastrous Suez adventure, will be increasingly concerned with its role in the European community; its UN policies will be influenced by the degree to which the Community is able to develop unified economic and security policies. France, which under de Gaulle moved to a marked degree away from a policy of even modest UN support, is not likely to revise radically that course in the near future. The Federal Republic of Germany, now a member of the United Nations, is likely to pursue a UN policy dictated on the one hand by interests shared with the United States and the members of the European Community and on the other by the requirements of its policy of improving relations with its eastern neighbors, and ultimately achieving German unity. The smaller states of Western Europe together with Canada, Australia, and New Zealand—the middle powers which in the past have been the dependable supporters of UN action in the full range of its responsibilities—have been somewhat disillusioned by the failure of peace-keeping to achieve its initial promise and by the persistence of the financial crisis. While they are likely to give full support to making the United Nations an effective means of giving financial and other support to the developing countries and of dealing with a wide range of technical problems, they are not likely to take initiatives, as in the past, to involve the United Nations in peace and security; nor will they show the same willingness to participate in peace-making or peace-keeping without convincing evidence of support from the major powers and some reasonable assurance that the operation will be successful.

On the basis of its past record, one would expect Japan to give the United Nations an important place in its foreign policy and to support measures for strengthening the Organization. One must recognize, however, that the circumstances that have produced this UN commitment in the past may change. When Japan, recovering from a disastrous military defeat, was seeking to regain recognition as a major power and to get accepted as a peaceful and law-abiding member of the world community, the United Nations provided a favorable setting for getting the desired recognition. Now that Japan has in a spectacular manner achieved the status of a major economic and financial power and is in the position, if it so chooses, to move back into the ranks of military greatness, it becomes particularly sensitive to slights or denial of proper recognition. The Western powers' willingness to accept Japan as an equal and Japan's success, by no means assured, in obtaining a permanent seat in the Security Council would undoubtedly go a long way to assure its continuing support of the Organization. Giving the Japanese the impression that their country is not being treated as an equal among the major powers may cause a decline of interest in the United Nations.

In defending himself against Khrushchev's attacks at the time of the Congo crisis, Hamarsksjöld made the point that it was not the big powers but rather the smaller states that had special need of the protection afforded by the United Nations.[10] To a certain extent that explains the special interests of the smaller states in the Organization. More importantly, however, the smaller states see in the Organization better opportunities for advancing their primary concerns than are afforded by other means, or at least they see opportunities for action which will increase their overall chances of success. More particularly, the new Asian and African states, along with other states that have felt themselves the objects of foreign exploitation, see in the Organization the best means of making known their special demands and bringing pressure to bear on responsible governments for remedial action. It is above all in the General Assembly, where these states have the majority of votes, that they seek to influence the United Nations and member governments to provide adequate assistance for development purposes, to eliminate the last vestiges of colonialism, and put an end to racial discrimination. Even though the resolutions adopted have often been too extreme to command the needed support of governments, the member states constituting this "new majority" have not given up hope. In the years ahead they can be expected to continue their pressure.

10. Wilder Foote (ed.), *Dag Hammarskjöld: Servant of Peace* (New York: Harper & Row, 1962), p. 319.

The chief enigma among member states is the People's Republic of China. Its acceptance in the United Nations has been so recent that we do not have much indication of what its UN policy is likely to be in the years ahead. Furthermore, its position as a major power with the potential of a superpower—but denying that ambition— and as an underdeveloped country, with the announced intention of aligning itself with the underprivileged nations of the world, makes it difficult to determine the direction in which its interests may lead it. Evidence to date would suggest that while the Peking government will support the causes of the new and developing states and will play an active role in the politics of the United Nations, it cannot be depended on to make the United Nations and the specialized agencies primary instruments of its foreign policy. Its primary concern in the years ahead will in all likelihood be to strengthen its security position, especially against the Soviet Union: it will see greater possibilities of doing this through bilateral negotiations and playing the interest of one major power against that of another, rather than by taking seriously the guarantees of peace and security that the United Nations offers. It will undoubtedly seek additional leverage against its potential enemies by aligning itself with the efforts in the United Nations to put an end to colonialism and imperialism, eliminate racial discrimination, and achieve a more equal enjoyment of the world's resources.

CONCLUSION

Such indications as we have from recent and present trends in UN activities, changes that are taking place in the world political system, and the policies of member states suggest that the role of the United Nations in the next decade or two, barring some unforeseeable upheaval, will not be as important as its more ardent supporters would like, or as inconsequential and minimal in importance as many pessimistic observers would have us believe. It is already close to attaining universality of membership, a condition that many have thought essential to maximum effectiveness. The nature of its membership—the extremes of size, population,

wealth, etc.—and voting arrangements make it highly unlikely that
the General Assembly will become much more than a continuing
international conference, primarily serving as a forum and as a
means of achieving the general agreement necessary to the handling of matters of wide, if not universal, concern. The Security
Council has been hampered in the past by the conflicting purposes
and policies of its principal members; whether with improved relations between East and West the Security Council will assume a
larger role in the maintenance of peace and security will depend on
the major powers—whether they find it in their interest to use it for
that purpose. Increasing the size of the Council, making it less a
reflection of the differences of power and responsibility among nations may reduce its attractiveness to the major powers. Also it has a
built-in weakness due to the fact that the Charter enumerates the
names of the permanent members, and consequently no change in
response to changes in actual power relations among states can be
made except by Charter amendment.[11] The possibility of greatly
developing the role of the Secretary-General to provide the Organization with something approaching executive leadership seems
remote; it would certainly require a radical change of attitude on
the part of the Soviet Union and other members who resist any
such development, particularly in respect to matters of peace and
security.

The United Nations is not likely to assume the prominent role in
the maintenance of international peace and security that the framers of the Charter accorded to it. The Charter provisions giving the
Security Council power to order collective military measures—initially proclaimed to be one of the special virtues of the new organization—will in all likelihood remain unused. The use of the Council's powers under Article 41 to order nonmilitary measures is likely
to be used more commonly in those cases where its real purpose is
to enforce respect for basic human rights enjoying wide support
among the new states than for the more limited purpose of defeat-

11. Japan for example can become a permanent member only by amendment of
Article 23, by adding Japan to the list of permanent members in paragraph 1. The
possibility of continuous membership could be achieved by eliminating the last sen-
tence of paragraph 2 which precludes reelection.

ing aggression, restoring peace, or dealing with an immediate and pressing threat to the peace. Such measures, generally within the competence of member states to take without Charter authorization, will undoubtedly continue to be used collectively as means of persuasion on General Assembly recommendation. The critical issues upon which peace or war depends will in all likelihood be handled principally by direct negotiations among the major powers.

It cannot be assumed that an improvement in relations between the United States and the Soviet Union will necessarily result in greater use of the organs and procedures of the United Nations for maintaining peace and security. It may have the opposite result if these powers see a great advantage in handling matters outside the Organization or in discouraging its use by others. However, there may be clear advantages for them in involving the United Nations and its membership. This may provide the means of mobilizing wider and more disinterested support for proposals that they have agreed upon, or it may be a means of providing a way out of a threatened impasse by having the matter considered and decided in a larger context such as the United Nations provides.

For the time being, peace-keeping, recently regarded as one of the major achievements of the United Nations, is under a cloud of doubt. Though talks regarding its basic principles of operation are presumably deadlocked, the possibility should not be excluded that the major powers, even if unable to come to an agreement on principles governing all future operations, will recognize the advantages of using the United Nations peace-keeping capability in a situation where their interests are not too deeply involved or where the involvement of disinterested third parties will help to relieve tension in their own relations. Whether it will be possible to remedy one of the shortcomings of peace-keeping—failure to produce an agreed settlement—will depend more upon the attitudes of members, and particularly the major powers, than upon new techniques of conflict resolution that may be developed.

In the increasingly important field of economic and social relations, the main focus of United Nations activity will continue to be on development; while its work in that area up to the present has been impressive, it has hardly been adequate to the need, considering that the gap between developed and developing countries has been widening. However, the United Nations has of late defined its overall strategy and greatly improved its operating procedures. It clearly justifies greater support on the part of members, some of whom, particularly the United States, have shown evidence recently of lessened interest and willingness to contribute.

Though matters of trade policy, currency stabilization, and foreign investments are related to development, and developing countries have sought to maximize their influence over them, the major developed nations continue to insist on discussing and reaching agreements largely outside the United Nations; GATT, however, may provide the setting for important trade negotiations and the Fund may be reorganized to play an important role in future currency management. The importance accorded to regional arrangements is likely to become more pronounced with the expansion of the European Community to include the United Kingdom. It is significant that the world balance of payments crisis of the early 1970s—in part the result of the inadequacies of the remedies provided by GATT and the Fund—has resulted in the tightening of cooperation among the members of the European Community and in talks and stopgap agreements between the major Western developed nations and Japan. The final outcome of these discussions hopefully will be agreement on new rules governing trade, currency management, and capital transfer, but there is no certainty that they will be integrated into the United Nations system.

In two areas—human rights and the future of non-self-governing territories—the United Nations will in all likelihood continue active, but this activity will show limited immediate results. The purposes of the Charter with regard to non-self-governing territories or colonies have already been largely achieved. Only a few major cases of colonial or white-minority rule remain: Rhodesia, South West Africa, and the Portuguese colonies of Angola and Mozambique. Asian and African members will continue to press for measures to achieve independence and self-government on the basis of democratic suffrage, which some members whose cooperation is needed will be reluctant to take. In the end, however, while perhaps not as soon or in as clear-cut a manner as the Asians and Africans would like, this pressure and the costs of maintaining their privileged positions will overcome the present stubborn resistance of the colonial powers and white rulers.

The remaining problem—that of the small and widely separated islands and enclaves—requires some solution other than that of full independence and membership in the United Nations. The present efforts of the anticolonialist majority in the United Nations—through the instrumentality of the Committee of 24 and General Assembly debates and resolutions—to apply to these territories the principle of self-determination and the terms of the 1960 Declaration on the Granting of Independence to Colonial Countries and Peoples, without regard to practical considerations and even the expressed desires of the peoples involved, serve no useful purpose and in fact damage the credibility and authority of the Organization. This is not to say that the United Nations does not have an important responsibility for seeing that the interests and wishes of the inhabitants of these small territories are properly considered and that practical arrangements are worked out for giving effect to Charter principles.

In the field of human rights, the approach of the United Nations has been selective and highly political. While it has succeeded in listing the basic human rights which should be protected and in drafting covenants for their legal protection, its concern with specific instances of violation has been dictated by political considerations and majority votes rather than an interest in securing wide and equal respect for recognized rights. The work of the United Nations in setting standards, and in providing information will continue to be of great value. Its efforts to correct inequalities have been too narrowly focussed and politically motivated, and too insistent on extreme measures, to achieve the desired results. One cannot question the justness of the objective, but for the United Nations to achieve credibility and effectiveness it is necessary that violations of specific rights be of equal concern no matter where or by whom committed, and that measures taken to remove such violations take into account practical considerations and the difficulty of achieving a quick change in the practices of an established community. Given the present differences in the state of development, values, and political and legal institutions of states, a world in which general respect is shown for the basic human freedoms will be a long time coming.

In the years immediately ahead, the UN will most certainly be concerned with the growing interdependencies resulting from science and modern technology. It is clear from the current trends in UN activities and the policies of governments that in this area adequate institutional arrangements will be needed and the UN and the specialized agencies are particularly well suited to perform the necessary functions. Assuring the peaceful utilization of atomic energy, regulating the uses of the sea and the seabed, protecting the environment against pollution, preserving limited natural resources for present and future generations are all recognized to be matters of common concern and to varying degrees require international cooperation for their attainment. Admittedly this cooperation in some instances may appropriately take the form of regional arrangements or arrangements among a limited number of states most directly affected. Experience to date indicates, however, that at some stage on some subjects, and for certain purposes the global approach becomes necessary; the UN system, with its close approach to universality, will undoubtedly continue to be accepted as providing the appropriate means of cooperation.

It is apparent from a review of the experience of the United Nations, and the League before it, that the importance of the UN's role in the years ahead and its effectiveness in dealing with the questions brought before it will be largely determined by the leadership and support provided by the major powers. It is also clear that, of the major powers, the attitude of the United States will be most decisive. If current disillusionment with the results of an active role of leadership and discontent with what is currently happening in the United Nations leads Washington to adopt a passive and somewhat negative policy toward the United Nations, this is likely to be the direction in which the Organization moves. If, on the other hand, the U.S. government, in spite of its disappointments, disapprovals, and occasional defeats, makes clear its commitment to the United Nations and provides strong responsible leadership in initiating and supporting programs and courses of action, the Organization will become a vital factor in international relations; and the United States' true interests will, from an enlightened and long-range perspective, be best served.

INDEX